MW00760507

# BEYOND
# THE BAR

RIVERDEL PRESS, L.L.C.

NEW YORK CITY

To Josh Markowitz —
who I care for deeply —
+ wish all the success and
fulfillment as he
travels beyond
the bar.

Albert Stark

# BEYOND
# THE BAR

*CHALLENGES
IN A
LAWYER'S
LIFE*

ALBERT STARK

Copyright © 2002 by Albert M. Stark.

| | | |
|---|---|---|
| Library of Congress Number: | | 2002096130 |
| ISBN #: | Hardcover | 1-4010-8364-1 |
| | Softcover | 1-4010-8363-3 |

All rights reserved. No part of this book may be reproduced or transmitted in any form or by any means, electronic or mechanical, including photocopying, recording, or by any information storage and retrieval system, without permission in writing from the copyright owner.

This book was printed in the United States of America.

**To order additional copies of this book, contact:**
Xlibris Corporation
1-888-7-XLIBRIS
www.Xlibris.com
Orders@Xlibris.com
17154

To Ellen,
my beloved partner for thirty-six years

Life must be lived forwards, but can only be understood looking backward.

KIERKEGAARD

And do as adversaries do in law. Strive mightily, but eat and drink as friends.

*As You Like It*

The law is good if a man uses it lawfully.

1 TIMOTHY 1: 8

# CONTENTS

# OPENING STATEMENT

## MAY IT PLEASE THE COURT:

*Beyond The Bar* is my testimony relating to persons and events during the fifteen years after I passed the Bar Examination. It does not profess to have the merit of biography, nor the accuracy of history, but is rather an album of snapshots–of cases, interesting incidents, judges and lawyers. It is hoped that the reader will find it relevant and material to the development and understanding of the life of a young lawyer.

*Beyond The Bar* is my story. I do not pretend to recall with absolute accuracy conversations, testimony, and events that occurred more than twenty years ago. I have taken the liberty to reconstruct some dialogue and testimony. In the interest of privacy and propriety, some names, dates, locations, and personal characteristics have been altered.

Proceeds from the sale of *Beyond The Bar* will benefit Leadership Trenton, a non-profit organization that trains citizens to improve the life of those living in New Jersey's capitol. Under the auspices of Thomas Edison State College and The Fund for New Jersey, Leadership Trenton is doing some of the work I set out to do.

# FOREWORD

YOU HAVE SEEN THE PRIME TIME LAWYERS AND JUDGES ON TV. You have read headlines that scream about lawyer's misdeeds and give the impression that lawyers are arrogant, shrewd, and greedy. John Grisham and other novelists who specialize in the legal scene expose you to fictional heroes.

But what really happens after the servile etudes of law school? After the toil of cramming for the state bar exam? And, after the dreaded test is passed. How do lawyers get started? What do they do all day? What challenges do they face?

To answer these questions, which I have been asked many times during my forty years of practicing law, I have written *Beyond The Bar*. My stories about perseverance, getting help from others, organization, thoroughness, compassion, following your instincts, and risk taking introduce you to everyday dealings with lawyers, their passions, their competitiveness, their wit, and capacity for hard work.

In the real world, many graduates of top law schools join elite firms and become associates, spend long hours on the road to partnership, accept assignments at ungodly hours, sleep little, and socialize even less. Others bump over rocky roads, wondering how to get business, who they must get to know, and how to compete. Still others take what is thought of to be a smooth and easy path, join the government and learn to navigate the bureaucracy.

It is my hope that my readers will enjoy the trip beyond the bar and achieve a better understanding of how being a lawyer fits in with having a life.

# PART ONE

*BEGINNINGS*

# FIRST ASSIGNMENT—LOST AGAIN

I TOOK THE OATH TO BE AN ATTORNEY AT LAW ON TUESDAY, SEPTEMBER 8, 1964, a day like my birthday, or the one when JFK was shot, a day I will never forget.

Janice, my father's secretary, hugged me the moment I returned from the celebratory family lunch. When, as a toddler, I used to spend Saturdays in my father's law office in the Broad Street Bank Building, Janice amused me by making necklaces and bracelets out of paper clips. Now, beaming with pride, she proudly showed me the supply of yellow pads and ballpoint pens she had placed in the drawers of a metal desk in my small office, which was once a storage room.

I sat down and read the instructions I received along with the engraved certificate that attested to the fact that I was now a bona fide member of the New Jersey Bar. At nine o'clock sharp on a Friday morning, I was to report to the Mercer County Courthouse where I would be assigned to represent someone who was charged with a crime and who could not afford a lawyer.

That Friday morning, lawyers were mingling in a large, mahogany paneled courtroom, waiting for court to begin. Not knowing any of them well and feeling too insecure to introduce myself, I eavesdropped. They were exchanging greetings and gossip, complaining about a new court rule, and inquiring after each other's families. I realized that I would have to prove myself before I could join their world.

I approached two other new lawyers with whom I had taken the bar exam. We talked about our swearing in, the feelings we had getting fingerprinted on Wednesday at the Sheriff's office, and our first real day of work on Thursday.

We weren't sure where we should sit. Just inside the rear entrance to the courtroom were several rows of benches for spectators. In front of this section, there was a low wall bisected by a set of swinging doors. This was the bar. Traditionally lawyers are permitted to sit in front of the bar, where there were two mahogany tables with matching wooden chairs, one on each side of the courtroom. The chairs faced a raised judge's bench with an ornately carved seal of the State of New Jersey. To the left of the judge's bench was the jury box, a low wooden enclosure surrounding twelve chairs. On the table closer to the jury box was a placard that read "PROSECUTOR." The other table had a placard that read "DEFENDANT." As nine-thirty approached, we noticed some of the lawyers taking seats at the table and in other chairs in front of the bar.

A Sheriff's Officer in a brown uniform with a yellow patch on his sleeve approached us. "Have some business in the court this morning, gentlemen?" he inquired. We told him that we were members of the panel, a group of new lawyers upon whom destitute defendants would have to rely. He raised his eyebrows, smiled, and instructed us to follow him. Leading us through the swinging doors in the bar, he cleared his throat, exclaimed "make yourselves comfortable right there," and pointed at several empty wooden chairs lined up beyond the bar. I sat down, still feeling that I was in strange territory.

I had visited courtrooms as a law student, always sitting with the spectators. In front of the bar for the first time, I was struck with the realization that I was a lawyer now. I had been given the secret handshake. When the judge entered the courtroom, everyone stood up. "All rise," the bailiff declared, "The Superior Court of New Jersey, Criminal Division, is now in session."

Hearing Judge Mark Light announce "State versus Mary Pittaro, Albert Stark, Esquire, representing the defendant," I looked at the Sheriff's Officer who beckoned by raising his hand.

"So you're Sidney Stark's son. You have a big pair of shoes to fill," the officer said as I approached him.

I nodded politely and smiled nervously.

"Counselor," said the judge," I am assigning you to represent Mary Pittaro. My clerk will give you a copy of her charges. Please contact the defendant and advise her that you are her lawyer." The judge leaned to his right as he picked up a green sheet of paper from the clerk's desk. "Have you ever had a client for whom you were responsible?"

"No, Your Honor." I responded.

"Let me tell you about Mrs. Pittaro's problems. A very serious matter indeed. She is charged with abandoning and contributing to the delinquency of a five-year-old boy. The boy is her son. She faces a long jail sentence if convicted."

My heart began to race. With the back of my hand, I wiped beads of perspiration from my forehead. I never expected to be called up to rescue a woman who had abandoned her child. I wanted to ask the judge if it would be better to have a more experienced lawyer handle Mrs. Pittaro's case.

Judge Light handed a green sheet of paper to the clerk, who then offered it to me.

The few steps I took to grab the statement of charges felt like a mile. I immediately began to read the words typed on the paper.

"Counselor," the judge snapped, "Read the charges at your leisure. I have many more cases this morning. You are dismissed. Thank you and good luck to you, Mr. Stark."

Judge Light called the name of another member of the panel. The Sheriff's Officer, who had earlier helped me to my seat, tugged my arm and led me back through the swinging doors of the bar, through the spectator's section, and into a hallway outside the courtroom.

A few hours later, seated behind the tan metal desk in my office, I carefully read the devastating charges which Mary Pittaro faced. After I wrote down her name and phone number on a message pad, my father and Janice came in to see how things were going.

I told my father that I was about to call my first client.

"Albert", he said, "Let Janice call her. That way she'll think she has a real lawyer." My father not only made a client feel more secure but a lawyer as well.

# A SIMPLE AGREEMENT—BAD WILL

TRYING TO LOOK BUSY DURING MY FIRST FULL WEEK OF WORK, I read municipal ordinances and poured out numerous cups of coffee from a pot next to Janice's desk. Finally, she asked me what I was doing. As I fumbled for the answer, she came to the more pointed question. "How are you going to get some business?"

"Any suggestions?" I asked.

"Be friendly and upbeat to everyone you meet. Get out and about," Janice suggested. "And, say hello to Doris, the elevator operator, and tell her a joke."

Soon Doris was referring people to me who wandered into the Broad Street Bank Building looking for a lawyer. Most of them were crazies. A disheveled looking man wanted to sue the President for cutting off his radio communication with God. A woman thought a plastic surgeon had made her look too young. So, when Sasha appeared, I didn't know what to expect.

Slightly stooped over and wearing a rain coat that was a size or two too big, she carried a red plastic shopping bag. A faded kerchief covered her hair. Her beady, black eyes and small nose were surrounded by wrinkles and sagging cheeks. "The goil in de elevader told me you did vills," she told me in the clipped accent of an Eastern European immigrant.

Sasha Borkowski reminded me of a Yiddish grandmother. She lived at 390 Bellevue Avenue. 'Near the schul,' she emphasized, making sure I knew it was near the synagogue and not on the 100 and 200 blocks where poor blacks lived.

"So, young man, how much is a vill for me?" she asked.

I walked over to Janice's desk. "What do we charge for a will?"

"Look in your Lawyer's Diary. It has suggested fees for all kinds of cases," she replied.

My red Lawyer's Diary contained a list of fees for everything from a real estate closing to defense of a criminal charge. A simple will for one person was one hundred dollars.

"Mine. It's a simple vill," Sasha assured me as she leaned over and pulled out two pieces of paper from the plastic shopping bag on the floor.

"It's a hundred dollars, yes?" she asked again, handing me the papers.

I nodded.

Sixty six paintings were listed, not by name, but by location, such as the painting over the hutch or the drawing next to the refrigerator. Next to each item was the name of the person she wished to inherit it. A notation at the bottom indicated that Sasha also wanted to leave five hundred dollars to each of her two children.

"Who, Mrs. Borkowski, painted these pictures?" I asked. "Do they have titles? What if you move them around?"

"Bennie," she replied. "He did dem. Bennie, he vas my nayber next door, in Roosevelt when I lived dere. Bennie, he vud give me a painting ven I did something for him like fix his pants, bake him a sponge cake, or a challah for shabbas, or let him kibbitz after he and his vife had a disagreement. Sometimes Bennie had not a dime. Sometimes, for him, money vas not enough. So he gave me the paintings. And don't you vorry about me changing vare day are hanging. I am old now. Dey have been in the same place for years and I don't change dem now."

I knew that Roosevelt was a New Deal community located in the rural area of central New Jersey. Many farmers relocated there during the 1930's and it was the home of many artists. However, I did not know that Sasha's friend "Bennie," who lived in the community, was the artist Ben Shahn.

Sasha agreed that I could drive her to her apartment to see the paintings. "You are a smart young fellow. I can see that. Just like your grandfather and his father, the rebbe," Sasha said as we got into my car. My grandfather, Lou, after having been forced to be a cantor because his tenor voice was so beautiful, had run away and worked in the theater. In the twenties, he became an entrepreneur and opened a supermarket and chicken business in Trenton, before losing everything in the Depression. I had fond memories of going with him to chicken farms where he brokered feed to the farmers, to Ebbets Field to see his Dodgers, and to parks to see bears, monkeys, and deer. I wanted to interrupt Sasha and ask her questions about my grandfather, but she kept rambling on about Bennie.

"Bennie. He was a vunderful man. Sometimes messhuga. Sometimes he vas angry. But Bennie, he cud be so kind and gentle. To me, he vas a good storyteller. Even me, I cudn't get in a verd ven Bennie vas in my kitchen. Bennie, he is famous. Ve saw Bennie ev'ry morning at the post office. Ev'ry morning at the Roosevelt post office, it was time for Bennie to talk."

As we walked into the small apartment, the smell of old things enveloped me. The dining room had a worn walnut table in the center that was covered with unopened mail and stacks of magazines. In the center, a cut glass bowl was sitting on a yellowing doily.

The walls were covered with paintings, drawings, and sketches. Some were framed, others were just canvasses hung with nails. The living room to the left was a bit brighter than the sullen dining area and the walls were completely covered with art work. Over a worn sofa, a tarnished mirror surreally reflected a painting of a fierce-eyed face with Hebrew letters around it.

In the kitchen, Sasha offered me a chair at a plastic table with aluminum legs. "Here," she said. "Here, you can make a list. A new list," she said, pointing to the paintings on the kitchen walls. On a yellow legal pad, I wrote a description of the colors and subject matter of each painting. After we finished inventorying the hallway, Sasha's bedroom, her dining room, and living room, I had a new list of sixty-six pieces of art.

"My father is an experienced lawyer. I want to go back to my office and get back in touch with you after I talk to Mr. Stark, Senior," I advised her.

Without a will, no one other than her kids would ever know of the paintings after she died. I wondered if I should do this will. A will might cause big problems with the IRS.

After I related Sasha's wishes to my father, he instructed me to get in touch with Morty Deitz, a tax lawyer on the 8th floor. It was obvious that Sasha's will was not going to be simple so I didn't tell my father I had quoted a fee of a hundred dollars since I planned to charge her much more.

"You shouldn't draft a will like the one she wants," Deitz informed me. "Those paintings are worth a lot now. If Ben Shahn dies, they'll be worth a fortune. The government will send a big tax bill and then the paintings will have to be sold to pay the taxes. If a number of paintings have to be sold, the price will go down because there will be too many on the market." Deitz told me that gifts to charity would avoid estate taxes and that the sale of some of the paintings at intervals would raise enough money for the children and lawyer's fees without hurting the market for the paintings. If Sasha wanted to give her friends some paintings, she could do that too.

A few days later, I told Sasha what I had learned.

"Too complicated for me. I vant a simple vill, one for one hundred dollars," she insisted. She was dead-set on giving the paintings to her friends and didn't want to hear why her will was not simple.

Frazzled, I wondered why law school professors spent so much time teaching cases and doctrine. I fretted that they didn't spend more time telling me about people.

"Who do you trust?" I asked.

"Rabbi Garfinkel. He vud never lead me wrong." Rabbi David Garfinkel had been the rabbi for many years at the Bellevue Avenue synagogue. I explained the situation to the rabbi and he then met with Sasha. He told her that she should listen to me, that Morty Deitz was a very well respected lawyer, and that she should sell some paintings, give her children substantially more than five hundred dollars, and give some paintings to the State Museum, as well as, of course, to the synagogue!

Deitz was waiting anxiously to hear how I had faired. When I told him what had happened, he congratulated me for asking for advice about something over my head, using information from a specialist, and charging a fair fee for the services that were being rendered. I lowered my head and admitted that I had not succeeded in changing the fee from the agreed upon one hundred dollars.

He suggested that I go to Sasha's apartment and photograph the work so that the list would be clear and consistent and that I draft the will in accordance with his advice and Rabbi Garfinkel's recommendations.

Two days later, I sat at Sasha's dining room table and read the will to her. I handed it to her, along with my bill for five hundred dollars.

"Five hundred? It was supposed to be a hundred." Sasha ripped up the will and the bill in front of my eyes. Sasha leaned forward, her eyes shooting lasers at me. What Sasha wanted was not in her best interest, but I felt it was my responsibility to redraft a will close to the one she wanted. I decided to allot twenty paintings to be sold to cover the inheritance taxes. I selected the twenty by writing her friends' names on small pieces of paper and placing them in a baseball cap. The friends whose names were still in the hat were to receive the painting Sasha intended for them. The others would not. I then accepted the one hundred dollars from Sasha.

When Sasha died a year later, her children hired another lawyer who sued to break the will, claiming I stole their inheritance by drafting a will that did not give them the paintings.

The lawyer hired by the children earned substantial fees even though the court upheld the validity of the original will. Sasha's unhappy children threatened to sue me for malpractice. Twenty of Sasha's friends were also upset when they were informed they were not going to receive the paintings that Sasha had told them would be theirs.

When Morty Deitz heard through the lawyer's grapevine what had happened with Sasha's will, he asked me why I acted as I did.

"I followed my client's wishes," I explained.

Deitz tapped his fingers on his leather-top desk.

Realizing he was waiting for a better explanation, I continued, "That's what it said in the book and I wanted to be chosen to represent her estate."

"That's not how to get business," he said, before he smiled and continued, "What's in the book is in the book. Reality is reality. Simply following your client's wishes will not always create good will."

# FIRST TASTE OF THE COURTROOM—HOLE IN THE HEART

FOR A FEW SECONDS, ERNEST GLICKMAN WAS DEAD SILENT. When he began to speak, his voice was flat and even. "That the prosecution has to prove someone guilty beyond a reasonable doubt is what they teach you in law school. You're dealing with a child with a hole in his heart, who's been left with a babysitter who tells the police that some woman dropped off her child without saying when she'd be back. In the real world, a defendant like your client had better prove that she is innocent if she wants to walk away free."

The books I had read at the state law library didn't deal with the realities of representing a prostitute who had abandoned her sick five year old son. Mary Pittaro's boy had a medical condition that decreased his body's blood flow, a potentially fatal defect. I turned to Glickman, a well known criminal trial lawyer, for advice about her case.

I wanted to argue that the reasonable doubt standard would always prevail. But as his words sank in, I conceded he could be right.

"You've met with your client, you've heard her story, and you say you believe her. If you want to help her, you will have to find a way to persuade the prosecutor and the judge to believe her as well."

The prosecutor? He had only one interest, to add one more conviction to his record. And the judge? He would apply the law, without prejudice or passion.

"If you try to rush straight to trial in every case, you only make the path more difficult. The prosecutor will become that much more obstinate, and the judge that much less willing to hear you out. Most important are the stages before the trial. That's when you have a chance to make or break your case."

This reflection sent me back to the notes I had made during my interview that morning with Mary Pittaro.

Her long, black hair and tight, black skirt had instantly reminded me of my seventh grade music teacher, my first real crush. Sitting in my worn swivel chair, I had looked down at the charge sheet, trying to mask my attraction.

"I've been assigned to represent you in court," I began. "The charges are very serious. Abandonment of a child. Contributing to the delinquency of a minor. A lot of jail time." When I looked up, tears were flowing down Mary's cheeks and black mascara was running from her eyes. I scanned the office for a tissue but saw none. I was hoping Mary would open her pocketbook, take one out, and get herself together.

When she didn't, I handed her a handkerchief from my back pocket. As I gave it to her, she was repeating over and over, "I love my little Billie." Her soft voice didn't fit a mother who had coldly abandoned a child. She slid my handkerchief over her chest and stuffed it under her blouse.

Before I could ask her about the charges, she began to ramble. "I left him with my girlfriend, Rosie, to babysit him. I couldn't take care of him. I work at night and live in just one room. He has trouble breathing sometimes and turns blue. Billie has a hole in his heart. Rosie panicked when Billie started to turn blue. She called the cops, told them that I left Billie with her, that I said I was running away, that he was using dirty words, that he was snuggling up to her like he wanted to put his thing in her. You know what I mean?"

I wasn't sure what Mary was trying to say so I didn't say anything.

Wiping her eyes, Mary pleaded, "Mr. Stark, I love my little Billie. I didn't abandon Billie. Believe me, won't you?"

She gazed at me for what seemed an eternity and then continued.

"Rosie promised me she'd take good care of Billie. I paid her good money. I have to work. It's the only thing I know that pays such good money. And those cops told her they had to charge me with contributing to the delinquency of Billie and abandonment, and she just told them what they wanted her to tell them."

The look in Mary's eyes made me want to help her.

"Tell me more," I said. "Will Rosie back up your story? Will she admit receiving money from you? I am sure she doesn't report it to the government."

Mary shrugged her shoulders, signaling her uncertainty. "You can talk to her, can't you? She's Rosie Giordano. She's at EX 3-1377. She's at 868 Melrose, over by Saint Francis." Saint Francis was the local Catholic hospital in Trenton. "Nobody's believed me. Will you?"

"I'll believe you until I have reason not to, and then I'll tell you. That's my job. One thing is for sure. If you're honest with me, I'll be honest with you. Okay?"

"That's okay with me," Mary replied.

"Tell Rosie your lawyer is going to call her. I'll get back to you."

I helped Mary out of her chair and noticed her slim waist and gentle curves.

I called Glickman and asked if I could see him again. He agreed. "What's on your mind?" he asked as I entered his office.

"If a mother knew that her son had a hole in his heart, why should she be charged with abandoning a child if she paid a babysitter to take care of him? Isn't that a good defense?"

"And what do you have to say about the contributing charge?" he asked. "If a child imitates a mother who is engaging in sexual intercourse in his presence, surely that is contributing to the delinquency of a minor."

"But what if a psychologist testifies that a normal five year old would naturally snuggle up to a babysitter? Then, she wouldn't be guilty of contributing to any type of delinquency. Using a child psychologist, I could discredit the cop's interpretation of what the babysitter told them," I suggested.

"Before I can evaluate your defense you have to interview the babysitter and talk to a psychiatrist to find out whether it is natural for a five-year-old boy to get an erection and press it against a woman. You also have to find out what the prosecutor is thinking."

After Rosie reluctantly agreed to meet with me, I drove to her yellow, aluminum sided row-house, which was smack in the middle of a low-rent, blue-collar neighborhood. A freckle-faced woman in her late thirties with her hair in curlers answered the doorbell.

Rosie ushered me into a kitchen that appeared to have last week's dishes in the sink and offered me a chair at a table covered with piles of mail, morning newspapers, and a few unwashed coffee cups.

While stirring a packet of Sanka into boiling water, Rosie glanced at me. "I spoke to Mary. You know Mary likes you, don't you?"

My lips tightened into a nervous grin. "That's very nice. I like Mary, too. But that's not why I'm here."

Rosie picked up a cigarette that was smoldering in a saucer. "Mary's telling the truth. I'm afraid of the police. My ex writes numbers. They want to get Mary. You know what I mean?"

Not sure that I did, I shrugged my shoulders.

"They've had a lot of complaints from her neighbors about the traffic that comes and goes from her place. The cops told me they'd lay off my ex if I gave them a written statement. If I tell the truth now the police'll hit me with false swearing. Of course, Mary paid me. She's good for the money. Billie's her life." Rosie turned towards me.

I looked at this woman, and wondered if I could I believe Rosie. I wondered if she was lying to the police or to me. The thought crossed my mind that the cops might have paid her off for a statement since I had heard that cops sometimes did things like that.

"Want some coffee?" she asked. "By the way, what is your name again?" Rosie asked.

"Albert Stark. You can call me Albert."

"Like Prince Albert. Just like the Prince? Now I can see why Mary likes you. Mary feels like she can trust you."

"Rosie, this is serious business. There's a lot at stake here. I need your help," I said.

"You lawyers are all the same. You need the truth. Sure. You just want to win. I know how it works," Rosie said flippantly.

"Push comes to shove, I'm going to get to the truth, Rosie. That I can assure you," I told her emphatically.

During the next week, the police showed me Rosie's statement, which was signed and notarized under oath. Clearly, Rosie was not going to change her story, expose herself to a charge of false swearing, and undo the deal she cut for her ex.

I arranged an interview with Doctor Freihaupt, a reputable forensic child psychologist. After I told him about my case, he said he would not testify "for all the money in the world," because he held the opinion that a five-year-old boy would not get an erection and press it against a woman unless he had seen that happen. "Five-year-olds don't hump their mothers unless they are imitating," Doctor Freihaupt instructed.

Following Glickman's advice, I contacted Joe Merlino, the assistant prosecutor who was handling the case against Mary. Before I could speak, he barked, "I'm a lover and a hater. I don't care about the abandonment charge. The police already have the matter under control. The kid's with a foster parent. Billie would be better off without Mary. You get your Mary to visit her Billie at the home of the foster parent. I might consider a lenient sentence if she agrees to leave him in a good home."

Merlino didn't give me a moment to react before he continued, "As the prosecutor, I have the right to make you an offer. The judges leave this privilege to me. A plea bargain is a good way to save everybody money. The state doesn't have to pay for a trial. The defendant doesn't serve as long a sentence so the taxpayers don't have to pay the bad guy's room and board."

When I asked him if I could tell him what I thought, he cut me off.

"If Mary pleads guilty to the Contributing charge and agrees to leave Billie in a foster home and not to reclaim custody, she will only get six months in jail. If she doesn't and is found guilty of Contributing, she will spend two years in prison. If she is found guilty of Abandonment, five more years will be added to the sentence."

I didn't tell Merlino that I felt Billie would be better off with his natural mother and that Mary would be better off if she was given the chance to get a job that benefited society and earned her a living wage. I didn't believe jailing Mary would do any good, but I was reluctant to say anything, afraid that if I did, I would risk seven years in prison for Mary.

Merlino explained why his approach was reasonable. If he punished Mary, she would pay for her misdeed. Perhaps if Mary went to jail, another mother wouldn't do what Mary had done. He thought Billie would be better off somewhere other than in the one room apartment of a prostitute. Merlino's goals–punishing Mary, deterring others and rehabilitating Billie–were similar to what I had been taught in my first year criminal law course.

"What do you think?" I asked Mary, after telling her what happened at my meeting.

Instead of telling me what she thought, Mary described the brutality inflicted on her by her father. She then recounted being raped and abandoned by a man who had promised to marry her but left her with the unborn child.

I went back to Merlino to tell him Mary's story and argue that if she were telling me the truth about her past, she should get a chance to be rehabilitated since she was the real victim.

He laughed. "All you young ones wear your hearts on your sleeves."

Even so, my heart told me to tell Merlino I couldn't make a deal. Merlino asked me why I couldn't.

"This case is going to be decided on the credibility of the witnesses. No jury will believe Rosie Giordano. What five year old boy could do the things she told the police Billie did? Who's going to believe that a five–year-old boy gets an erection and wants to have intercourse with a babysitter? Besides, if I prove that Rosie took money and didn't report it, the jury won't accept her testimony."

"Have it your way. If I don't try this case with you, I'll be on my feet with another. It's all in a day's work." Merlino's lips curled into a skeptical smile, then a frown.

I recalled reading an article in the local paper about a child being brought over from Poland to Deborah Hospital in Browns Mills to have a hole in his heart repaired. I called Deborah Hospital and got the name of the doctor who helped children with bad hearts.

I asked Joe Merlino if I could meet with him again. "So she's ready to plead?" he asked when I entered his office.

I shook my head and explained my desire to get Billie a heart operation.

"You're a defender, not a doctor," he pointed out.

"If I write a letter to Deborah Hospital asking for the operation to be performed on behalf of the state, will you sign it?" I asked. "I think your signature would help me convince Deborah Hospital to authorize the operation."

"You have to plead to Contributing."

"Why should she plead if she didn't contribute?"

"But she did, and you know it," Merlino replied.

"But that has nothing to do with the heart," I said, agreeing to go see her if he would sign the letter.

"What the hell," he replied. "You write it. I'll sign it. You send it to Deborah. But she has to plead to the Contributing charge. I've got nothing to lose signing a letter. You and I know that there is no chance that Deborah Hospital is going to give a hooker's son a free operation. You're just like the rest of the kids getting out of law school. Nobody's guilty. Jail's no good. It doesn't help anyone. But guess what? The law is the law, and if you break it you've got to be punished. Those are the rules."

I went directly to Mary's apartment. Emory Street was about a five minute drive from the Courthouse. Looking sullen and pale, Mary answered the doorbell. I explained what I wanted to do and what she had to do.

"How come all of a sudden you're telling me it's all right to give up Billie?" Mary asked. When I told her she would probably have to relinquish her right to see Billie and only be able to visit Billie at the foster home, she turned away, put her hands to her face, and began to sob.

"Isn't it worth the risk to try to get Billie the heart operation? That's what you told me you wanted most," I reasoned.

"I'll go to jail for two years," she said haltingly. "If you can get my Billie an operation, I'd be happy to go. But I have to be able to keep my Billie and have him with me when I get out."

The image of Mary framed by bars brought on that uncomfortable queasy feeling again. I was giving up Mary to the jailer too easily and I knew I would regret it for years. I considered looking for another psychologist to testify.

Finally, Mary agreed to the plea if Billie got a heart operation. I typed the letter to Deborah Hospital. Merlino signed it. But when I dropped the letter into the stack of outgoing mail I still felt uneasy. I should have been happy to get Mary's son the operation, but the decision to have Mary plead guilty was still weighing heavily on me.

To my surprise, the following Wednesday Doctor Sheldon Cook, the children's heart doctor, called from Deborah Hospital. "I received your letter about William Pittaro. I have discussed it with the Medical Director. Can you arrange for me to examine the child?" he asked.

Merlino was even more flabbergasted than I was.

The notice said the plea date was set for the second Friday morning in January, 1965. After I told Judge Light that Mary had promised to appear, he looked down from the bench and said, "I'm sure she did."

I looked around. A Sheriff's Officer barked, "Mary Pittaro. Is Mary Pittaro in the courtroom?" There was no answer.

"I order you to go to her residence, get her, and bring her back so I can put her in jail today," the judge said.

"What if I can't find her?" I asked Judge Light.

"You will find her," he said sternly.

"You promised to come to court," I snapped when Mary came to her door.

Mary could hardly talk. "I tried to reach you. I called the office. Doctor Donato told me I had the flu and not to go to court. He's at the Courthouse. He told me he was going to see you there and tell the judge that I was sick," she explained apologetically.

"Sure," I said, thinking what a slim chance there was that a doctor would arrive at court to give a sick excuse for a prostitute.

"Does anyone know a Doctor Donato?" I asked a Sheriff's Officer after I returned to the Courthouse and scurried up the stairs.

"Over there," he pointed. "The man in the black coat."

"Did you tell Mary Pittaro not to come to court?" I inquired.

"Yes, I did. Who are you?" he asked.

"Her lawyer."

"She has an infectious disease, and I thought it would be bad for her to come here today," Doctor Donato told me.

"Would you tell that to the judge?"

"Certainly. I was planning to do that after I finished testifying in the trial for an accident case I am here for."

"I can't wait that long. I'm going to go see the judge. Just wait here, will you, doctor?" Feeling even more committed to Mary's cause, I made my way up the aisle through the spectator's section, and stood behind the swinging doors in the bar. "May I approach the bench?" I asked Judge Light during a pause between cases.

"Certainly, Mr. Stark. Is Mary Pittaro with you?" The judge nodded and winked playfully to Merlino.

"Your Honor, I spoke to Doctor Donato. He's in the hallway. He said he told Mary Pittaro to stay home."

"So, since when is Doctor Donato, Judge Donato?" The courtroom burst into laughter. " And what is her condition?"

"She has, according to Doctor Donato, an infectious disease."

Judge Light scanned the courtroom with a sly grin, raising and lowering his bushy eyebrows. When he stopped, his deep socketed eyes appeared ready to shoot out at me. "Mr. Stark, are you telling me that Mary Pittaro has the clap?"

Too stunned, ashamed, and embarrassed to turn around, I snuck a glance sideways. In the jury box, black men dressed in green prison garb, convicted criminals waiting to be sentenced, were howling with laughter. One, a big bear of a man, had jumped from his chair and was beating his thick, paw-like fists on his stomach.

"Your Honor, may I say something?" I inquired. The sound of shoes kicking inside the jury rail rapped like thunder. Appalled that a judge would be so rude to anyone in open court, I was about to go on a tirade, castigating the judge's behavior. It was fortunate the judge spoke before I had a chance.

"You'd like to say something before you bring Mary Pittaro here, before I put her in jail where she can get excellent medical care at the expense of our county's taxpayers, and before she can infect someone else?" Judge Light's sarcasm bespoke the satisfaction he was enjoying, displaying his cleverness and entertaining those in his courtroom.

"Good morning, Doctor," Judge Light called out when Doctor Donato entered the courtroom, treating him as though he knew him well. "Come here. Tell me about your patient for whom my patience is waning."

The judge leaned over. Doctor Donato stepped back after he and Judge Light whispered something to each other. "The case of State versus Mary Pittaro will be adjourned for two weeks. We will see Mary Pittaro here two Fridays from today. Thank you, Mr. Stark. And you too, Mr. Merlino."

Seeing the anger that was building in me, Merlino grabbed my shoulder and pulled me toward the spectator's section to keep me from yelling at the judge.

Two weeks later, Mary entered a plea to contributing to the delinquency of a minor. Judge Light never took his eyes off of her while Mary told him how happy she was to be able to get her Billie a heart operation. Suddenly, he tossed aside the probation report, which had been prepared to determine whether a defendant was a risk to society, evaluate his or her transgression, and recommend punishment. The report had recommended a year in jail. "Are you ready for sentencing?" he asked Mary. "Is there anything either of you gentlemen wants to say?" Joe Merlino and I shook our heads.

Mary raised her hand.

"Do you want to say something?" Judge Light asked softly.

Mary nodded. "Am I going to lose my Billie if I go to jail?"

"Mr. Stark," Judge Light said, "I heard your client's question. We'll deal with that later."

"What are you saying, Your Honor?" I asked.

"Just listen to me, counselor." Judge Light paused for a moment. "Okay then." His voice cracked. "I am going to sentence Mary Pittaro to five years of probation under supervision of the probation department. The juvenile, William Pittaro, will remain in the custody of the foster parent and the natural mother will be allowed reasonable visitation. She will receive no time in jail unless she violates the terms of probation, which will include prohibition from the commission of any crime of any nature whatsoever during the time of probation."

Mary was nodding as he spoke.

"Are you sure you know what the judge means?" I asked, loud enough for all to hear.

Mary whispered back. "He means I'm out of business."

She wiped tears from her eyes and cheeks with a tissue that a Sheriff's Officer had handed her.

The judge smiled from ear to ear. "Indeed, the defendant knows what I mean," Judge Light said. "Good luck to you and your son."

Numb, I shook Joe Merlino's hand which he had extended to me.

When the doors of the courtroom shut behind us, a Sheriff's Officer approached, grasped Mary's hand and led her to the Probation Office. I put my briefcase on the floor and leaned against the hallway wall.

She didn't glance at me while she waited to get into an elevator with the Sheriff's officer. I was left alone in the courtroom with a hole in my heart.

At the time, Mary's case was the most important thing in my life. Searching for the truth, it led to a powerful epiphany. I found there was no single truth.

The prosecutor had a different view from me and my client and, in the end, different even from the judge. While emotion had almost blinded me, I'd been exposed to a different view of justice than any I had thought about before I became a lawyer.

I burst with joy when, in September, 1965, Billie Pittaro had a heart operation at the Deborah Hospital under the sponsorship of the Mercer County Prosecutors' Office.

My first taste of the courtroom was bittersweet. The lesson I learned from my mistake in Sasha's case paid off for Billie.

# IDEALISM MEETS REALITY—DOWN AND ALMOST OUT

Following Janice's instructions to get out and about, I volunteered to help at the Mercer Street Friends Center, a settlement house that serviced poor families. Soon, I was going to Mercer Street at eight in the morning to take in the orange juice and milk that had been delivered for the children's day care program.

The director learned that, after graduating from law school and before I took the bar examination, I had been a Ford Foundation fellow. Working for Richard J. Hughes, Governor of New Jersey, I had drafted laws that encouraged the construction of middle income housing and established the Department of Community Affairs, an assignment that fit in perfectly with my ambition to be an urban development lawyer.

When the director asked me to form a non-profit housing corporation for the Center, I formed Mercer Housing Associates, which was the first non-profit housing corporation in New Jersey. While fulfilling my obligations as a panel lawyer and working on cases that my father assigned me, I was fulfilling another dream: using the law to make life better for people who grew up, as I did, in Trenton, a city facing social problems and decay. If I did a good job, I anticipated developing a law practice that would allow me to become financially successful while promoting social good.

For a year and a half, I worked a few hours almost every day in the office and nights at my kitchen table, designing and promoting a high-rise housing project to be built in an urban renewal area which had been cleared of slums.

Following my usual routine of reading the morning newspaper after I put the juice and milk in the Center's refrigerator, I picked up the morning newspaper. My eyes popped with excitement when I saw a headline, KINGSBURY PROJECT FUNDED. As I read the article, I learned that the legal work had been awarded to a political lawyer.

The devastation and disappointment that I felt that day were eclipsed when, a few days later, I learned that my wife and newborn son were paralyzed and that my wife might lose the use of her right leg and that my son may never be able to move his right arm. I called my father and mother to give them the bad news. Wanting to be alone and regain my composure, I refused their offer to come and get me. After a quick bite at the Nina, Pinta, and Santa Maria restaurant, I would return to see Ellen, who was scheduled to be out of the recovery room in two hours, and Jared, who was being put into an incubator.

Johnnie Puccinella's Nina, Pinta, and Santa Maria was on a busy street separating the downtown business section of Trenton from the posh, residential section on the west side of town. An Italian immigrant, Johnnie began his career dishwashing in center city eateries and learning to cook. After he bought the Nina, a run-down working man's tavern that was going out of business because the factories in the neighborhood had closed down, Trentonians flocked to the Nina for Johnnie's porcini manicotti, veal Neapolitan, lasagne flavored with anchovies, ravioli stuffed with pumpkin, and crusty Italian bread speckled with olives.

After dinner, while I nursed a coffee at Johnnie's, I started crying. A waitress was soon at my side, asking, "Something wrong? Do you want another coffee?"

I looked up. "Nothing. Nothing really."

A rotund man, dressed in a white shirt and a food stained apron, sat down next to me. "My food. Does it make you cry? Is it too spicy?"

"You're Johnnie Puccinella. Yes?"

His head nodded and through my glassy eyes I saw his warm, caring eyes.

"No, Johnnie, it's not your food. It's my boy." He listened attentively as I told him what had happened. While I talked, the waitress put a tartuffo and an espresso coffee mixed with a sweet liqueur in front of me.

"Are you OK to drive? I drive you home," Johnnie offered.

"No, no, I'm OK," I assured him.

Johnnie whispered something in the waitress' ears. She returned to the kitchen. A short time later, out of the corner of my eye, I saw her push open the swinging doors. In her arms was a carton which she handed to Johnnie.

"Here," he said, opening tinfoil containers one by one. "Eggplant parmesiana. Some veal parmesiana. Some spinach. With garlic. And some pasta." He pointed inside the box to things wrapped in waxed paper. "Meatball sandwiches. Here," he said, handing me the carton, "Give them to the nurses. They'll take care of your boy better. Tell them they're from Johnnie at the Nina. They love my food."

"You know my name?" I asked.

"No. What I know is you cry," he replied.

"It's Albert Stark. And my wife's name is Ellen. And we will never forget you."

After Ellen got out of the hospital, she was fitted for a leg brace so she could walk with a cane. We traveled to New York to see a physical therapist for Jared. Some tough days ended at the Nina, which became our escape from life in a one-bedroom apartment. We got to know the Pucinellas, Johnnie, his wife Nora, his sister Jennie, and his sons, Johnnie, Jr and Salvatore. When Johnnie would not let me pay for a meal, I left a large tip for the waitress. After I threatened to stop coming to his restaurant unless I could pay, Johnnie reluctantly gave in, but would always find a way to bring an extra salad, a special dessert, or a Sambuca on the house.

In two years, Johnnie's was transformed from a neighborhood saloon into a regional hotspot for businessmen, bookies, retired folks, young couples, and singles on the make. The dining room's worn, brown linoleum floor was replaced with shiny black and white marble. The drab walls were covered with rich fabric and a beat-up bar was removed to make room for a disco floor. It was a toss-up whether the food or the renovation was the more interesting topic of conversation.

After Johnnie found out I was a new lawyer in town, he asked me about some problems he was having with vendors. I helped him without hesitation. Before long, I seemed to be calling vendor after vendor to get Johnnie more time to pay his bills. When I asked Johnnie why he was a late payor, even though business seemed to be booming, he always had the same answer, "Expanding too fast. Alberto, why should they be unhappy. The bigger I get, the more they sell me." His belly shook and an ever-present cigarette hung between his thumb and forefinger as he spoke.

To help Johnnie out, I made the Nina, Pinta, and Santa Maria my lunch spot, where I met potential clients. Janice was fond of making derogatory remarks about Johnnie Puccinella's because it had a reputation as a gathering place for the mob. She subtlely suggested I select more upscale eateries. Anything, but the Nina.

Once I was one of the regulars, I began to get calls from some street criminals and from people who had been hurt at work or in auto accidents. Many told me they had been referred to me by Johnnie.

My dream of becoming an urban renewal lawyer seemed to be just that, a dream. I thought about leaving the practice of law. It wouldn't be the last time I felt that being a lawyer wasn't meeting my expectations. But I had a wife and child to support and I didn't want to disappoint my father. Plus, it wasn't my nature to give up.

One day, my father walked into my office unexpectedly. I wondered if he had sensed my despondency when he said, "You're evolving from an idealistic law school graduate to a lawyer who is getting a taste of reality. From your indigent cases, helping the street criminals, and the accident cases, you are tasting the richness of getting to know a client. And Johnnie's place is really giving you a dose of the human element, isn't it?"

After I nodded, he said, "It's not always being a good lawyer that gets you business. You'll have your bad days. When you're young, everything looks like a bigger deal than it is."

"I'm thinking seriously of doing something else with my life," I replied.

I saw his eyes water. And, as he turned to leave my office, I noticed him raise his hand to his face. It was then that I began to cry.

# CAUGHT IN THE WEB—BY ALL MEANS

MY FATHER WAS SMILING WHEN I LOOKED UP AT HIM after taking the oath to be an assistant prosecutor in Mercer County. I was not sure whether it was a proud smile or whether it was an expression of relief because he was free now to pursue his pressure free, risk-averse practice as he had before I had joined him.

I had followed the advice given to me by Jefferson Fordham, Dean of the University of Pennsylvania law school, who had taught me state and local government and had encouraged me to work for the Ford Foundation. After I told him about what had been happening to my dreams and how I didn't want to hurt my father, he told me, "Get trial experience and become active in local politics. You have learned the hard way that political connections are necessary to get legal work pertaining to public projects. Trial experience will be important if you become a lawyer for developers. If agreements are disputed, it is vital to know how the litigation process works. Without that knowledge, you will be at a disadvantage." I had applied for, and obtained, a job in Prosecutor Mario Conti's office, taking advantage of my father's ties with the Democratic Party.

After the swearing in ceremony, Conti got right down to business. He began my orientation tour by saying, "If you want to get promoted, you have to learn to play within the system. The means don't always justify the ends; and the ends don't always justify the means." I followed him into a file room where he yanked open a file drawer full of yellow dossiers. "I assign these cases to assistant prosecutors who are wet behind the ears. They deal with misdemeanors and lesser crimes that usually end up with fines or imprisonment for less than a year. You get some courtroom experience without the opportunity to do much harm."

Conti stepped back, rolled the drawer shut, and sidestepped to another file cabinet. "Try to avoid these. They're the "C" cases, and they are predominantly minor election day violations allegedly committed by political candidates. They die a slow death, because they are usually filed by sour grape losers."

In front of a cabinet labeled "A," Conti pulled out a drawer full of red files. "When you get promoted, you get one of these. Felonies. The real thing. Crimes punishable by imprisonment for more than one year or even death. The cases include murder, rape, arson, burglary, and fraud."

Seventeen yellow files after my orientation tour, the red file on my desk had a note which read, "Here's one right up your alley." It was my first felony case. I had been promoted.

The file revealed the details: a burglar had looted the Greenwood Avenue home of Doctor Julius Castelli who was a well-known local physician. Greenwood Avenue separated Chambersburg, an Italian section, from a Puerto Rican community. It was a dangerous place to live. The stately homes, which had been the pride of Trenton's wealthy at the turn of the century, were now deteriorating as they were broken up into tenement apartments.

In the investigative reports, I came across a statement from a mole, an informer who was looking to exchange information in return for clemency for crime that he had committed. The mole had helped Detective Brushman find the culprit who robbed the doctor's house, and he assisted in recovering the doctor's wife's jewelry and photographs. The photographs showed doctors, some of whom I knew, and other females in acts of fellatio and multiple sexual activities and combinations thereof; they clearly portrayed the crime of adultery.

Brushman barged into my office. "You look at the Castelli case yet?"

"Look at it? What are you doing? Playing a practical joke on me?

This can't be for real," I exclaimed.

"Stark, this is no fucking joke. I wouldn't play a trick on a young fellow like you," Brushman said.

"If it's for real, how can I handle this case. I know some of these people. They're friends of my family." I was on the outside looking in, afraid that I was being intimidated by an older, savvy detective.

"It's simple. Get rid of those," he snapped, pointing to the photographs on my desk.

"What do you mean, 'get rid of those'?" I asked, looking up nervously.

"Use your head. Let's see how smart you are," Brushman replied with a wry grin.

"What do you want me to do? Tear them up? Throw them in the wastebasket? Isn't that a crime, John?"

Brushman stood mute, then sauntered to the side of my desk and picked up the photographs. He slowly leafed through them, one at a time, smiling, laughing, and making lewd comments. He suggested that I think of a way to do what was just.

"A prosecutor has a duty to turn over evidence that would vindicate a defendant. But this evidence implicates someone. Wouldn't I be destroying evidence? Why should I risk being disbarred and losing my lawyer's license? Jesus, John! You can't do this to me," I exclaimed.

"So," he uttered slowly.

"What the hell am I supposed to do with these damn photos? I can't destroy them, can I?"

"What does an honest prosecutor do with recovered stolen goods? Return them to their rightful owner. Right? Who is the rightful owner? The doctor. Right? You don't need every piece of evidence to get a conviction. Why implicate innocent parties? You wouldn't want to embarrass those other doctors, would you? Or their wives? Or maybe someone who isn't their wife? Right?" Brushman tossed the stack of photos on my desk, wheeled around on his heels, and, just as he was about to exit the door, did a snappy about-face. "No one has ever been prosecuted for adultery . . . not in my lifetime anyway." He clicked his heels and combed his crewcut with his fingers as he exited.

Being told how to handle things with a wink and nod without being told very much was exasperating.

"Doctor Castelli," an unsuspecting voice said a long minute later. Following Brushman's orders, I had reached for my telephone directory and looked up the office telephone number for Doctor Julius Castelli. I had given his receptionist my name, but I did not state the location from where I was calling. I peremptorily told her I was calling on a "personal matter."

"Thanks for taking my call. I'm calling from the Mercer County Prosecutor's Office. My name is Albert Stark."

"Why are you calling me?"

"Doctor, I have been assigned a case involving a burglary that occurred at your home. We have been fortunate enough to recover the goods that you had reported stolen."

"Fantastic," Castelli replied.

"Doctor, among the goods recovered are some photographs."

Dead silence filled the telephone line. Then, Doctor Castelli muttered, "Photographs, photographs, oh my God . . . . Oh my God, I never . . . . " Doctor Castelli suddenly stopped speaking.

"Doctor, I can't destroy the photographs. That would be improper. You understand that, don't you?" I waited for his reply.

"Of course. Of course."

"Doctor, I have been asked to return them to their rightful owner. I am located in the lawyers' section on the third floor of the Mercer County Courthouse. I go to lunch from twelve to one. I will leave the pictures in an envelope with your name on it. If you would like to come to the courthouse to pick up your property, you are welcome to do so. I will instruct the receptionist to show you where my office is located."

"What about my wife's jewelry?" Doctor Castelli asked.

"Unfortunately, Doctor, I have to keep the jewelry for a while to use as evidence."

"I understand. Thank you. I can't believe it. I just can't believe it. I just . . . . " I heard the doctor repeating as I hung up.

The envelope with the pictures was gone when I returned from lunch. I had followed instructions. Nevertheless my stomach was churning.

I scampered to Brushman's office where I anxiously told him, in no uncertain terms, how disturbed I was.

Brushman smiled mischievously. "I'll look for a good one for you," he said.

A week later, another red file appeared on my desk. Detective Brushman's scribble on a sheet of yellow legal paper read, "Here's another one that's up your alley."

John Hart, a senior at Ursinus College, had come home during the Christmas recess with a friend, Charles Avanti. He had shown Avanti three cars owned by friends of his parents. Avanti paid Hart two hundred dollars for each car he had identified and then stole them. The New York District Attorney's Office records revealed that Avanti had taken the vehicles to a chop shop in Brooklyn. The owners, his friend's parents, had collected insurance money to pay for the stolen cars. Avanti tried to shift the blame to John Hart to get a lenient sentence for himself. Now Hart faced three felony counts of Fraud On An Insurance Company and fifteen years in State Prison.

The Hart case seemed too simple. Known in the office as a "slamdunk," it was one you could not lose. Thinking that Brushman's idea of a reward was an easy case that would give me a felony conviction, a notch in my belt so to speak, I looked through the typed investigation notes for the name of the lawyer who represented Hart. In accordance with the Rules of Court, I had to send the attorney evidence. Because I found no name of a lawyer for Hart, I prepared a letter requesting him to advise whether or not he would be hiring a lawyer.

While in my office, I received a phone call. The shaky voice that said "the judge told me to call you" was one I did not recognize.

"With whom am I speaking?" I asked.

"You sent me a letter. You don't know me. My name is John Hart. I got your letter, and the judge told me I should meet you, because you are handling my case. You see, I want to go to law school."

"Law school," I thought to myself. "Jail, yes. Law school, never."

I was confused, because Hart's case had not yet been assigned to a judge, nor had it been presented to the Grand Jury for an indictment. I responded carefully. "Mr. Hart, I have written you to find out who would be representing you. You're in a lot of trouble. I suggest you get a lawyer and have the lawyer get in touch with me. If I do not hear from a lawyer in two weeks, I will assume you will be representing yourself. Truthfully, I do not think you have a defense to the charges. If I don't hear from you, you will hear from me. An indictment will be served on you by a sheriff, and you will be taken to jail until you post bail. Do you understand what I am telling you? I hope I hear from your lawyer."

A few days later, while I was walking through the reception area of the prosecutor's office, I heard someone call my name. I turned and saw a strong young man, neatly dressed, sitting on one of the wooden benches that lined the wall.

"Mr. Stark, can I see you, please?" I slowed down my hurried pace. "I'm John Hart."

"Do you have a lawyer, Mr. Hart?" I inquired sharply.

"Not yet," Hart answered apologetically.

"Then what brings you here?"

"The judge told me to come up and make sure I see you. I must see you. He said that if I called again without a lawyer you would hang up."

"The judge, whoever that is, is absolutely right."

Hart's chin dropped to his chest and his eyes peered blankly at the floor.

A door, with a sign above it, designating "Lawyers' Section," closed behind me. Through the glass panel in the door, I saw Hart walking down the set of three steps on his way to an elevator. I turned around.

"Mr. Hart, Mr. Hart," I called after I pushed the door open and stuck my head out.

Hart stopped, looked back over his shoulder, and turned around.

Hart complied when I waved him back. "I have some questions for you." Maybe Hart had information about bigger frauds? I assumed that the judge, whoever he was, had told him to come to see me to work out a deal for leniency in return for leading me to a "big fish." I hoped that Hart would help me crack a large Mafia theft ring.

Instructing Hart to sit in a chair in front of my desk, I settled in my high-backed chair and tried to size him up. Well groomed, he did not exhibit signs of drug use, nor did he fit the profile of the juveniles and young adults I had seen behind bars. "I assume you have something to tell me," I said, exploring my hunch that Hart was a "mole."

Hart nodded.

Leaning forward, anxious to hear what Hart had to say, I took a fountain pen from the pocket inside my suit jacket and prepared to take notes. "I gather you don't have a lawyer yet. So I presume that what brings you here must have some importance. Anything you say to me can be used against you. You have a right, under the Fifth Amendment, to remain silent."

"I understand. What I'm going to say is important. That's why the judge told me to come see you. I'm a college senior. Varsity wrestler. I've had my heart set on being a lawyer all my life. Judge Huggins told me you were an understanding prosecutor. I apologize for coming up without an appointment. But this guy, Avanti . . . he's the son of an underworld boss. He pressured me. Believe me, I knew it was wrong, but I didn't know what to do. Avanti and his friends threatened to beat me if I didn't show them the cars. A buddy of mine had his leg broken. Avanti told me nobody would get hurt, that the people whose cars were stolen would have insurance, and that they could collect what they lost. I was plain scared of what would happen if I refused. Wrestling season had started and I was looking to be All American in the 190 weight class."

"This fellow is scared of some New York punk," I muttered to myself after looking at Hart's broad shoulders. "You here to give me info on a mob story or a sob story? I'm not interested in a sob story. You understand what I'm telling you," I said, standing up from my chair.

After Hart told me that he was not there to give me information about the mob, I ushered him out of my office. I wanted to call Judge Huggins. If Judge Huggins was acting improperly, I was going to make him pay for his indiscretion. But before I jumped to that conclusion, I had to find out if Hart was making up his story about Judge Huggins. I had some other concerns, too. Had Huggins asked Brushman for a favor? Had John set me up to do another "favor"? Was I on the road to becoming the assistant prosecutor who would become the "patsy," dishing out deals for detectives and politicians who would collect their booty later at my expense?

"The college prankster," Judge Huggins responded after I asked if he had instructed Hart to call me. "He's a good kid. I've known him all of his life. The Harts are a nice family. If there is anything you can do to help him, I'd appreciate it. Rehabilitation is as important as punishment in many cases. He has a lot of potential."

"Rehabilitation?" That was the goal I sought as a defense lawyer representing Mary Pittaro, a prostitute, who was charged with abandoning her child who had a heart defect. After I found out that she was just trying to get her five year old boy an operation, I helped her obtain a heart operation which fixed the hole in the child's heart. Listening carefully to what Judge Huggins had said, I could not find that he had done anything improper. He had not asked for anything other than a close look at all of the factors in a case. He was not a judge before whom I would appear in the case, nor did I think there was anything I could do to rehabilitate John Hart.

"I will look carefully into Hart's case, but I can't give you any assurances; there doesn't seem to be anything I can do for Hart. The facts and the nature of the crime seem indisputable," I told Judge Huggins as I tried to perform my prosecutorial duties without violating any ethical rules.

Mario Conti's words resounded in my head. "Always remember the power you have over someone's life. Never hesitate to 'go out of the box' to solve a problem," he had told me the day I began working in the prosecutor's office.

If I was going to give the case a careful look, I wanted to be sure I had used all the leverage that I could. I called Hart back into my office, talked some more, and tried to wring out information that would lead me to a big fish in the stolen car scheme. Hart convinced me he would not be able to entice Avanti into giving up the upper echelon car thieves. Avanti was in New York. He had already been convicted. He had squealed on Hart to get leniency. If Hart had been intimidated by

Avanti, perhaps he had succumbed to pressure that he now regretted and wanted to address. Was there "something outside of the box" that would be appropriate?

"OK, here's what I'm thinking of doing," I began, after I brought Hart back into my office. "I'll put this case in the "C" drawer. That's where we put cases that are pending further investigation. I have five years to indict you so I don't have to rush your case. It's a slam dunk if I do decide to prosecute. And, I hope you know that."

Hart nodded his head in agreement. His eyes were locked on mine.

"Anything I have to do, I'll do," Hart replied. "But I was arrested by the Trenton police on these charges. How can I get rid of the arrest record?" Hart asked.

"I have no control over that. But an arrest without a conviction is explainable and cannot be used against you."

"So what do I have to do?"

"You sit right here. I want to check something out." I fingered the books in the law library until I came to the letter "P." I flipped to the page labeled "Prosecutorial Discretion," and read, "A prosecutor has discretion not to prosecute if the public interest would be served." Examples of decisions not to prosecute had a common theme: when the defendant has been unduly influenced and deviates from usual behavior, a prosecutor has the opportunity to cast a blind eye if the benefit to society outweighs the risks.

Concluding that prosecutorial discretion was not a black and white concept, I was not confident that I had the right to let Hart go without being accountable. I considered the possibility of Hart's pleading guilty and then expunging or erasing his recorded conviction. I thought that would accomplish what I wanted. I side-stepped to the "E" book. Expungement would take at least five years. Afraid that I might not get Brushman's approval, I decided not to discuss the case with him. I was going to take responsibility for the Hart case and call the shots.

"You have to apply to law school, pay back the insurance companies the thirty–three grand they paid out, and graduate within five years," I announced after I returned to my office.

Hart had a puzzled expression. "I haven't applied to law school yet. I didn't think it was worthwhile with all this going on. You think I ought to apply?" he asked.

"Do you have a choice?"

"I guess not," Hart responded. "I have a job in June with an investment firm. I'm going to be making twelve thousand a year. Maybe I can go at night. You know of any night law schools?"

"Seton Hall in Newark. Hofstra in New York," I responded.

"I'll take the law boards, apply to law school, and I'll do it. I promise. I won't disappoint you," Hart cried out.

My eyebrows rose as if to say, "Sure you will." Then, in a serious tone, I said. "As an added incentive, if you do it, I'll get you a judicial clerkship." I even had a judge in mind. His name was Huggins.

Four years later, I received an invitation to Hart's graduation at Hofstra University Law School. "I'll be damned," I said to myself.

A woman answered the telephone number on the response card. Her name was Jennie Hart.

After I told her who I was and congratulated her on her son's achievement, she told me, "He paid back every last penny to the insurance company. All of it. Over thirty thousand. John worked and went to law school at night for three years and every summer. He paid almost a thousand a month with a little help from us. We were so disappointed in our son. He made such a big mistake. He's scared to death, even today, that after three years of law school he won't be able to be a lawyer. He told us about what you did. Thank you. Thank you. Bless you. He was so young."

Judge Huggins answered the telephone.

"Remember the college prankster?" I asked.

"Who?"

"Remember John Hart, the young man who was charged with fraud on the insurance companies?"

"So?" he inquired, trying to sound unsuspecting.

"Judge Huggins, I made a deal with him. He appears to have kept it."

"Mr. Stark, I know about the deal. John has kept me abreast of everything."

"So then, what about a clerkship for him?"

"He's got it," he responded.

I breathed a sigh of relief. The worries I had had about violating legal ethics that had been drilled into my head in law school evaporated. An experienced prosecutor, detective, and judge had exposed me to reality: a decision you make as a lawyer can make or break a life, even your own.

In 1972, I removed the Dr. Castelli and Hart cases from the "C" drawer. The doctor is a respected member of the medical community in Trenton. The law student is an outstanding trial lawyer in Massachusetts.

I had been given the opportunity to take a chance, and I risked it. My experiences with Mary Pittaro, Julius Castelli, and John Hart whetted my appetite for helping people caught in the web of the legal system. The uneasiness I felt vacillating between my responsibilities as an attorney and as a human being still stays with me today. Not crossing the line from ethical to unethical behavior is often difficult, but the challenge of finding a result that is ethical and practical is worth the effort.

# LET'S FIX THE SYSTEM—MY SECOND DEGREE

PROSECUTOR MARIO CONTI, GRAY-HAIRED AND BESPECTACLED, was sitting in shirt sleeves behind a mahogany, Chippendale desk when I obediently responded to his call. "I hear you did good jobs on the Castelli and Hart cases," Conti said as I entered his office. He instructed me to sit down on a leather sofa. "Stark, we are going to see what you're made of. We got this case here. It happened at the State Hospital." He turned toward a man sitting in front of his desk who had the physique of a Paris Island Marine, a square jaw, and an expression that said, "Nobody messes with me." "Meet Frank Hutchinson," Conti said.

Hutch leaned over. I could not tell from his half-smile what he thought of me. Even though I was more confident in Conti's office than I had been the first time I had been invited to see him, I was uneasy. Hutch fingered a thick red file that rested on his lap. "It's gonna be a bitch. Here's what happened. Hunter, an asshole of an attendant at the loony bin, killed this patient, an old, helpless man. Jimmy Byrd was his name. I know Hunter killed him. But you know what? I gotta prove it. And you know what? Nobody here, except me, gives a shit. Who the fuck cares about some poor old geezer who's nuts? It's just one less the taxpayer has to pay for. I care about these poor fuckers. Christ, one of 'em could be your own mother, or, God forbid, one of your kids." A former Trenton cop, Hutch boasted about the time he gave the mayor a parking ticket. "Fuck, I even gave one to myself when, like an asshole, I ran a stop sign and hit a lady with my cop car." While Hutch continued to discuss the case, I remembered that I knew something about that hospital; it was something my mother told me.

Teasingly, she used to tell me that if I did not stop driving her crazy, she would end up in the nut house. The nut house was the New Jersey State Hospital, an asylum for the insane, located a few miles from our home in Trenton.

Driving together, my mother took her right hand from the steering wheel and pointed toward the somber buildings we were passing. "The nuts in there," she continued, "are crazy in the head and they are cooped up like dogs. They bark, but they can't run around like you and me."

"Come on mom, they're not dogs."

"Right, Albert, not dogs. Underdogs," my mother exclaimed.

That is how I was introduced to the State Hospital when I was nine. For many years we often passed the monolithic buildings that sat on a hill on Sullivan Way as we went out of town. They were reminders of something I did not understand. I knew only that something bad happened in there. When my mother was exasperated, she would say sarcastically, "Either you're going to drive me to drink, and I'll end up in the insane asylum, or I'm going to hit you on the head and knock your brains out." Neither alternative sounded too good to me.

As a teenager, I caddied at an exclusive country club golf course located across the road from the State Hospital. Walking up the sixth fairway, I would hear screams and moans coming from open windows, and every so often, I would catch a glimpse of a gaunt face gazing out.

In 1956, during my first semester at Dartmouth College, I took a required psychology course. Fascinated with the fantasies and delusions described in the case studies, I chose to do a paper on schizophrenia during my winter break. Schizoids sounded extreme to me, and I was always fascinated by extremes. Because I was a good student, my professor, Doctor Philip Brown, helped me arrange to visit the wards at the State Hospital.

On a gray, winter day, a psychiatrist, Doctor James Tobin, using a chart to diagram the ego, id, subconscious, and the superego, explained why people were schizophrenic and described three different types of schizophrenics: the manic-depressive, the catatonic, and the narcoleptic.

Doctor Tobin believed that mental illness was based on the chemical makeup of the brain. He was certain that schizophrenia was in part a physiological illness of the brain, not a psychological problem. He believed that psychiatrists who tried to analyze such a patient often ended up doing great damage.

He led me through corridors with yellow-tiled walls, brown linoleum floors, and faded white ceilings that were lit with incandescent light bulbs encased in wire mesh. We went into the ward where insulin shock and electroshock therapy were being administered. The environment was so dismal that I asked, "How can society put anyone in here and hope they can get better?"

When Doctor Tobin shrugged, I did not know if he was expressing cynicism or frustration. Then, he opened a door in front of us and motioned for me to go through. In front of me, I saw Peter Angelini, a boy who had sat next to me in my tenth grade homeroom at Trenton High School. Instead of the friendly, smiling Peter that I had remembered, a young man sat rigidly in a catatonic state. He wore a white gown that resembled an apron. His eyes stared into space. I turned to see what he was looking at. There was only a blank wall. I caught his eye and he blinked back. Otherwise, he did not move.

The smell of perspiration in the warm, unventilated building was putrid. The moans, screams, and ranting patients, clad in dull robes and shirts, presented a scene that overloaded my sensibilities. One middle-aged man in diapers, who looked like Jesus Christ, stalked about the ward, pounding his chest with his thin hands and clenching his fists. He professed that he was the Lord and that he had been sent to lead us to eternity.

Inside the Treatment Room, men and women, tied to padded wooden beds, were hooked up to wires. Their arms and legs twitched when electric current passed through their bodies. "According to the 'theory,' they are being relieved of their memory of painful situations and frustrations," Doctor Tobin chuckled. He was cynical, just like my professor. I could picture their shared interests.

Another section of the treatment room was reserved for patients being given insulin. They were strapped down to the hard, thinly padded beds that looked like examining tables in a doctor's office. Rubber hoses were inserted in their noses. The smell was so sweet that I tasted vomit rising in the back of my throat.

After my visit to the State Hospital, I was conscious of the importance that environment played in keeping people from needing hospital treatment. I felt that society's rules and the pain of trying to belong was a frequent contributor to driving people to drink or insanity. I had a desire to change conditions in mental hospitals, but I did not know where to begin.

Hutch coughed. His tough tone changed dramatically to that of an understanding school teacher after we were settled in his office. "We're going to do this as a team," he assured me. "You just listen to me. I've been around. I know people. We're gonna put William Hunter behind bars. It ain't gonna be easy. There's a cover up going on over there at the nut house. Justice is my job, and I'm damn good at it. I don't give a fuck who this ends up hurting, even if it's the superintendent of the hospital."

Filled with fear and dreading a foray into court, I took a deep breath before I asked Hutch, "What's the defense look like?" I hoped that by remembering what Ernest Glickman asked me when I explained my first criminal case. I would impress Hutch.

"That the dead patient, Byrd, Jimmy Byrd, fell and hit his head," Hutch said, shaking his head incredulously.

I had learned that after I established what I had to prove, I had to figure out what the defense to the charge was going to be. That was not always easy. The defense did not have to release its information to the prosecutor because a defendant was innocent until proven guilty.

"How do you know Hunter was the killer? Any other witnesses?" I inquired.

"Good question, Stark. Some other patients 'fessed up' that it was Hunter who hit Byrd and then pulled him off a chair. He left the poor guy on the floor to die," Hutch replied. I was not sure from Hutch's expression whether his remark was one of admiration or whether he was merely being patronizing.

"Who's going to believe the patients? They're insane, aren't they?

Otherwise they wouldn't be there? Right?" An uncomfortable silence made me ask why Hutch had not thought of that.

"And there are some employees who have told the administration at the hospital that Hunter was the only one in the ward during the time when Byrd was found dead on the floor," Hutch added. "Look here." Hutch pointed to autopsy photos, the first I had ever seen. My stomach flipped. "See these marks on the chest. That's a blow. That's a fist mark. Hunter was in charge of the ward. Byrd was a pathetic schizophrenic confined to a hospital. He was supposed to be tied to his chair all day for his own safety. He was delusional. So how could he fall to the floor? What Hunter told the investigators for the hospital administration was that he was trying to pick him up from the chair. He claimed that he had one hand on his back and the other hand on his chest, and as he lifted him, Byrd fell. Hunter's a fucking liar. Where did this fist mark come from?"

I always was intrigued by puzzles. I wanted to find out.

Hutch told me Hunter had been assigned not just one lawyer but two: Richard Ross and Lionel Mann. He explained that murder cases against indigents, people who could not afford lawyers, or state workers, like Hunter, were usually assigned to lawyers to whom politicians owed a favor. The fees for defending murder cases were not very good since the state's budget for indigent work was small. The patronage lawyers usually padded their bills. No one in the court system ever reviewed them to see if they were accurate because the "padding" would just later be used to contribute to election campaigns. Ross and Mann were powerful political lawyers. Ross was a black accountant who specialized in real estate tax appeals and estates, and Mann was a real estate broker who became a lawyer when he was in his forties. Neither, Hutch said, had any extensive criminal trial experience, so I did not have to be concerned about my inexperience.

Reflecting on the day about ten years before when I saw my friend Peter Angelini in that ward, I asked myself, "What if that happened to Peter?" What must Jimmy Byrd's family be feeling? They had trusted the state with his care. Scenes from *One Flew Over the Cuckoo Nest* floated around my head.

I arranged a meeting with Ross and Mann. They told me that they believed their client was innocent, because even if he did overreact and hit Jimmy Byrd, he did not intend for him to die. They questioned why their client should have his life ruined because he overreacted in an ugly, pressure-packed environment that was understaffed with incompetent people.

Hutch and I discussed the evidence and agreed that Hunter probably did not intend to kill Byrd. We determined that he was reckless and used too much force on a frail old man. "Byrd was left alone on the floor," Hutch argued. "The bastard should have given him medical attention once he saw that he was injured. If he hadn't hightailed it out of the ward, Byrd would be alive today."

"Second degree murder is something you can prove," Hutch counseled. "But you don't have a chance in a million to win a first degree conviction. Stark, let me show you how good a guy I am. Offer 'em manslaughter. Let's save the state some money that a trial'll cost, and we'll give the poor bastard the benefit of the doubt. What do ya think?"

"Tell you the truth, I think Hunter deserves second degree," I stuttered. Second degree would bring a sentence of thirty years, with parole available after twenty years. Manslaughter was a minimum of five years and maximum of twenty years in jail.

"Offer 'em manslaughter. Call 'em and give 'em forty-eight hours. Fair enough?"

I had mixed feelings when the manslaughter plea was rejected. Although I felt Hunter deserved the second degree, I was intimidated by the thoughts of going to court, even though Ross and Mann were not experienced criminal lawyers and Hutch was sure that we would win.

A few days later, as I prepared a witness at the State Hospital, an attendant approached me and told me that Hunter had confessed to him the day after Byrd was found dead that he had punched Byrd because he would not get out of his "fucking chair." The attendant refused to give me a written statement, which he had the right to do, and insisted that he would not testify under oath, because he could be the victim of revenge by his fellow coworkers. He was worried that his life would be made miserable by the hospital administration, which did not want the case to lead to bad publicity. He informed me the administrators were standing behind Hunter and that was it. I passed on the information to Hutch and suggested that, because I had the right to subpoena the attendant, I should use my power to bring out the truth. Hutch poo pooed my idea, telling me his experience had taught him that an uncooperative witness would most likely hurt my case. I accepted his argument.

As the day of trial was approaching, I was looking at the autopsy photos. They were normal 5x7 prints from a still camera. The fist mark looked like a black-and-blue mark; however, it was an odd looking black-and-blue mark, because it was a line and not a circle. I wondered why Hutch had not picked up on that before. I rang Hutch's telephone. Hutch answered. "Hey, Hutch," I said. "I got an idea. You have a minute? Can I come over and see you?"

Excitedly, I passed the photo to Hutch as soon as I entered his office. "Hutch, look at this mark. See something odd?"

"Seen a million of these. A blunt hit by a fist. Nothing special," he said.

"Hutch, this looks like a line. It's not round. I wonder what it would show if I blew it up to life-size. I would bet my week's pay that it would show knuckle marks. And I bet next week's pay that they would match Hunter's knuckles."

Hutch looked at me. "Let me take another look at that." He looked at it very closely. Without responding to me, he picked up the phone, called the head of the photo lab, and asked if a 5x7 could be enlarged to life-size. "Shit." said Hutch, and he hung up. "Can't be done. We don't have the equipment here."

"But Hutch," I exclaimed. "How am I going to prove Hunter did it?"

"I think I can get that attendant to sing. I won't let you down. But good thinking, though." Hutch smiled confidently as he headed out the door. He threw on his jacket and grabbed his car keys.

I thought about why Hutch rejected my ideas. Was his ego too big to give me any credit? Was I too intimidated to stand up to Hutch?

Was I afraid to pursue my ideas, because I was afraid that I would look foolish?

As the trial approached, I got word that the defense was trying to get the hospital employees to recant their statements claiming that Hunter was the only attendant in the area of the ward at the time Byrd died. The witnesses were hospital employees who, while they did not see "anything," knew that Hunter was in the ward at the time. I relayed the information to Hutch who said, "Somebody's bullshitting you."

When I told Mario Conti how nervous I was to go to court, he gave me a book by Rothbard about how to try a criminal case. I went into the bathroom, looked in the mirror, fixed my tie, and wiped my forehead with a damp paper towel. I nervously walked into the courtroom. When our case was called for trial and jury selection began, the two political lawyers sat with their client who was dressed neatly in a crisply pressed suit, shined shoes, and an ivory white shirt and dark blue tie. The book by a famous criminal trial lawyer had a chapter about picking a jury, and a process called "voir dire," French words meaning "to speak the truth." During voir dire, lawyers have the opportunity to ask the jurors questions about what they know of the case, or if they had read or heard about it in the media. The purpose of the questioning is to find out if any of the jurors are prejudiced against the state or the defendant. I memorized the name of each juror. When I addressed them as "Mister" or "Miss" or "Misses" as appropriate, the defense lawyers went nuts and objected to my tactic. After the judge overruled them, I took control of the courtroom just as Rothbard wrote I would. I felt strong, and I thought the jurors liked the confidence I displayed.

After the jury was selected, I stood in front of the jury box. The courtroom felt warm. My knees felt rubbery as I began my opening statement, which I had written out. I glanced at the judge and said, "Your Honor." He looked bored. I turned to the jurors. "Ladies and Gentlemen of the Jury," facing twelve people with blank expressions. Comparing the case to an enigma, just as the book had advised, I confidently said, "You will find that this case is like a puzzle. Throughout this trial, you will be provided with pieces of the puzzle, and it is your job to put them together." I delivered an opening statement, outlining that I would prove that William Hunter was an attendant responsible for the welfare of Jimmy Byrd and that he did not fulfill his responsibility. I told the jury that I would present facts that would show that Hunter alone had the opportunity to injure Byrd and leave him lying on the floor of a ward to die. "All the pieces, ladies and gentlemen of the jury," I declared, "Will come together to form a picture. This picture will show that William Hunter is guilty beyond a reasonable doubt."

Lionel Mann gave an impassioned opening, raising and lowering his voice, waving his hands, arguing that the prosecutor had the burden to prove guilt beyond a reasonable doubt. He told the jury that Hunter was clothed with the cloak of innocence, which the evidence in this case would not be able to remove. He assured them that at the end of the testimony the jury would see that the prosecutor would not be able to keep his promise about what he told them he would prove. I started to sweat.

The judge leaned over his bench and asked, "Mr. Stark, are you ready for your first witness?"

"We are not prepared to begin this morning, Your Honor. Our witnesses are at the State Hospital. Jury selection took a lot less time than I anticipated. I did not know if we would be reaching them today so I tried to save the state the time and expense of having patients and staff wait in the hallway of the Courthouse." Scared, I sat down, waiting to be chastised by a judge who had a reputation for running a tight ship.

"Very considerate of you, Mr. Prosecutor. Given the sensitivity of this case, I understand perfectly." The judge smiled at the jury. Hutch turned toward me and winked. I was relieved.

"All rise," the bailiff yelled. "The Superior Court of the State of New Jersey is now in recess until nine-thirty in the forenoon tomorrow."

Hutch and I rose from our chairs. Mann and Ross were whispering something to each other. They turned toward us. "See you tomorrow morning, gentlemen."

Hutch put his hand on my shoulder forcefully. "Let them go. I have to talk to you about somethin.'"

"What's up?" I asked.

In a hushed tone, Hutch said, "Got word that those two are planning to meet the employees on our witness list outside the hospital tonight at eleven. That's when their shift is over."

"That's goddamn illegal! They can't do that. They could get disbarred and lose their license. Why would they do that for a guy like Hunter? What the hell are we going to do? Without those witnesses my case sinks."

"What do you mean, what do we do? That's simple. We're at the door of the hospital at eleven, and we give them a surprise welcome."

Hutch, unbeknownst to me, had assigned detectives to follow the defense lawyers. While they chomped on steaks at Lorenzo's Cafe, the detectives would hear of any plans to interview witnesses that night.

At Lorenzo's, where anyone who was anyone in New Jersey politics sipped martinis, manhattans, and good scotch, the detectives sat at the bar peering into the mirror behind the late nineteenth-century mahogany bar, spying on defense counsel.

After I closed the courtroom door behind us, I looked around the hallway and saw no one. "Hutch," I said. "Remember the autopsy photos? I took them to a professional and got them blown up to life-size. Hutch, it shows f . . . . ing knuckle marks. Four of them. And a thumb print. From a right hand. Just where Byrd, sitting in a chair, would be hit by a guy standing in front of him. Remember my bet. I'm going to collect. If those guys get to our witnesses, I'll show that Hunter's knuckles match the black and blue mark, " I said excitedly.

" Fat chance. You ever hear of the Fifth?" Hutch snapped. His lips were pursed. His cheekbones vibrated. "And besides, why the hell didn't you tell me about it? That's not our deal."

"Truthfully. I was afraid. You know I am duty bound to turn over any exculpatory evidence, and I was afraid that if the knuckle and handprints didn't fit that I would have to dismiss the case. I know that they fit. You know how? This morning, when Hunter was sitting at the counsel table, I watched him as he pushed himself up from his chair. I waited. I walked over to the table and looked at his knuckle marks left on the table. His imprints are in the wax. When I went back to my office, I got the negative of the life-size and took it to the courtroom and put it over his imprints. They match exactly." I was breathing heavily as I spoke, not knowing how Hutch was going to react. He had not been impressed with my idea of the blowing up the photograph before.

He looked me in the eye. "You son of a bitch," he said with a whimsical smile. "Bruise marks are like fingerprints. Once a guy is dead they are there for life." He raised his right hand. I raised my right hand, and I can still remember the loud clap of the high-five he gave me.

Hutch and I picked up some ribs and chicken wings for dinner at Bud's Barbecue on Prospect Street. "We're goin' to go home and dress up in black," Hutch informed me. "We're gonna meet at the point. You know the point?" It was where Sanhican and State Street met, just about five blocks from where I had grown up in the western section of Trenton.

When I got home, Ellen was reading on the couch.

"How'd it go today in court?" she asked as I entered the apartment.

"Can't talk now. Got to meet Hutch. We're going to work tonight," I responded as I went into our bedroom. When I came out dressed entirely in black, Ellen was in the kitchen cooking.

"What's this outfit all about?" she asked.

"We'll talk about it later. Hutch has set a trap for the defense lawyers. They're trying to intimidate some of my witnesses," I said as I hurriedly left the apartment. "Don't worry. Everything's all right. I'll be back later. I'll be with Hutch. Working on the case."

At the point, Hutch was waiting for me. He threw his lit cigarette onto the sidewalk and stamped it out. He opened the passenger door of his car and told me to get in. When he was behind the steering wheel, he filled me in on his plan. He and I would drive over to the country club across the street from the hospital. By walking across the golf course and up the hill to the hospital, we would avoid the gate to the hospital in case the administration was in on the meeting that the defense lawyers had arranged. Hiding behind a hedge that lined the driveway, we would be able to see the defense lawyers driving through the gate. We knew that the defense lawyers had vintage license plates. One was LEM 1 and the other RRR1.

When the employees exited, I would approach them, introduce myself and thank them for agreeing to come to court in the morning and ask if they had any questions. If the defense lawyers got to them first, I would just walk over to them and say, "Greetings, gentlemen," and Hutch would take care of the rest. I was permitted to approach the witnesses legally, but it was improper for the defense lawyers to attempt to discourage them from testifying.

In Hutch's unmarked car, we proceeded to the parking lot at the county club. When the lawyers' cars arrived just before eleven, I was surprised. They parked just outside the exit door to the ward, blocking our view. Neither Ross or Mann got out of their cars. Hutch put his hand forcefully on my shoulder. He whispered to me. "You just stay here. It's mine now." I remained crouched behind a hedge. The exit door opened. Employees began to leave. Suddenly, the lawyer who was in the driver's seat of LEM 1 opened the door and began to yell, "Sammy, Sammy." He jumped out of the car and began running to catch a black man who was talking to a woman. The black man turned, but continued to walk. "Sammy, it's lawyer Lionel Mann, Billie Hunter's lawyer." The black man hesitated, but then continued walking. The lawyer picked up his pace, looking back. Ross had gotten out of his car and was running to catch up. All of a sudden, Hutch leaped over the hedge and put on a high-powered flashlight. "Is that you, Richard Ross? Is that you, Lionel Mann?" Hutch yelled. The two lawyers froze in their tracks as Hutch shined his light first at one and then the other.

Hutch walked slowly toward Lionel. "Gentlemen," he said, "Fancy meeting you here at this time of the evening. Working after hours, are you? Billing by the hour, of course. I'm looking forward to reading your billing records after the case is over. Good night, gentlemen." Hutch turned and walked over to the lawyers' cars. He took out a small camera and first took a picture of the license plates and then took a picture of the exit door from the ward.

The black man got into a car and pulled out of the hospital driveway. Hutch walked around the hedge and stood watching the two lawyers walk back to their cars and pull away. "Time to go home to the family," Hutch said as he returned to where I was standing. I gave him a high-five. He grabbed my arm and guided me back to the golf course. I saw the lighted country club parking lot in the distance.

When we got to the point he turned toward me. "All in a day's work. Tough day in the courthouse tomorrow. Get a good night's sleep." His chiseled face was a silhouette in the dull light from the interior of the car.

Early the next morning, I went to my office, took the life-size photograph out of the closet in which I had stored it for security reasons, and looked at the image of Jimmy Byrd, lying on a cold autopsy table. I wondered what Jimmy Byrd would think if he knew he was the subject of so much fuss and emotion. "If only I knew more about this man?" But, for the time being, I didn't know anything about him or his family, so I focused my angst at Ross and Mann. I also wanted to win my first felony case.

Should I bring the photo into the courtroom? Or ask Hutch to get it at an opportune time?

Shortly after nine-thirty, the judge took the bench and the testimony began. My first witness was a patient who could hardly speak or respond to my questions.

"Do you know this man?" I asked, standing behind William Hunter. He nodded affirmatively.

Ross and Mann followed me to the foot of the judge's bench. From my inside coat pocket I pulled an autopsy photograph. "May I have a few minutes to retrieve a blowup?" I asked.

The judge looked at the photo and asked me what I was going to do with it.

"I am going to ask the witness if he saw the person in the photo struck and, if so, by whom."

The judge instructed me not to use any life-size photos since they would be too inflammatory, but did allow me to show the small 5x7 print to the witness. My stomach fell to the floor since I anticipated that the judge's ruling would preclude me from showing the life-sized photo later and matching the knuckle and thumb print to William Hunter.

I questioned three patients and each of them identified William Hunter and Jimmy Byrd and motioned with their hand how Jimmy Byrd was lifted and struck by William Hunter. Would the jurors believe these insane witnesses? I looked at the jurors. Their faces were expressionless. Clearly I could not rely on them alone.

My next witnesses were Sammy and Mike, two attendants who had given statements that William Hunter was responsible for the ward in which Byrd was a patient. They also said that they saw William Hunter enter and leave the ward that night. I planned to explore whether they had had any conversations with William Hunter after Byrd was found. Both Sammy and Mike denied having any conversations with Hunter. They looked at William Hunter and his lawyers. Ross and Mann looked at each other and smiled Ross and Mann had spoken to Sammy and Mike prior to the trial. After Sammy and Mike testified, they walked from the witness stand. Hunter nodded to them. His two lawyers began to whisper to one another. Ross and Mann were not paying attention to me when I called out the name of my next witness, "William Hunter."

Mann jumped to his feet. "Objection, Your Honor. Wait a minute. The prosecution cannot call a defendant to the stand. A defendant has the right to remain silent."

"Mr. Prosecutor. The defense is absolutely correct. You cannot call the defendant to the witness stand. A defendant is innocent until proven guilty. There is no confession in this case, is there? I have not been told of one at any rate. Mr. Prosecutor, you should know better. I am not going to permit you to call the defendant. If he wishes to testify on his own behalf, he may do so. Mr. Hunter, you may be seated. Mr. Prosecutor, do you have any more evidence to present?"

"No, Your Honor. I apologize to the Court, the defense counsel, and Mr. Hunter for my mistake," I said. I knew that the judge was not going to let me put the life-size photo into evidence in my case. There is no more evidence to be presented by the State at this time."

"Then the State rests?" the judge asked.

"Yes, Your Honor," I replied and turned toward Hutch. I expected him to be staring at me in disgust. Instead, he was smiling.

"Is the defense ready to proceed?" the judge inquired.

"May we have a few minutes recess?" Lionel Mann inquired.

"Yes, Counsel. The Court will go into recess." Turning toward the jury, the judge explained, "The State's case has been presented. The defendant is innocent until proven guilty, which means that the defendant is innocent until all of the evidence is presented. The defendant has the right to present evidence. If the defendant chooses not to present evidence or to testify, that failure to either present evidence or testify cannot be used against him." The judge asked the bailiff to provide coffee and tea for the jurors and ordered a thirty-minute recess.

Hutch's hand was on my shoulder, a cue not to get up. Ross, Mann and William Hunter walked out.

"You sure put it to them," Hutch said to me after they left.

"What are you talking about? I looked like a jerk off," I said.

"Uh, uh. They have to put ol' Willie on the stand now. He was identified. The jurors want to hear from him. He can't risk the jurors believing the loonies. And he is confident that he can sway them his way. Look how he is dressed today. See the gold cuff links on his shirt sleeve. He's ready. He's not going to let ol' Lionel and Dickie boy take away his day in the sun. And guess what . . . those boys are appointed. They're not experienced enough to have the balls to convince him not to take the stand. If they don't call him to the stand and he loses, Hunter will appeal on the grounds that he had incompetent counsel. That's the last thing these political lawyers want." Hutch paused. "Guess what. Time for the blowup. Either the knuckles fit along with the thumb, or we'll all be saying 'Gee you're dumb,'" Hutch said teasingly.

"Come on. I only bet a week's pay," I responded, knowing the knuckles and the thumb would fit perfectly. Hutch gave me his familiar wink when I asked him if Hunter would take the stand.

I nervously waited in the empty courtroom. The door next to the jurors' box opened. The bailiff looked in, saw me, and smiled. I smiled meekly back. He looked at his watch, and said "The judge is ready."

The rear door of the courtroom opened. Hutch walked past the six or seven rows of benches where the regular observers–retired men and disheveled bums—spent their idle hours. Hutch was not carrying the life-size photo. When he approached me I leaned forward. "Where's the life-size?" I asked.

"Who do you think I am? A magician who shows his secrets? Give me a break? You think I have an IQ of 50?"

"What the hell are you talking about? I need the life-size when Hunter gets on the stand."

"If they saw the life-size in this courtroom, the chances that Hunter would take the stand are minus zero plus infinity," Hutch exclaimed.

"You're a goddamned genius," I told him.

Hunter came in with his lawyers. They were talking. Ross went up to the clerk's desk and looked at the 5x7 photo of Jimmie Byrd. Hutch sat poker-faced.

Court reconvened. Hunter took the stand. Hutch was right.

"Mr. Hunter," the judge said. Startled, Hunter turned toward him.

"Mr. Hunter, you have the right to remain silent. Before you testify, I want you to know that the United States Constitution has a Fifth Amendment. You are presumed innocent until proven guilty beyond a reasonable doubt. Do you understand me?"

Hunter eyed his lawyers. They nodded.

"Yes, Sir," Hunter replied.

"Do you wish to testify?" the judge inquired.

"Our client will testify," Lionel Mann said emphatically.

Hunter mouthed everything that his lawyers had said in the opening statement and denied hitting Byrd. He testified that he had unstrapped Byrd from his chair and lifted him up into a standing position. He showed the jury how he had his left hand on Byrd's back and his right hand in an open position on his chest, palm toward the chest. As he lifted him up, Byrd fell to the ground. He said he left the area to get help and could not find any. When he returned to the ward about a half-hour later, Byrd had no pulse. On the way back from the medical unit someone stopped him and told him that one of his patients had been found dead.

Hunter's lawyers finished their direct examination. Hutch turned to me.

"Where's the blowup?" I asked.

He leaned over and whispered in my ear. "Ask for a few minutes to prepare your cross examination. The judge will give it to you. It's regular procedure."

"Your Honor, may I have a few moments to prepare my cross examination?" I asked.

"Certainly, Mr. Prosecutor. I see very well that you need it." The judge smiled at the defense lawyers. A few jurors looked at each other. "How long will you need, Mr. Prosecutor?"

Hutch raised five fingers.

"Five minutes, Your Honor."

Hutch rose and left the courtroom in a hurry. Everyone watched him leave.

In a few minutes, Hutch returned carrying a life-sized photo of Jimmy Byrd.

"What have you got there?" Mann and Ross asked excitedly. Hutch turned the photo toward them and continued walking toward me.

"What are you going to do with that?" Richard Ross asked.

"You wait and see," I replied.

"I think we better get the judge," Ross said, hoping to stop my next move.

Ross called over the bailiff and instructed him to get the judge, which he did with haste.

"Gentlemen," the judge said after he entered from a door behind his high-backed chair, "the bailiff advised that you need to speak with me."

Ross, Mann, and I stood next to each other and said, "We do, Your Honor."

"Your Honor, I am going to show that the knuckle marks and thumb marks match those of the defendant. I will disprove the defendant's testimony that his right hand was palm side up to Jimmy Byrd's chest. The life-sized photo will show the jury that William Hunter made a fist with his right hand. Then he directed it to the chest of Jimmy Byrd. The knuckle marks and thumb mark will line up perfectly. Had William Hunter put his hand on Byrd's chest with the palm facing the chest, then the finger marks and thumb marks would be different. There will be no controversy over how Jimmy Byrd died or that William Hunter was the last person to touch him before he died."

The judge looked at the defense lawyers and asked, "Well, gentleman. How do you respond to the proffer of proof by Mr. Stark?"

Ross argued it would be prejudicial and inflammatory for me to use a life-sized photo of an autopsy. When the judge rejected the argument, saying that the probabilities that the photo might reveal truth may outweigh the possible prejudice, Mann took up the fight.

"Counsel," the judge interrupted, "you are well aware that while the jury is the God of the facts, and while it is their duty to find which facts are probably true and which are not, I am the God of the law in this courtroom. The rules of evidence are very clear. If there is a question as to admissibility of evidence, I can hear what the prosecutor seeks to prove out of the presence of the jury. If I think it is probative and will help the jury find the truth, without being unfairly prejudicial, I will permit the jury to hear the prosecutor's evidence. A little extra time spent now will not hurt anyone."

The faces of Hunter's lawyers reflected their disappointment.

During the demonstration, I took Hunter's hand and lifted it toward the blowup. I turned his hand slowly. The judge had a clear view of the black and blue marks. Slowly I placed Hunter's knuckles and thumb on the black and blue marks. They matched perfectly.

The judge ruled that the demonstration was proper. After the jurors reentered the courtroom, I repeated the demonstration. I put the life-sized photo of Jimmy Byrd on an easel and asked William Hunter to come forward. The jurors were on the edge of their seats as they watched me put William Hunter's fist on Jimmy Byrd's chest.

Second degree murder was the verdict. I was elated, but also exhausted. I looked over at Lionel Mann and Richard Ross. I saw two lawyers who were wiped out from the stresses of the adversary system, which I thought had unfortunately brought out some of the worst in them. Their behavior made me feel that I could not always trust fellow members of the bar or the people who ran our public institutions.

Alone in the courtroom, I fell into Hutch's outstretched arms. "We showed the bastards, didn't we?" he whispered. I saw the bailiff behind him, smiling.

"Thanks, Hutch," I said. "You taught me a lot about teamwork. You really fight for what you believe." I felt his gentle squeeze." Victory was thrilling. Putting together a puzzle had been fun. But what had it accomplished? Mario Conti knew the State Hospital would not change.

Otherwise, he would have involved the administrators. Deep down, perhaps he wanted me to lose. Why else would he have assigned me to the case? If I lost, he would have won the favor of those in power. No one could bring Jimmy Byrd back to life. But who cared other than Hutch and me?

A few weeks later, I saw Ross and Mann eating at Lorenzo's. I tried to avoid them, but could not help seeing Ross waving to me. I sauntered up to their table.

"You can talk to us. We fought you in the courtroom. But outside we're friends," Mann said. "Sit down, let's talk."

"We know you're angry at us," Mann began. "You think you can save the world and do justice. So did we when we were younger."

"I fought for what I believed. So did Hutch," I said.

"So did we," Ross replied.

"That's right. We thought that Hunter shouldn't have taken the fall for the boys in the front office. You should have been trying them," Mann interjected.

"As lawyers we don't always have the luxury of representing our own values. We were assigned to represent him. We didn't believe what he did was right. Not by a long shot. But we had a job to do. It was the system that made him do what he did," Ross added.

I felt like I had been hit over the head. I heard my mother's words about how an environment can effect someone's behavior.

"Thanks for calling me over. I feel better having heard your side of the story. Someday I'd like to talk to you about the night we met at the hospital."

"So would I," Mann snapped. "I didn't appreciate being spied on by your detectives."

On my drive home that evening, I was not as anxious to try my next case as I was to try to fix the system. When I had walked out of law school, I was confident that I knew what I wanted to do and had an enthusiastic attitude. When I arrived at the prosecutor's office the next morning, I had it again.

# A SENSE OF SOCIAL JUSTICE—I
# RESIGN

RENNIE DAVIS, ABBIE HOFFMAN, AND DAVID DELLINGER, who were later to become part of the Chicago Seven and would be charged with the federal crimes of crossing state lines to incite a riot, delivered anti-establishment speeches at an Unbirthday Party for Lyndon B. Johnson to celebrate the president's decision not to run for reelection in 1968. Their views jived with mine and Ellen's. They argued that the American soldiers' involvement in Vietnam was futile. They discredited the Humphreyites who preached that the so-called domino effect would lead to the spread of Communism throughout Southeast Asia. They accused Secretary of Defense Robert McNamara of using the war to test his mobile army.

We had felt frustrated and helpless after Martin Luther King was assassinated in March of 1968. The shock of seeing Bobby Kennedy murdered in front of our eyes in June added to our angst. When we watched Russian soldiers drive tanks over Czechs in Prague to snuff out a revolution against communism, we were mortified.

Ellen strummed her guitar and sang along with Phil Ochs, Arlo Guthrie, and Peter, Paul, and Mary as they entertained anti-war protesters in Chicago's Grant Park.

Charismatic Bobby Seale, the chairman of the Black Panthers, passionately encouraged people to defend themselves by any means necessary if attacked by the police after the concert.

Ellen's outrage toward the Vietnam War reached its boiling point during the police attack on that Wednesday evening, the last week in

August of 1968 when, during a commercial break, I went into the kitchen to pour some cold drinks and dish out some ice cream. "Look, honey, they're dragging people. They're kicking them. They are going to make Rennie Davises out of all of them, " she exclaimed. She was alluding to an incident the day before when the Chicago police, seeking retribution for an anti-establishment speech Rennie Davis had delivered to a cheering crowd in a Chicago park, had kicked the anti-war advocate until he was unconscious. Davis had said that unless the delegates at the Democratic National Convention were willing to go to Vietnam to see what was going on and not let their sons evade the draft, they should be jailed for murdering innocent Americans and Vietnamese.

Leaving the ice cream container on the counter, I scampered back to the sofa. The veins in Ellen's neck were ready to explode. "It's horrible. I know that. But calm down. Calm down. I know how you feel," I said after a few moments of watching uniformed policemen, wearing gas masks and holding plastic shields with one hand, beat demonstrators and bystanders with clubs held in the other hand. Tear gas canisters were being tossed into a crowd. Black mace guns were pointed at anyone close to a cop.

I also knew that Ellen was thinking about Everett Covington, a close friend who had been killed. during the race riots in the summer of 1967 while running from a policeman who falsely alleged Everett had "drawn a gun on him."

"What do you mean, 'calm down'? What you do mean 'you know how I feel'? Aren't you outraged?" she asked. "Just look. Just look." Ellen's glare was sharp and piercing. "Why can't you cry? Dammit. Are you becoming just like them?" she continued, abruptly turning toward the television and pointing to the screen. "Are you one of those male chauvinist pigs? Dammit. Cry. Yell. Dammit. Cry. Show me you feel something. I'm your wife. I'm not one of those cops you have to kiss ass to every day." She wheeled around, her brow creased, her eyes glassy, her nose red and running.

To escape her anger, I looked away from her and toward the television. Ellen jumped up, crying out frantically, "Can you believe this? Can you believe it? Those male chauvinist pigs. I want to kill them. Every last one of them."

Nothing I said could make things any better. If I appeased her, she would probably ask me why I was a prosecutor and not out there with them.

I thought of Henry Thoreau's response to Ralph Waldo Emerson when Emerson visited him at Walden Pond. Thoreau, an advocate of civil disobedience against the tyranny in Boston, was inside his cabin. "What are you doing in there? Emerson asked. "Ralph, what are you doing out there?" Thoreau replied.

I began to feel mad. I suddenly felt "out there," isolated from Ellen, wondering if I still had any beliefs of my own. "I've had enough. Let's call it a night. OK?"

"Oh no. I'm not going to let you off that easy," Ellen said forcefully.

"You're tough," I remarked.

"Maybe so, but when I married you I thought I was marrying someone who was for the real people, spelled with a small 'p'. I don't want to lose that person. You understand," Ellen said. "Call it a night? Uh. Uh. You can argue in the courtroom. But when it comes to your feelings, oh no, you can't confront them. How could you watch what has gone on tonight and go to work tomorrow with a clear conscience? You're going to let King and Kennedy die in vain? And let Eugene McCarthy stand out there alone? And let more guys die in the jungle? And protesters being run over by tanks? Where are you, my husband?"

I could not reply to Ellen.

"Have you forgotten why you went to Selma or Tuscaloosa?" I had gone south to register voters during the Christmas recess in 1957. When I boarded a bus in Trenton, my father had said, "I never thought my son would become a Communist."

I had told Ellen how, at a synagogue in Selma, a girl my age urged me to go home. "You can live with integration up north," she had said. "We like it just the way it is here."

"You tell me police twist their stories. But what are you doing do to get rid of the cops who lie? Not a goddamn thing. After you won the State Hospital case, you were going to try to fix the system. What happened? You like it the way it is. You like getting your name in the paper. You like not being your father's son. You're just as caught up in winning as Johnson and Daley."

"Of course, I'm upset," I finally replied, "But what can I do? I didn't incite a riot. Why can't they get what they want through the courts? Look, we got Brown versus the Board of Education through the courts," I responded.

"And it took the president and federal marshals to get those kids into school in Little Rock, didn't it?" Ellen snapped back.

"It sure did. So where would we be without law enforcement?" I responded, sounding like a lawyer countering the argument of the adversary.

"Now I see why you're so good in court. You have a quick answer to everything. But is that really how you feel? I hope not. Maybe we should call it a night," Ellen conceded.

"You're right. This conversation is going nowhere fast."

All night I tossed and turned. Images of the Chicago police beating people, leaving them prostrate on the streets, and dragging them off to jail raced around my head. I woke up the next morning feeling like I had been hit over the head with a hammer.

Driving to work, the radio announced that Hubert Humphrey had enough delegates committed to win the 1968 Democratic Party's nomination for President. As I listened to the reports about the riots that occurred the night before in Chicago, Abbie Hoffman's bulging eyes danced in front of me and his exclamations echoed around me. I stopped listening to what was being said on the radio.

While I tried to concentrate on where I was driving, I thought about Dean Johnson, a seventeen-year-old Sioux Indian from South Dakota, who was killed by the Chicago police a few days before. It brought back memories of Everett Covington. A white policeman, Joe Quinn, swore that before he pulled the trigger of his police revolver, Everett had pulled a shiny object from his pants pocket and had pointed it at him. But the gunshot had entered Everett's back and eyewitnesses reported that Everett fell forward as he tried to run away from the policeman who was chasing him. Just as no weapon had been found near Dean Johnson as alleged, no weapon had been found near Everett.

Everett had helped me run two programs, the Youth Employment Service, which found jobs for high school dropouts, and After School Study in School Topics, which tutored inner city youth.

After Everett was killed, I stood with mourners on a hot New Jersey day outside a Baptist church and heard the Reverend S. Howard Woodson plead with the crowd to stay calm. I cried with the others who were wailing. Vengeance toward Joe Quinn built within me. But I could not do anything. I worked for the cops.

When I stopped thinking about Everett, my mind flipped to how upset I had been toward callous, racial remarks about the Johnson killing by some of the red-neck detectives in the Prosecutors' Office. I was furious that I had not been able to express my feelings.

The Mercer County Courthouse is an imposing Federalist building at Broad and Market Streets in downtown Trenton. From the dank, parking garage, I took a slow elevator to the third floor.

Drinking coffee from Styrofoam cups and chatting about the cases they were presenting for indictments, uniformed policemen and detectives were huddled outside the Grand Jury room. They looked different to me. They were no longer like friendly George, the policeman, who had helped me across the street every day on my way to third grade, or the dedicated and caring detectives who helped me with the cases during the past eighteen months. They looked like the cops who had shot Dean Johnson and Everett Covington and had beaten Rennie Davis.

Charlie Bernstein, Challie, as he was known to everyone in the office, was a career prosecutor in charge of presenting cases for indictments to the Grand Jury. As he walked toward me, he said, "Hear you've been doing a good job, winning cases. You know, filling up the jail," he said as he approached. Instead of smiling as I would have the morning before, I stared at him. "Keep it up, kid." he said. Catching my unfriendly look, Charlie asked, "I say something wrong?"

"No. No." I responded curtly.

"So, what's up? I thought you'd like to hear a nice thing or two from Challie," he said.

"Challie, since you've always been honest with me, I'll tell it to you straight. I had a rough night. What happened in Chicago really got to me," I said.

"Good for you. Those cops did a hell of job out there with those pinko hoodlums. Did you hear that Brillo top talk? That Hoffman chump. Yippie. I'll Yippee him. I'd love to get my hands on him. I'd shake him like a rag. The law is the law. Who the hell do Hoffman and company think they are to disobey the cops? What right do they have to tell the President of these United States to stop a war before we win and let our boys who gave their fuckin' lives die in vain? He's the commander in chief, God dammit." Challie patted me on the shoulder and leaned over toward me. "You'll get over it. Tomorrow's another day. You've got what it takes," he whispered in my ear.

"Thanks Challie. But I'm thinking about leaving. "

Challie stepped back. "Getting out of here? Is that what you're telling me? What do you have? A big offer from one of those Newark firms?"

"No. No big offer. It's about last night. That's all."

"Last night, what about it?" Challie pried.

"Challie, did you see those cops beat the living shit out of innocent people? The Constitution was desecrated by their acts. Speech. Assembly. It's all bullshit."

Challie sidled up next to me and took me by the hand. "Let's get out of here and go somewhere where I can make sense out of this conversation." I followed him into his office and sat in a green leather chair that was catty-corner to his desk.

"So you think that the cops should have just let those pinkos like Rennie Davis and Bobby Seale run roughshod in Mayor Daley's city? Let me tell you, I'm not a violent man. I couldn't kill a fly. But Martin Luther King and Bobby Kennedy were out of order. Plain out of order. In World War II, I fought in the South Pacific. It was hell. Let me tell you. Now you have soldiers fighting for their lives in Vietnam. You don't cause riots and undermine the President of these United States.

Nope, this country is built on law and order. There's no freedom of speech or assembly when it comes to national security. I know how you young folks think. You lose a few battles, see some blood on the TV, and you turn on your heels and run for cover. You, so idealistic, are you? You didn't go to Vietnam, did you? You were one of the 'smart ones,' went to law school and joined the reserves. Now you go on your merry way and think about what Uncle Challie just said, and you do the best goddamn job in the courtroom that you can. You'll make our Constitution what it was meant to be. Something to protect the people. You hear what I'm saying?"

Opening his top desk drawer, Challie took out two fat cigars. He put one in his mouth and bit off an end and spit it into a waste paper basket. "Here's one for you. Chew on it. It'll get you ready for the back room at Lorenzo's where everything isn't black and white. You understand?"

On the way to my office, I threw the cigar he gave me in a waste container. Thinking about Charlie Bernstein, red-neck detectives, lying cops, and the scene at Lorenzo's, I got angrier and angrier.

Pete Lorenzo's Cafe sits across the street from an old inner-city cemetery and across a side street from the run-down Trenton railroad station. The street is "home" to prostitutes and drug dealers. Within easy walking distance of the restaurant are some of Trenton's very worst residential neighborhoods.

The building is rather nondescript: a four story construction with a vertical sign for the restaurant on the corner from the top three stories. A parking lot is to the rear. The attendants expect to be well tipped and they are. The cars are the very best. Mercedes. Cadillac. Lincoln. Saab. Porsche. Jaguar.

The front door is usually locked. You are admitted only after being cleared by Mike, the bartender. You walk into a dark room that has a bar that runs the length of it. There are small clusters of well dressed men and women drinking cocktails. At the end of the bar, Tony holds court at a little desk admitting you to the dining rooms, assuming you have a reservation.

During Prohibition, Lorenzo's was a speakeasy and legend has it that the upper floors house Pete Lorenzo's ghost. The dining rooms are relatively small but the tables are separated enough to allow semi-private conversations. They are clean, with white linen tablecloths and napkins. The walls are usually adorned with art for sale. The wait staff knows you by name.

Almost every face in the restaurant is recognizable. The governor, state legislators, the most prominent lobbyists, the most successful doctors, the most affluent business people, financiers, and state movers and shakers all eat at Lorenzo's.

They accept cash, and, if you are well known to them, your business check. You will need a big wad of cash or a hefty check book balance. The prices are not in the least modest or even reasonable, but they are worth it.

I often wondered why people went to such a bad neighborhood, to a restaurant that will not take credit cards to eat a meal. The people that went there did not need to be seen. The menu is moderate with usually five or six specials. There are some things that are not on the menu that the regulars know about. The Herbie Gross salad with three kinds of lettuce, crushed bleu cheese, anchovies, and Jersey tomatoes, is reputed to be the best salad on the East Coast, maybe in the country.

The specialties of the house are the steaks. They age their own meats and they are perfectly presented. The bread is warm, crusty, and served with very cold butter. There are specialties on the menu such as spaghetti with chicken livers.

A lot of state political business is conducted at Lorenzo's. Many lawsuits are settled there. Many a client is wooed there. With its understated luxury, Lorenzo's is a hidden power center in the Northeast.

My mind spun like a top. I was upset that I didn't have the courage to weed out cops who liked to clean up the streets by fabricating lies, or, worse yet, those who planted drugs on black kids who hung around the corners of North Trenton. I questioned why I was spending my time being a trial lawyer and not fulfilling my dream to change cities. Why this? Why that? Rat-a-tat. Questions, one after another.

The image of police brutality, society's anger and violence, and the verbal beating I had taken from Ellen the night before had knocked the wind out of me. I was concerned about what the Democratic party would think if I resigned from my role as prosecutor. I was afraid I would be kissing any political ambitions I had good-bye.

Following the advice of Challie Bernstein I decided to go about my business. The Tuesday after Labor Day, the fall court session began. While trying a rape case against a hardened criminal, I had a hard time telling the jury that I "proudly stood before them as a representative of the State."

I came home and told Ellen what I had felt addressing the jury. The six o'clock news was on. Mayor Richard Daley appeared on the screen at a press conference and said, "The policeman isn't there to create disorder. The policeman is there to preserve disorder." The camera swung to show the faces of reporters who were roaring with laughter and back again to Mayor Daley who by his expression did not know that his tongue had slipped.

"Honey, I'm going to resign tomorrow."

"What? I hope it's not because of me. It's not, is it?" she asked. "Please don't do anything rash without talking to me about it."

"OK," I assured her. "But I can't get Chicago out of my mind."

Ellen got up from the sofa and approached me with a serious expression on her face. "Okay, let's see if you can write it?"

"Write what?"

"Your letter of resignation."

"My what?"

She reached over the arm of the sofa and picked up a yellow legal pad resting beside the blue lamp.

We read my letter of resignation over and over again.

The letter was in my jacket pocket when I arrived at work the following morning. I stood while Mario Conti read it out loud:

Dear Mr. Prosecutor:

While I have enjoyed the time I have spent in your employ learning trial law and winning convictions, I must tender my resignation, because I have lost my ability to prosecute due to my convictions. Thank you for the opportunity to serve as Assistant Prosecutor. I came here with ideals and leave with the same ideals. I will do what I can to help preserve the Constitution of the United States and the State of New Jersey.

Yours truly,
Albert Stark

After he finished reading, he looked up at me. "I understand," he said. "You have my best wishes."

Ellen and I went to the Nina for dinner. "I see you differently tonight," she said after we finished our dessert.

"I'm scared to death. Sure, we ate good tonight. But how am I going to put bread on the table for us tomorrow?"

"Don't worry, everything will work out. You'll call your father. Tell him what you did, and I am sure he will help you out," Ellen said.

"My father? He'll be so pissed at me. He wasn't that disappointed when I left him to go to work for Conti. I think, in a way, he was relieved. He could practice without the burden of having me around. He'll be devastated when he hears what I did today. I was afraid to tell him I was resigning. I was afraid he would convince me not to. How do think he will feel when I crawl back to him?"

"You should be proud you lived up to your convictions. He will be too," Ellen said.

"Proud. I'm not so sure. 'Disappointed' might be a better word. I should have tried to fix the job, to fix the system, to make it meet my expectations."

"I understand. You're anxious. Apprehensive. You're wondering how you're going to feed your family and be true to yourself."

"I am overwhelmed. I have nothing in the wings. I'm going to have to start pounding the pavement. You think that's going to be fun? I'm not so sure I even want to be a lawyer."

"So what else do you want to do?" Ellen asked.

I looked at her. While she said nothing, I asked myself what else. What would I do with my renewed sense of self?

# RED LIGHT GREEN LIGHT—SCORE ONE FOR JUSTICE

ELLEN PUSHED THE MORNING PAPER TOWARD ME. Pointing to an article, she asked, "Isn't Joe Quinn the same cop who killed Everett?"

According to the story, a drunk black man named George Isaacs had run a red light, struck a police van on its way to an emergency call with its red roof lights flashing and its siren wailing, and killed a popular Irish cop by the name of Bobby Cunningham.

While it was true Joe Quinn was the name of a Trenton policeman who had shot Everett Covington, I had so much on my mind having to do with the day-to-day of running a legal practice, that the story was not important to me.

A few weeks later, Janice transferred a call to me. George Isaacs' sister wanted me to help her brother. When I met with George in the county jail where he was being held on one hundred thousand dollars bail, I turned the case down because he didn't have enough money to pay my fees for representing him. I was also apprehensive about facing off against the police who I had recently represented. After I told Ellen how ironic it was that I got a call about the Quinn case, she begged me to take it.

At her urging I conferred with George again. He agreed to pay me fifty dollars a week towards the two thousand dollar fee. After his sister and mother put up their houses as security, George was released from jail. The next day, he pulled ten five dollar bills from his wallet and gave them to me.

I went to Al's Auto Body where I took pictures of the police van and George's Plymouth. Making my way around the dirt lot filled with wrecks and mountains of worn-out tires, a black man wearing a green uniform with a patch on his that said "Willie" approached me.

"You the lawyer for George? Or for the law?"

"George." I said.

"George. A good man. A brother hanging out at the Blue Note was on the corner, smokin' a cigarette when he sees George go by in his car. Hearin' the crash, he looks up. Light was green for George. Watchin', he was. He didn't hear no siren. No lights neither. A cop jumps out of the one that hit George and runs. Busts the window with his gun. Then another cop car comes ablazin'. Sees a heavy cop jump out. Goes over to the cop with the gun. The two of them go over to the driver door of the banged up cop car. The heavy cop gets in. The light on top goes on, it did. Then stops, it did. The same with the sireeen."

"How do you know that?" I asked.

"Driving the wrecker that night, I was. Havin' a shot and a beer at Blue Note after work one evenin'. A brother comes up to me, asking was I one of Al's men. He tells me what I just tells you. Says George bein' lynched."

"Willie, you know the brother's name?"

"Sapp. Thurston Sapp. Used to work at Amtico. On the fly now."

"On the fly?"

"Words out Sapp's got trouble brewin'."

"Thanks, Willie. I may need you some day."

"Not me. Told Al about Sapp. Said to keep my mouth shut, he did. Al. He works for the law. They bring him wrecks, they do. This just between you and me. Hear?"

Willie's boss, Al, was a square-jawed, no nonsense fellow who knew everything that was happening in Trenton. Every day he sat in an easy chair in front of his auto body shop where all of the wrecks in the city seemed to be towed.

I understood Willie wanted to help George. What he told me wasn't admissible in court because it was hearsay. What someone else tells another is not respected as credible evidence of the truth. I needed Sapp.

I thought about what Willie had told me. If the roof light was not flashing when Quinn entered the intersection, why would it have been put on afterwards? To warn traffic traveling on Southard Street of an accident? To falsely imply that George had had ample warning that an emergency vehicle was approaching Brunswick Avenue? But why would it go off? Why would the siren go on, then off?

Samuel J. Lenox, Sr., whose office was on the tenth floor, was in the elevator when I got on at the fourth floor. Lenox was a well respected Trenton insurance company trial lawyer, a Scotsman known for his penurious payments to injured defendants.

"What are you doing here so late at night? Don't you have a family to go home to?" he inquired.

"I'm working on a complicated case. The one involving the accident where Bobby Cunningham was allegedly killed by George Isaacs."

Lenox looked me in the eye. "Son, you know the story of Sherlock Holmes?"

I nodded.

"You ought to learn from Sherlock. He said the brain is like an attic. There is only so much room in the attic so you must choose what to store up there wisely. That case is a loser. If you want to support your wife and family, you better choose your cases wisely. Otherwise, you won't have the time to handle a good one when it comes in."

I tried to heed Lenox's advice, squeezing the work I did on George's case between meetings I set up with developers, public officials, and city planners, interviewing injury victims, and trips to the county jail to answer the call of someone who was arrested and needed an attorney and bail arranged.

A few months after I had run into Willie at Al's Auto Body, I was coming home from New York. Douglas Ponder waited for a fare behind the steering wheel of his cab in the curved driveway in front of the Trenton train station. While he drove me home, we chatted. He told me he grew up in South Trenton, dropped out of high school, worked at Acme Hamilton, a rubber hose factory near the Blue Note, before deciding that being a cabbie was better than factory work. After I told him about the case I was handling for George Isaacs, I offered him a "few bucks and some free drinks" to hang out with me at the Blue Note while I hunted for Sapp. After three frustrating nights of drinking shots and beer, shooting some pool and playing pinball with Ponder, Thurston Sapp stumbled in. "That's him," Ponder whispered. "I'll make some small talk and find out what the brother knows." Ponder slid off the bar stool, waded through wisps of smoke, and sidled up to Sapp. I sat alone self consciously, glancing every now and then to see what Ponder was up to at the far end of the bar. I tapped my fingers on the counter and stared at the mirror behind the bar wondering what was going to happen next. Ponder, holding Sapp by his arm, walked toward me.

"Sapp. This is lawyer Albert Stark. Representin' George," Ponder said.

I tried to make eye contact with Sapp, but his eyes, bloodshot and bulging, wandered aimlessly. He reminded me of a sad soul who needed a square meal and a cup of coffee.

"The brother could use a drink on us. What d'ya think, boss?" Ponder asked.

"No problem," I responded.

"What'll it be, Sapp? Jack Daniels and ginger ale? Somethin' high class. Not the usual Wild Turkey. Whitey's buying." Ponder threw his head back and laughed.

Sapp's lips smacked against each other as if they were parched from thirst and his eyes widened enough for me to see, even in the dim light, that his pupils were dilated.

Ponder put Sapp on a stool beside me and stood between us. Sapp slurred as he told me one thing at a time. Ponder put his hand on Sapp's shoulder and shook it softly, prodding Sapp to repeat what he had told Willie.

From what Sapp said, George was slowing up to make a right turn. From his left, the police van entered the intersection at a high rate of speed with no lights flashing or siren going. The houses on Southard Street came close to the corner so George didn't see the police van until the last second. That's why the Plymouth was damaged on the left front and why it came to rest on an angle in the northbound lane of Brunswick Avenue. Quinn probably tried to swerve to his left when he saw the Plymouth. But traveling fast, he lost control and hit the brick building. Cunningham died when his head hit the dashboard. The impact from the Plymouth couldn't have been very severe because the passenger door window of the police car wasn't broken. Quinn had used his gun to break it.

If I had put the puzzle together correctly, George Issacs was not guilty of a vehicular homicide. But Sapp was certainly not someone who would have credibility in front of a jury. I doubted whether even a master lawyer could get Sapp to testify clearly in a courtroom filled with cops and a judge.

"Sapp, why didn't you tell the police what you saw?" I asked.

"A warrant be out for me," he replied.

"A warrant? For what?"

"B and E. Three."

"Breaking and entering?"

Sapp shook his head up and down.

"I understand," I said. "If I need you to testify, you with George?" I asked.

"You a lawyer. I know better, I do," he mumbled, shaking his head from side to side.

"Sapp, where do you live?" I asked, contemplating a tactic of last resort. I could issue a subpoena to order him to appear as a witness. I wasn't sure Sapp would remember what he had told me and, even if he did, whether he would stick with his story.

"33 Rossell," he said, referring to an apartment building in a public housing complex catty corner from Blue Note.

"Got a telephone?" I asked.

He shook his head from side to side again. "Got just enough for day to day."

"When I need you, you there for me?" I asked, trying once again to change Sapp's mind and get him to cooperate. Maybe, I thought, I could get him to sober up to testify at a trial.

"You be taking care of the B and E's?" He asked, looking at me with questioning eyes.

"Buy yourself a couple of good meals on George," I said, handing Sapp a twenty dollar bill. I didn't answer his question, since if I answered in the way Sapp wanted, it would have constituted improperly influencing a witness.

"Sapp. I know we can count on you," Ponder broke in. "Ready for another Jack Daniels?"

"I is," Sapp replied.

Ponder put a five spot on the bar in front of Sapp.

"What do you think, Douglas?" I asked Ponder after we had left the Blue Note.

"You a slick dude for a leisure class whitey."

"What do you mean?"

"That brother thinks you're going to take care of the B and E's. He took the twenty as a payoff for his help."

"Are you kidding me? No way did I intend to bribe him."

"You could have fooled me," Ponder chuckled.

"The man's telling it the way it was."

"But who's gonna believe a drunk with three B and E's out on him?"

"You got a good point there. I was thinking the same thing. I wondered why you were wasting a twenty. A couple of good meals. Who are you trying to bullshit? You know you can't bullshit a bullshitter," Ponder said.

I pulled out the only bill left in my pant pocket, a fifty. I palmed Ponder.

"Good doing business with ya. See ya around." He slid into a green-and-white Buick Riviera and drove off.

The trial of State of New Jersey versus George Isaacs began the Monday after July 4, 1969.

Frank McGuire, a feisty, experienced prosecutor and long-time ally of the predominantly Irish Trenton police force, outlined to the jury the facts on which he would rely to prove George Isaac's guilt. "The emergency dispatch, red roof flashers, and a wailing siren are proof that the police van was three quarters through the intersection. George Issacs struck the passenger's side door because he failed to obey a traffic signal. It all adds up to guilt beyond any reasonable doubt that George Isaacs is responsible for killing Bobby Cunningham."

I got up, trying to hide my shaky knees, when it was my turn to speak. "Ladies and Gentlemen of the Jury," I began slowly. "You are going to hear that the slam dunk case Mr. McGuire described to you is actually a legalized lynching. I am aware that this is a time, not yet two years after race riots ripped this city apart, when blacks are singing 'We shall overcome' and whites are saying 'No you won't.' Emotions and passions are intense." So were mine.

I paused and then picked up my cadence. "George sits before you in a cloak of innocence. He is innocent until proven guilty. Until that cloak is completely removed by evidence that convinces you beyond a reasonable doubt, George Isaacs is not Bobby Cunningham's killer. You have taken an oath to listen with an open mind. I ask that you keep that promise." Twelve white jurors listened with blank expressions on their faces.

Patrolman Thomas Doolan, round-faced, with broad shoulders and a barrel chest, stood up, smiled, and strutted to the witness stand when he heard McGuire announce his name.

A son of a former Trenton Police Chief, Doolan had been a patrolman, the lowest rank for a cop, for over thirty years. I had first met Doolan when he was doing guard duty at the local municipal court. I had arrived early, and stood in the line of lawyers waiting to tell the Court Clerk who I represented. I was third or fourth in line. Nine or ten lawyers were behind me. After I introduced myself, Doolan said, "You're a new one. Seniority counts in my court. You go to the back of the line." I humbly walked to the end of the line.

Nancy Karlosky, my secretary, and my wife, Ellen, sat in the front row of the spectator's section. Nancy took shorthand almost as fast as a court stenographer recorded testimony. Since I couldn't afford to pay for daily transcripts, I asked Nancy to take down as much of the testimony as she could. When I was an assistant prosecutor I could not observe everything going on in a trial and relied on the detective I worked with to observe and take notes on the witnesses. Now that I no longer had a detective in the spectator's section, I asked Ellen to watch and tell me what she saw. Neither Ellen nor Nancy had ever been to a trial before.

"Patrolman Doolan, how long have you served the citizens of Trenton?" McGuire asked as he began his interrogation.

"Twenty two years as a policeman and ten years as the head of the union."

"The union?" McGuire inquired.

"Yes, sir. The Patrolman's Benevolent Association," Doolan added.

"Patrolman Doolan, were you the first policeman to arrive at the scene of the accident? McGuire asked.

"Yes sir, I was. I heard Car 40, driven by Patrolman Quinn, dispatched to an emergency domestic violence call. I was about a half-mile away and proceeded to the call as back up. When I approached Brunswick and Southard, I came upon the accident scene."

"What did you observe when you arrived?"

"The police van was up against a brick building, approximately fifty feet from the northeast corner of Brunswick and Southard, facing east. The police van was damaged at the right front passenger door and the front was crushed. The Plymouth was in the center of the intersection, in the northbound lane of Brunswick, with severe front-end damage, more on the left than the right."

Nancy noted that he mentioned nothing about observing flashing lights or hearing a siren when he arrived at the scene.

"When you arrived at the scene, where was Patrolman Quinn?"

"Patrolman Quinn was at the right front passenger door trying to tend to Bobby, Patrolman Cunningham."

"What did you do?"

"I ran over to Joe and tried to help him save Bobby. But it was no use. There was no movement. I reached in and took a pulse. There was none." The jurors' eyes were glued to Doolan.

"After you went to Patrolman Quinn, did you make observations of the siren on his police van?" McGuire asked very slowly.

"Yes, sir. I did make observations."

"What did you observe?"

"It was operating."

"And what about the roof lights?"

"The roof lights flashed," Doolan replied. Had he given a literal answer to avoid committing perjury?

I wrote on my yellow legal pad. "Was he referring to the roof lights flashing when he turned them on after the crash? The same with the siren?" As a prosecutor, I had observed how cops split hairs to obscure the truth.

McGuire walked toward Doolan. When he was arm's length away, he stopped and asked, "When you approached the intersection, before you went to assist Patrolman Quinn, did you hear a siren and see flashing lights?"

"Yes, sir. I did," he answered authoritatively.

"Are you sure?" McGuire continued.

"Very sure," Doolan testified.

"After you made those observations, did you go to the Isaacs vehicle, the Plymouth?" McGuire inquired.

"I did, sir. He was slumped over the steering wheel. He appeared to be unconscious." He was about to continue when I stood up, anticipating what he was going to say.

"Mr. Stark, why are you standing?" Judge Thomas Shusted, a no-nonsense, jurist, asked.

"I would like to approach the bench with the prosecutor, Your Honor."

"Very well, gentlemen. Please come up," Judge Shusted instructed, pointing to the side of his raised chair.

McGuire and I walked past the court clerk to the side of the judge's bench furthest from the jury.

"What is it that concerns you, counselor?" Judge Shusted inquired in a soft voice so the jury could not hear what we were saying.

"Your Honor, I suspect that Patrolman Doolan is about to testify that he smelled a strong odor of alcohol on Mr. Isaacs' breath. Before the trial I made a motion to exclude evidence of alcohol consumption. My investigation turned up an important fact. The vial of blood taken from George was mishandled by the hospital personnel. I thought there was a strong probability it was contaminated when it was tested. Under the rules of evidence, procedures must be strictly adhered to."

"Is what Mr. Stark argues correct, Mr. McGuire?" Judge Shusted asked.

"Unfortunately, it is, Your Honor," McGuire replied.

"Very well then, Mr. McGuire. Please instruct your witness not to mention any observations he made of an odor of alcohol on the defendant's breath," the judge ordered.

Thrilled with the vital ruling in my favor, I watched McGuire sidle past the jury as if nothing important had happened.

"Thank you, Patrolman Doolan," McGuire emoted.

McGuire looked at the jurors, nodded, then turned toward me. "Your witness, counselor."

Nancy had taken down every word on her shorthand pad.

If Sapp's version of what happened was correct, McGuire had very cleverly interrogated Thomas Doolan. Doolan had told the truth literally. The red roof light had worked when he tested it. The red flashers he saw as he approached Brunswick and Southard were the ones on his police van. It became clear to me that McGuire had every move Tom Doolan made clearly engraved in his mind. Willie and Sapp had talked to the prosecutor.

I had to make a decision whether or not to cross examine Doolan. I needed to show that Doolan had hedged, split hairs, obscured the truth, or worse yet, lied.

If Sapp was telling the truth, the red flashers and the siren on Quinn's police wagon were not on when he entered the intersection. I could ask Doolan if the red lights he saw and the siren he heard were the ones he had activated on his own police car on his way to the domestic violence call. I could also ask Doolan if, upon seeing that Quinn's flashers were not on and not hearing a siren, he decided to test them to see if they worked.

Doolan had testified many times in cases. If I tried to expose gaps in his testimony, I didn't know how he would answer. In prior trials, I had learned the hard way that asking a question on cross examination to which I didn't know the answer was very risky. I also strongly suspected that the jury would not believe Thurston Sapp, an alcoholic, wanted for three felonies. I sat at counsel table feeling McGuire had trapped me.

"I have no questions of the officer at this time," I announced. McGuire grinned with satisfaction.

Patrolman Quinn resembled a bantam weight fighter. His wavy, red hair, deep set eyes, chiseled cheeks, broad shoulders and narrow hips gave him a devilish and dangerous look that I hoped would go against him in the eyes of the jury. Quinn had killed Ellen's friend Everett Covington. I didn't want him to destroy the life of George Isaacs. But, in the meantime, I had to keep my inner hatred under control and methodically rip Quinn's story apart.

Quinn swore he approached the intersection of Southard and Brunswick with his siren blasting and his red lights whirling. He was then violently struck on the passenger's side door and pushed into a building. When he described how he got out of his police van and desperately tried to revive his partner, the jury responded sympathetically.

"What did you do after you struck the brick building?" I asked, moving slowly toward Joe Quinn.

"I turned off the engine. I was afraid the van would catch fire," he said, conveying to the jury that he was a careful person.

"Did you turn off the switch which activated your flashers?"

"No, I didn't turn it off. I didn't have to," he replied wanting the jurors to believe they were on.

"Did you see Patrolman Doolan turn on the red lights of your police van?

"I think so," he answered.

"You think so?" I had brought out a fact consistent with Sapp's version.

"I think so."

We were almost nose to nose, ready to butt heads.

"Did you see him put on the siren?

"I think so. I'm not sure," he muttered.

If I got Sapp to testify, I could argue he wasn't lying because Quinn admitted he saw Doolan put on the flashers and siren after the crash. I quickly turned to the jury to see their reaction. The jurors were shaking their heads from side to side. I wondered whether they were shaking them in disbelief or whether my combative tone had enlisted the jury's sympathy toward Quinn and ignited anger toward George.

I needed to show that turning the engine off wouldn't shut off the flashers or the siren.

It was difficult to let Quinn leave the stand without wanting to discredit him. But I followed the rule not to ask a question to which I didn't know the answer.

Detective Danny Babashak was the next witness for the State. He had examined the police van after it was towed to Al's Auto Body.

Babashak testified that the sirens and roof lights were operable when he tested them.

I had prepared a line of questions that would allow me to argue that George's Plymouth was going slowly, turning right and that Bobby Cunningham died because Joe Quinn was going too fast. If Quinn wasn't telling the truth about the impact, maybe he wasn't being forthright about the lights and siren. The principle of "Falsus in uno, falsus in omnibus" means if you tell a lie about one thing, you've told a lie about everything.

Without Thurston Sapp, this approach was my best hope.

"Detective, did you observe the damage to the front passenger door of the police van?" I asked.

"It suffered direct impact," he answered.

I had taken three photographs of the police van at Al's. "Do these photographs accurately depict the damage to the door?"

Taking the photographs from me, Babashak looked at them carefully and acknowledged that they did.

I placed the photographs into evidence. They showed an elongated dent, not particularly deep, in the door just beneath the passenger side window, which had been shattered. The dent showed no evidence of heavy impact.

I needed to show that the window glass was broken by a policeman's pistol. Babashak verified the accuracy of the photographs that showed a broken windshield and a large dent in the dashboard of the police van. He examined the photos I had taken of George's car that showed moderate damage to the right front fender and bumper. The moderate damage to George's car made it clear that something other than the impact of the accident had broken the window.

McGuire rested the State's case. Whether the traffic light at Brunswick and Southard was red or green, or whether the damage to the police van was major or minor, or whether George's Plymouth was damaged only on the left front did not matter as far as McGuire was concerned. What mattered to him was that George Isaacs should have yielded to a police van with its red lights flashing and its siren wailing. Failure to do so was reckless disregard for the safety of others. In plain words, vehicular homicide.

George Isaacs ambled to the witness stand. A tall, light-skinned black man in his mid-thirties, George seemed respectable, even demure. The type of brain injury George suffered was difficult for an ordinary person to detect. His short term memory was affected. Unless he wrote down what he needed before he went to the store to buy something, he might forget what he wanted once he got there. His long term memory was intact from about two weeks before the accident. The brain injury had also left him with a slightly slurred speech pattern, but even that could be easily mistaken for someone having had had one too many drinks .

Hesitantly, he told the jury that he had always been employed since he dropped out of school in the ninth grade, that he lived above the Blue Note, and that his garage was in the alley behind the bar. He swore he didn't remember the events of the night of the accident.

McGuire asked him only one question. "Mr. Isaacs, where were you coming from before the accident?"

George replied, "The Spot Cafe."

"A bar?" McGuire asked. McGuire had not only researched the accident scene but also had traced George's after hours habits.

George shrugged his shoulders. "Yea," he admitted.

McGuire looked at the jury, then at me.

After fighting to keep evidence of alcohol out of the case on a technicality, I now found that the alcohol was before the jury. Worse yet, George appeared to be lying when he claimed he didn't remember what happened at the corner of Brunswick and Southard. If he remembered he was coming from the Spot Cafe, why couldn't he recall whether the light was red or green? My stomach turned over.

McGuire, mocking my histrionics when I had turned to the jury after my confrontation with Joe Quinn, imitated me. The jury smiled at him.

George appeared to be in a daze.

"You are excused, Mr. Isaacs," the judge said.

George didn't move.

"Mr. Isaacs," Judge Shusted said. "You are excused from the witness stand. That is all."

A Sheriff's Officer walked over to George and was ready to take his hand when George rose from the witness chair and walked toward me, his shoulders slumped.

I was devastated by what had taken place during the past few minutes. I didn't know where Thurston Sapp was, but when Judge Shusted asked if I had any more witnesses, I answered, "Yes, Your Honor, I do."

I had a gap of a few days because court was not in session on Friday. Judges usually spent Fridays hearing motions, doing research, writing opinions, taking pleas, conducting arraignments of recently arrested persons, setting bail, or pronouncing sentences.

The night before, Ponder and I had trudged up a dimly lit cement stairway covered with graffiti to the fifth floor of 33 Rossell. We knocked on a door with the name "Sapp" in a tin frame. There was no answer. We rang the neighbors' door bells. Sapp hadn't been seen since the weekend.

I didn't know that Willie from Al's Auto Body had told Al what he told me and that Al had tipped off McGuire that Sapp witnessed the accident and had talked to me. McGuire put out on the street that the police were looking for Sapp, hoping it would prompt Sapp to leave town.

Ponder picked me up after dinner Thursday evening. When we returned to 33 Rossell, a woman dressed in a wrinkled flannel housecoat, her dyed red hair in curlers, opened the door. I didn't know who she was. She looked too old to be Sapp's wife. Perhaps she was his sister. The heavy smell of cooking oil hit us in the face. She told us Sapp was in Allentown, Pennsylvania, at his sister's and that she didn't know the address, telephone number, or when Sapp would be back. "Left suddenly. Monday afternoon. Took a bus to New York. From there he was headed to Allentown. That's what he told me. Said somebody'd be looking for him. Didn't say who. Said 'the law' gave him bus fare."

"Ponder, that McGuire is a no good son of a bitch," I barked as we skipped back down the dimly lighted stairway.

"Boss, that dude done did you a big favor. He done bribed brother Sapp. If brother George does time, so will that ol' red-neck."

How was I going to prove McGuire obstructed justice? Who would believe Sapp?

Nancy typed up her notes from the trial. I read them to her.

"You know what we should do," Nancy said.

"What's that?" I asked.

"You play Sapp. You testify the way you think Sapp's going to. Then we can match up what he says and put it together with what Doolan told the jury. We can make a diagram. We'll put what Doolan said in black and what Sapp said in red. I'll bet you they'll fit together to allow the jury to see the gaps in Doolan's testimony. If Doolan's telling the truth and Sapp is telling the truth, we can show the jury the whole truth."

"Good suggestion," I said. While Nancy made independent decisions about what to put in a letter to a client or a judge, she seldom played this active a role. She was as involved in the case as I was. We were a team. "But there's a problem. We don't have Sapp. I've been to Allentown, New Jersey. But Allentown, Pennsylvania? Never. I'm afraid Sapp's a goner."

"Maybe so," Nancy said. "But let's do it anyway."

Exhausted and frustrated after the events of the week, Ellen and I went out to dinner at Lorenzo's Cafe.

I pulled into the parking lot and was greeted by Joey, one of the big parking lot attendants. He offered a hand that looked like a meat hook and pulled me from behind the driver's seat. "You're one of the new ones. I heard about you." His bloodshot eyes, bulbous nose, and oversized front teeth filled my eyes. "Welcome to Lorenzo's," Joey continued.

"What are you going to do about Sapp?" Ellen asked.

After putting down two Chivases on the rocks while standing in front of the mahogany bar, my foot on a brass rail, I answered, "Nothing. You're not going to believe this one. McGuire paid Sapp to skip town. He's pretty slick. I'm going to expose the bastard and make a deal for George. He'll get probation or a suspended sentence with no jail time."

"Are you out of your mind? You think McGuire will admit to such a thing? Are you so naive to think he gave Sapp an office check?" Ellen asked.

"Maybe you're right," I told Ellen in a clipped tone.

Ellen smiled, happy I had listened to her. "Let's head up to Allentown, Pennsylvania. What do we have to lose? You've gone this far."

"Allentown. I don't know a soul there. I've never even been there," I responded, still doubting that a trip to Allentown would be worthwhile and worried that it might actually ensnare me in an ethical problem.

"Let's check directory assistance. Maybe they have a Sapp? We'll make some phone calls," Ellen suggested, sensing I didn't have the energy to do everything she wanted me to do for George.

"If you say so. What are the chances Sapp has an unmarried sister, let alone one with the same last name?" I inquired dejectedly.

Ellen got up from the table and went to the pay phone. After the waitress brought me the check and I paid, Ellen returned to the table and gave me a thumbs down sign before she sat down.

"I've been thinking. We really need Sapp. Without him, we don't have a chance," I said.

As we were leaving I got an idea. Allentown probably had a section where blacks lived. If Sapp got there last Monday, the day his sister told me he went to the bus station, he would probably be at a bar. I would need Ponder to find him. I looked directly across the street at the Trenton Train Station. As luck would have it, Ponder was working the night shift.

When he saw us Ponder jumped out of his cab. "What's up? You find him?" he asked.

"No, but we're going to," Ellen said. "You fellows are heading up to Allentown in the morning."

Saturday morning I picked up Douglas Ponder and we headed west on the Pennsylvania Turnpike to the Northeast Extension. We found a room at a Howard Johnson's near the entrance to Dorney Park, a well known amusement park in Allentown. We looked for a telephone book but couldn't find one in the room. I went to the front desk and came back with a piece of paper with the numbers for four Sapps.

Lillie Belle Sapp answered on the first ring. She told me she was Thurston Sapp's sister and that Thurston was at her home.

Thurston Sapp was waiting outside a rundown, faded Cape Cod style house. A large red "BEWARE OF DOG" sign hung on the gate to the yard.

"What you want from me?" Sapp asked after we got out of my car.

"The truth. The truth. That's all," I answered.

"You must want it real bad. How'd you find me?"

I looked at Ponder.

"Brother Sapp," Ponder said, pointing to me. "Stark doesn't think the police are telling the truth. If you were George, and George was standing on the corner, I am sure that George would testify for you."

"Look here, Ponder. George ain't facing three B and E's."

Ponder didn't have a chance to say a word when an attractive, middle-aged woman wearing a full-length leather coat, tight black jeans, and bedroom slippers ambled toward us. "What's the problem here, Thurston? Who are these folks?" she asked.

Ponder told her that I was a lawyer for a brother up in Trenton and that I needed Sapp to testify.

"I'm cold out here. We'll talk in there. It's warmer." Lillie Belle Sapp opened the gate to the fence and started walking toward the front door.

Ponder sat next to Lillie Belle on a worn velour sofa covered with a white sheet and thanked her for letting us into her home.

"Is what the brother is saying right?" Lillie Belle asked Sapp.

He nodded.

"The brother is right, Thurston. Us black folk have to walk together even if the coals is hot."

Sapp looked at me. "The B and E's?"

"They're there whether you testify or not. Sooner or later . . . . " I said.

"He's right, Thurston. You can run but you can't hide. Do the right thing, brother," Lillie Belle insisted.

Sapp had indeed thought I had offered to help him with his B and E's. Since he was doing the right thing at the urging of his sister, I wanted to help him even more. Sapp wouldn't be swift enough to deny any claims that I induced him to testify. He probably had already told McGuire about the money I slipped him at the Blue Note and that I had promised him future legal services in return for testimony. I shivered as I thought of the consequences. Disbarment was even a possibility. I wished I had never met George Isaacs or Willie. I was angry at myself and Ellen for urging me on. Reality had once again brought me face to face with the rules of professional conduct.

"Sapp, the law gave you bus money, right?" I asked.

He nodded.

I took a chance and asked another question. "Had he promised to drop the B and E's?"

Another nod.

"So I guess you're afraid to testify."

Sapp's silence told me I was right on the mark.

Ponder, Sapp and I returned to the Howard Johnson's. We checked out and brought Sapp to Trenton. Ponder was given a job to deliver Thurston Sapp to the courthouse Monday morning. When I got home I reported to Ellen what had happened.

"I've been thinking," Ellen said while we ate breakfast Sunday morning.

"Thinking? What now?" I snapped. "I've been thinking too. How can I call Sapp to the stand? What if McGuire gets him to tell about the cash I slipped him or about helping him with the B and E's?"

"Come on now. Sapp had already told you the truth before you gave him a little something to help him get a meal. And the B and E's. You haven't, from what you've told me, made any promises. If I were on the jury, I'd understand that completely. Sapp has to tell the truth, the entire truth. Even about the B and E's and the drinks and the twenty. That's the only way the jury will understand why he didn't tell the police what he saw and why he went back into the Blue Note the night of the crash. If I were you, I'd even have him tell the story about how you found him in Allentown. It would make him more believable. The jury will see you are a real fighter. If I'm not mistaken, the jurors are all white and there's a woman from Princeton sitting in the back row. She may be a liberal. Who knows?" Ellen responded.

"Maybe so. But I'm still scared. I never should have given him the twenty. Maybe I should have him say that Ponder gave it to him?"

"You want the truth. Let the truth come out."

"If you say so. I hope you're right."

"How do the flashers and siren work?" Ellen inquired out of the blue.

"What do you mean 'How do they work'?"

"Just that. Nancy and I read over her notes of Doolan's testimony. Do you know what Quinn had to do to activate them?"

"No. Do you?"

"How would I know? Maybe you should find out."

Holding Sapp's elbow, a Sheriff's Officer opened the swinging door that separated the spectators from the lawyers, jury, and judge. He led him to the witness stand. Frank McGuire stared straight ahead as Sapp walked by the counsel's table. Sapp, wearing a plaid wool shirt, dungarees, and work boots, stood, looked around nervously, then placed his hand on the Bible and swore to tell the truth.

"Mr. Sapp, where do you live?" I began.

"33 Rossell Avenue, Trenton, New Jersey. Fifth Floor," Sapp testified.

"Mr. Sapp, where did you meet me?"

"The first time or this weekend?"

"The first time."

"The first time. Blue Note."

"What did I ask you at Blue Note?"

"If what I told Willie over at Al's was the truth" he said.

"The truth about what?" I asked.

"About George and the police."

"Are you going to tell this court and jury the truth here today?"

"I is. God be my witness."

"What did you observe at the corner of Brunswick and Southard?" I asked.

Sapp pointed at the expressionless man sitting beside me. "George. He had the green light, he did. I know. I be smokin' a cigarette. Outside Blue Note. Had a few, I did. But not so much. I be hearin' a loud noise. I turn around. I look. I see the light for Brunswick. Green, it was." Sapp stopped talking. He coughed.

"Does Mr. Sapp need a glass of water?" Judge Shusted asked.

The Sheriff's Officer poured water into a paper cup from a pitcher on my counsel table and took it to him. Sapp drank it slowly.

"Continue, Mr Sapp," I said.

"Then I heard a bang. A big one. I run to the corner. The paddy wagon. It was up against the drugstore. It was real quiet. I be spooked. A cop gets out. He runs over to the side of the paddy wagon toward me. I hear glass breaking. I see him put his gun in his hip. He reaches in. He jumps like he's trying to dive in. I hear a sireeen. Then red lights. A cop car pulls in. A fat cop jumps out. He goes over to the number one cop. The one with the gun. They go around the back of the paddy wagon. The fat one gets in. The red lights go on. Then go off, they did. Then the sireeen. On, then off." Sapp took a deep breath and put his hands on his head.

"After you told me what you saw, what did I do?" I continued, trying to preserve the drama of the moment.

"You done buy me a Jack Daniels."

Laughter echoed throughout the courtroom. I glanced at Frank McGuire. His face flushed red as he tried not to join in the laughter. Judge Shusted banged his gavel. "Order. Order. Order in the courtroom."

The spectator's section was filled with uniformed policemen, all friends of Doolan, Quinn, and Bobby Cunningham, who had come to see George Isaacs found guilty. The section was so quiet you could have heard a pin drop. When I turned around, I saw Nancy in the back row holding her thumb up and grinning.

I took Sapp through a line of questions about finding him in Allentown, his breaking and entering charges, why he talked to Willie at Al's Auto Body and not the police after the accident, and finally about his fear of testifying and being arrested. I turned to McGuire. "Mr. Prosecutor. Your witness." I had asked nothing about the bus fare. I knew McGuire wouldn't.

McGuire put Sapp through the ringer. He mumbled when McGuire asked him where he was standing, "How could you see there were no red flashers on when the police van entered the intersection if you were looking at George's Plymouth approaching from the left?" McGuire challenged. "How long after the crash did you see the light?" McGuire turned to the jury, hoping it would imply it could have been red when George went through it and green when he turned around. McGuire attacked Sapp's credibility with questions whose answers informed the jury that Sapp was an alcoholic who had been through seven treatment centers with no success.

"No further questions," McGuire said. As Sapp left the stand, aided by the Sheriff's Officer, McGuire grinned at him mockingly. I nervously watched the jurors' heads turn, their faces still void of expression, as Sapp passed in front of them.

"Any further witnesses, Mr. Stark?" Judge Shusted asked.

"May I have a few minutes, Your Honor? I may have one more," I responded.

"This is a good time to take our mid-morning break. The coffee is waiting in the jury room. We'll take a fifteen minute recess. If you have no further testimony, we will begin with summations when the jury returns," Judge Shusted said, indicating he was getting impatient and wanted to bring the case to an end.

McGuire's face had a puzzled look.

Nancy ran up to me. "You were right."

Danny Babashak sat in the spectator section with the other police officers. I had subpoenaed him to appear in court.

Judge Shusted settled into his high backed chair. "Your next witness," he said gruffly.

"I recall Detective Babashak to the witness stand."

I let him sit for a few moments while he squirmed, obviously uncomfortable, before I asked, "Detective Babashak, if the engine is off on a police wagon like the one Patrolman Quinn was driving, could the siren be wailing?"

I hadn't known how the siren or the flashers worked when Babashak had testified earlier in the trial. On Sunday night I had contacted a policeman from another town. He explained that the sirens would work even if the engine was off, assuming the switch had been activated. Joe Quinn had turned the engine off, but not the flashers or siren. He didn't have to. They weren't on. He had lied. I wasn't surprised.

"Yes," he answered.

"Detective, I'm going to show you this photograph of the siren switch in the police van. Is it in the off or on position?"

Babashak looked closely at the photograph I had taken at Al's. "Off," he said. Tom Doolan had turned the siren on, then shut it off as Sapp had testified.

"And Detective Babashak, what is the position of the red flasher switch?"

He looked at the picture I handed him. "Off." He looked at McGuire. If Quinn had his flashers on when he entered the intersection, why would the switch be off unless the flashers were not activated. Tom Doolan had tested them, saw they worked, and turned them off. I looked at the jury. Two of them, including a woman in the back row, were whispering to one another.

I worked all weekend on my summation. It was Monday morning. It was time to put the puzzle together for the jurors.

"Ladies and Gentlemen," I began, "On a moonless October night, with the houses dark and the streets nearly empty, George Isaacs drove his 1958 Plymouth slowly north on Brunswick Avenue from Five Points, the intersection of five streets on the north edge of downtown Trenton. George intended to go home to his one room apartment above the Blue Note Tavern, a dank bar that catered to men who worked in the nearby floor tile, rubber hose, wire rope, and pottery factories. Blue Note Tavern is two long city blocks north of Five Points at the corner of Brunswick and Southard.

After crossing the frozen Delaware River on a frigid Christmas Eve in 1776 and marching twelve miles through deep snow, George Washington's brave soldiers passed through Five Points minutes before they surprised the Hessians, won the Battle of Trenton, and turned the tide of the American Revolution. A monument memorializes the 'few men' who in Thomas Paine's words, 'did so much for so many.'

Lined with small businesses, bars, and run-down brick front homes, Brunswick Avenue is a street cops hate. Now, brave men of a different ilk than George Washington pass through. After dark, hookers stroll while drug dealers hide in the dim shadows cast by the street lamps. Men drive slowly by while others saunter on the cement sidewalks, waiting for an opportune moment to make a deal.

George glanced at a few hookers, and turned his attention to the traffic light at Brunswick and Southard where he would park his car behind the Blue Note Tavern.

At the same moment, Patrolman Joe Quinn's police van raced east on Southard Street, responding to a domestic violence call. His radio had crackled with directions to break up a squabble between an inebriated husband and his wife. Ignoring the red light at Brunswick, Quinn caught sight of George's turning car and swerved to the left. The police van and George's Plymouth collided. Joe's partner, Bobby Cunningham, a popular Irish cop who coached youth baseball and basketball teams, was thrown forward into the dashboard.

George's head hit the steering wheel of his Plymouth. He suffered retrograde amnesia, a condition that causes people who experience severe, sudden trauma to forget what happened not only during the moments before an accident, but also what they did for days, or even months, before. Injury to his brain permanently erased any memory of the accident.

Tom Doolan, operating a police van about a half mile away, heard Quinn's car Number 40 being dispatched to the domestic violence call and proceeded as back up, his siren wailing and red roof lights flashing. He came upon the accident scene a few minutes after the crash, noticed that Quinn's red roof light was not operating and didn't hear a siren. He pulled up behind Quinn's police van, jumped out and ran over to the front passenger door, where Quinn was frantically trying to help his dying partner. When he realized he could not help Quinn save Cunningham, Doolan circled behind Quinn's police van, got into the front seat, turned on the flashing red roof light to see if it worked and tested the siren. The siren wailed for a moment before Doolan turned it off. Why did Doolan do what he did? Because he expected to see lights and hear a siren when he pulled his police van behind Quinn's.

Thurston Sapp, a patron at the Blue Note who had gone out to get some air and have a smoke, watched George go through a green light and get smashed by the police van. He witnessed what happened." I paused and looked at each juror.

"Ladies and Gentlemen, do you remember the promise you made to George Isaacs when you took the oath to be a juror? If you have kept that promise and kept an open mind, you will prevent this lynching. Neither you, nor I, nor the Prosecutor, nor the judge can bring back Bobby Cunningham. All you can do is bring back a just verdict, a verdict that is consistent with the evidence and not one based on speculation. Or bias. Or prejudice. Or sympathy. I am aware of the passions that fill this courtroom. You are now aware that a police van siren works when its engine is not running. When Patrolman Doolan approached the scene he may have heard a siren. But it was his own. Not that on the police van driven by Joseph Quinn. Why? Because Joe Quinn told you he had turned off the engine to avoid a fire.

If Thurston Sapp is correct, the red flashers went on and then off after the heavy cop got into the paddy wagon. Didn't Doolan test them because they were not flashing when he arrived at the scene after the crash? Patrolman Doolan only told the literal truth, but not the whole truth. If Sapp has told the truth, that the siren and the red flashers went on and then went off after the heavy set cop got into the wagon, were the lights flashing and siren blaring when Joe Quinn's patrol wagon went through the intersection? No. The lights and flashers Doolan saw and heard were the ones on his own police vehicle, not the ones on Quinn's patrol wagon."

I banged my fist on the table when I heard the words, spoken by the jury foreman: "Not Guilty."

"We did it, boss," Ponder said as we skipped down the Courthouse steps after the jury acquitted George Isaacs.

Shortly after the case was over, Joe Quinn resigned from the police force. It was my opinion he was too filled with guilt to continue a career in law enforcement. A few years later, George was arrested for using heroin and put in jail for five years.

While I was working on George's case, Alvin Gershen, a city planner, hired me to do the legal work on an apartment house that he was going to build under the provisions of the housing law I had drafted for Governor Hughes. He reignited my desire to be an urban development lawyer. The five thousand dollars Gershen paid for work on a senior citizens high-rise apartment next to a synagogue which my great grandfather founded in 1883 kept me from going into the red. However, it didn't allow me to start building my team.

Nancy, Ellen, and Ponder were the teammates who helped me win for George. I looked forward to having legal teammates as qualified as Hutch and as dedicated as Nancy, Ellen, and Ponder, not in criminal law, but rather in urban development.

# DEAD END—TAKING ON THE BIG GUYS

"I NEED HELP FOR ONE OF MY CAB DRIVERS," Douglas Ponder said when he called me on the telephone.

"Mr. Slim's in trouble. His real name is Alonzo L. Parker. He's in the federal lockup on East State."

"Drugs? An accident?" I asked.

"Nothing like that. This is big. Stealing bonds from the bank."

After Douglas helped me successfully defend George Isaacs, he referred cabbies and Trentonians for criminal and accident cases. Referrals from people and clients who perceived me as a caring lawyer and fighter had steered my practice into the courtroom, hospitals, and jails, and away from urban development. I had hired a lawyer fresh out of law school to work at a low salary with a promise of a good future if we succeeded. The satisfaction of helping an injured person as well as the financial rewards of the injury cases were tugging me away from the challenge of the criminal cases. Seeing how blacks and Hispanics were treated by the police and the courts, my sense of social justice and idealism made criminal work attractive. Unfortunately, most of the criminals didn't have the funds to warrant the time and effort I had to put into their defense. My father took pride in good legal work and did not cotton to the charity work I accepted. Paying the rent and payroll and supporting a wife and two children made me think twice before I undertook a criminal defense.

Because it was Douglas calling, I responded immediately. I knew that the federal lockup at the Post Office building, which was a few blocks from my office, was by no means Alcatraz. But the large room with two or three cells probably made Mr. Slim feel like he was on that island.

The forsythia were abloom in the cemetery of the Methodist Church as I walked as quickly as I could to the Post Office.

A middle-aged man with a crew cut who could have passed for Superman asked me what I wanted at the FBI office. Agent Stewart Donaldson proceeded to tell me that Alonzo L. Parker had been arrested that morning. He was charged with extorting one hundred thousand dollars for the return of three million dollars in bonds stolen from a courier working for the Philadelphia Trust Company.

"Oh my God," I exclaimed. "There's a lawyer-client meeting room down on the second floor, isn't there?" I asked.

"So what if there is?" Donaldson replied, seeming not to care that Alonzo had a right to an attorney under the Sixth Amendment to the United States Constitution or about the sanctity of a client's right to communicate with a lawyer privately.

Donaldson reluctantly picked up the phone and made arrangements for me to go to the lockup. "Tell your client that it would be a lot easier on him if he came clean now and avoided a lot of trouble," Donaldson said as he after I had been cleared to go downstairs.

Alonzo was sitting on a metal stool and holding his head in his hands. The long–sleeved orange pullover shirt with the big white letters PRISONER on the back was at least two or three sizes too big for him.

After the Federal Marshall selected a key from a chain hooked to his black leather belt, and opened the cell door, Alonzo turned his head over his shoulder. I told him who I was and that Ponder had sent me.

The Marshall went into the cell and put his large, right hand around Alonzo's upper arm. He lifted him effortlessly from the stool and ushered him to me. I shook Alonzo's hand. His crooked, tobacco-stained front teeth, unevenly spaced, were framed with gold. My hand almost slid from his grip because it was so clammy.

"Call me when you're finished," the Marshall instructed as he slammed the meeting room door behind him.

The small meeting room was furnished with only two wooden chairs and a small metal table.

"I be so happy you came to see me," Alonzo whispered. "Can he be listening?" he asked, pointing to the door.

"No. No. Everything is private. What you tell me is strictly confidential," I assured him.

"You sure?"

"Trust me," I replied. "But whether I can help you out of this one is something I'm not sure about," I continued.

"What you mean?" he asked.

"What I mean is that extortion is a heavy crime."

"That's a lie. Believe me. It's a lie."

"So what's your side of the story?" I asked.

"What 'd they tell you?"

"That you stole bonds. And that you extorted a hundred thou to return them," I said.

"Ain't true." He began to talk faster and faster about how he came upon the bonds.

"OK now. Slow down and tell me what happened."

"It was two or three weeks ago. I was drivin' my taxi to the station. A man stopped my taxi. He gets in at the center of town. From State and Broad, I drive him to the station. He gets out. I go to the trunk to get his suitcase. It be black leather. The size of a gym bag. I work all day. Cleanin' up at night, under the back of my seat, I be seein' a brown paper bag. Thinking it has some food in it, I take it to the trash can. It not be smellin'. Not like food wrappers. So I open it and these papers be in it. Cash! Big cash! I never be seein' nothin' like it before. I put the bag in my trunk. A few days later a man from Hiltonia gets in my cab. You know Hiltonia? Where the houses are big. A businessman type wearing a couple of hundred dollar suit. I drive him to the station, open my trunk to get him his suitcase and see the bag. I think, 'Maybe this dude knows what be in the bag.' So I ask, 'Hey mister, you know what is in here?' His eyes go bonkers. They open up wide. Like this." Alonzo rolled his eyes back so that they looked like freshly laid eggs.

"Tell me more," I urged.

"I be showing them to a few more customers and they tell me they are United Airlines bonds worth a bundle. I keep a lookout for the man with the gym bag. I remembered he be carryin' a paper bag like it was his lunch. I never see him again. Through the grapevine at the station I be hearin' that someone be lookin' for a bag left in a taxi. That there be a one hundred thousand dollar reward. From the FBI."

"When you heard about the reward, what did you do?" I inquired.

"You know Miss Priscilla?" he asked.

"Miss Priscilla?"

"She's a downtown reader on Stockton Street. She is readin' my cards and she is seein' a hundred thousand dollars in my future and a limousine. I ask her where the hundred thou be comin' from and she is tellin' me from an award I be gettin'. So I call Trenton. I'm switched to Newark. They tell me that I be a rich man. A man calls, says he from the FBI, and tells me to bring my paper bag to Pat's Diner on South Broad Street, at nine o'clock in the morning."

From my travels in Trenton I know Pat's Diner. I guess Pat's Diner has always been there. I went there growing up in Trenton. It sits on South Broad Street, right at the border of Trenton and Hamilton Township. Hamilton is the largest suburb of Trenton but South Broad Street at that location is a combination of commercial, retail and residential streets.

Pat's is open 24 hours a day, seven days a week. Breakfast is served at any time. Parking is good. Lighting is good and the neighborhood is safe. It is a typical New Jersey diner with a combination of counters and booths. It is always busy. The clientele is eclectic. It changes depending on the time of day or night. There are always cops there. At any time. Cops know where the good food is at reasonable prices.

"I be parkin' my taxi and go into Pat's. These two white guys be comin' up to me. Be flashin' a badge. All of a sudden it be 'Hands up'. Five guys with guns pointed at my head, be yellin', 'You be under arrest. Don't be movin'. Don't be sayin' a word. It can be used against you.'"

Alonzo was talking fast. The hundred thousand dollars. The reward. I wondered why Alonzo had told me about the reader who saw the hundred thousand in his future. I thought that perhaps Alonzo L. Parker was a conniver and that he schemed up the extortion. That there was a reward offered by the Philadelphia Trust Company caught my attention. A call to the FBI would be easy to verify. The call from Newark would be on a federal telephone system bill. Whether he did not make the calls would be easy to ascertain. I thought about what the courier would say about the leather bag and the paper bag.

"So what happened after that?" I asked.

"I be taken here. Yesterday afternoon. I be sitting' here. One of them. Donaldson. He told me I'd be better off telling. Telling what? I be askin'. He be coming to see me every so often," Alonzo explained.

"You mean Donaldson? Agent Donaldson?" I asked.

Alonzo nodded.

"Agent Donaldson. Can I speak with you for a moment?" When Donaldson saw me enter the reception room, he turned his chair away so that all I could see was the back of his head. He was talking on the telephone. After he hung up, he turned his chair toward me.

"Certainly, counselor," he answered formally.

"Are you interested in what Parker told me?"

"I thought that what your client tells you is confidential," he replied.

I winked at him. "He agrees with everything that you told me. Except for one thing."

"What's that?" Donaldson asked, tilting his head to the side.

"He said something about a reward."

Without letting me finish, Donaldson snapped. "He's full of shit. He was trying to sell them on the street. I got a call from an informant. I set up the sting."

A federal grand jury indicted Alonzo L. Parker, charging him with attempted extortion of one hundred thousand dollars from a national bank. For four months I investigated his story and Agent Donaldson's allegations.

I verified that the bonds were not stolen. I read a statement given to the FBI by a Philadelphia Trust bank courier from which I learned that he had taken the Reading Railroad train from center city Philadelphia to West Trenton. He was carrying three million dollars in United Airlines bonds to the Chase Manhattan Bank in New York. He got off the train at West Trenton and took a bus from the West Trenton station to a stop downtown. He planned on taking another bus to the Pennsylvania Railroad station in Trenton to catch a train to New York. Instead, he hailed a yellow cab. While on the train to New York, he opened the black leather bag he was carrying. To his surprise the paper bag with the bonds was missing. He reported the missing bonds to the conductor, who called the railroad police. The police got on the train in Newark and began questioning people, thinking the bonds were stolen. The courier told the railroad police that, in accordance with bank regulations, the black leather bag was on his person at all times. A small note in the FBI file indicated the courier had been given a lie detector test.

The FBI, the railroad police, and the Philadelphia Trust's security personnel began to work together. The FBI had put out the word out that a reward of one hundred thousand dollars was being offered for the return of the stolen bonds or for the arrest and conviction of the person who had stolen the paper bag from the courier's black leather bag.

Something didn't jibe with what Alonzo had told me when I interviewed him in the federal lockup. He had told me that he had taken the black leather bag and put it in the trunk. He even described the size and shape with his hands. He had remembered that the man he picked up had a lunch bag. I reviewed my notes. Informer? Sting? Somebody was not telling the truth, but I didn't know who.

I filed papers in the court proceeding to get the name of the informer Agent Donaldson had told me about. My request was denied because, according to the law, if an FBI agent files a sworn statement that an informer has provided reliable evidence in the past it is not necessary to reveal the identity of the informer since it would compromise the effectiveness of law enforcement.

I assumed the sting Donaldson referred to was the information that was being put out on the train. I thought it was crucial that Alonzo told me he thought he was calling to get a reward. If he was calling for a reward, he wasn't trying to extort anything from anyone. I wondered why the FBI didn't just follow up, get the bonds, and give Alonzo L. Parker the reward.

I considered interviewing the courier. If he stuck to his story that the bag was in a leather bag that Alonzo had put into his trunk, that would lead to the conclusion that Alonzo lifted the paper bag from the courier's pouch. Was Alonzo L. Parker skilled enough to sense that something valuable was in that black leather bag, skilled enough to lift it from the bag, and clever enough to call the FBI to collect a reward for a crime he himself had committed? I had my doubts. I called the Philadelphia Trust security department and arranged a meeting with the courier.

Shortly thereafter, I received a call from Thomas Rose, the Assistant United States Attorney handling United States of America versus Alonzo L. Parker. He told me that he had received a call from the Philadelphia Trust asking for his permission to let me interview the courier and that my request had been denied.

The trial was three weeks away.

What was the result of the lie detector test taken by the courier? I called Tom Rose and asked for the results. He told me that lie detector tests were not admissible in court because they were not considered to be reliable and that he was not at liberty to give me the results.

"How about if my client were to take a lie detector and pass?" I asked, believing that lie detector tests were accurate if properly administered.

He informed me that he had never had such a request but that he would consider it. I offered to give a test administered by the FBI office in Washington. If Alonzo failed, I would plead him to the charges. If he passed, the case would be dismissed.

Tom called me back a few days later and agreed to the first part of the deal, but not the second. We agreed however that if, after a trial, Alonzo was convicted, the result of the lie detector test would be given to the judge before sentencing. That way, Alonzo would not be subject to the maximum penalty of fifteen years imprisonment and could get the same leniency that he would if he had pled.

I discussed the deal with Alonzo. "Mr. Albert. You be selling me out," he exclaimed. The more I spoke with Alonzo and watched his reactions, the more I was convinced he was telling the truth. He had been in jail for over four months. If he wasn't telling the truth, he would have been asking me to get him out one way or the other or to get the case over with so he could do his time.

My office telephone rang. I picked it up. A voice on the other end began to speak. I did not recognize it. "I can't tell you who I am. You are the lawyer for the taxi driver. The bank is going to pay the reward. One hundred thousand dollars."

" Great. To whom?" I asked. The phone clicked. The caller had hung up. How was I going to find out who the mystery caller was and whether the information was truthful?

I arranged to put Alonzo through a private lie detector test with a reliable operator who had retired from the New Jersey state police. He passed.

Later, I watched while the FBI lie detector operator put electrodes on Alonzo and asked him some simple questions, which he could only answer truthfully, such as his name and address and the name of the President of the United States. A baseline for truth was shown to the United States Attorney and me. We were then asked to leave the room.

After an hour of testing, the door to the room where the test had been administered opened. "May I talk to you gentlemen?" the lie detector administrator asked.

We walked into an office adjacent to the waiting area. "Mr. Parker shows no signs of fabrication," the lie detector operator told us.

I asked Tom Rose to drop the case. I was confident he would. He called to tell me he had set up a meeting with the trial judge, Judge Kinsman Clark, to discuss the case. At the meeting Judge Clark, a stern but fair jurist who was a United States Attorney before he was appointed to be a federal judge, told us in no uncertain terms that he would not accept a dismissal because a major bank was involved. He wanted a jury to decide on guilt or innocence. He informed us discreetly that it was not our job to second guess a grand jury's indictment. We informed him of the results of the lie detector test. as we left his chambers, the judge leaned back in his chair and stared at the ceiling.

Since the judge knew the results of the lie detector test, I decided to waive the right to a jury trial and let Judge Clark decide the case. My experience with juries told me that they would most likely believe FBI agent Donaldson rather than Alonzo L. Parker. Clearly, there was a risk of having Judge Clark hear the case. If I lost, the chances of overturning a verdict on appeal were slim to none. But, being a lawyer means making decisions based on risks. I didn't think a judge would ignore a lie detector result. A jury would not know of the test's existence because lie detector tests are not evidential unless the prosecutor agrees to admit them. Tom Rose had not agreed. His consent to waive the jury was a message to Judge Clark that he believed Alonzo was telling the truth.

I had the right to interview witnesses who were not government employees. Tom Rose agreed to let me interview security personnel and the courier. We went to Philadelphia and met with them

The courier entered the plush conference room at the Philadelphia Trust. I introduced myself and began to talk to the courier. As he responded to my questions, I noticed that his voice sounded very familiar. I asked him if he knew of a reward that was offered for information leading to the arrest and conviction of a person that led to the return of the three million dollars in United Airlines bonds. He hesitated. The United States Attorney looked at me. I stared back at him. I waited for the answer to my question.

"I think it is about to be paid," he said.

"To whom?" I asked.

"Don't know for sure," he responded.

I asked him to relate his version of the taxi ride from downtown Trenton to the station. I asked him where his black leather bag was when he got into the taxi.

"The black leather bag?" he asked. "The bonds were in the taxi on the seat next to me," he replied.

"That's not what I asked you sir," I said.

He looked at the bank security chief, who was sitting across the table from him. "I don't want to answer any more questions," he said.

Tom Rose suggested that we stop the interview.

Unexpectedly, the courier began to talk again. "OK, here's what happened. The cabbie offered to take my black bag from me. He was a nice man. I took out the paper bag before I gave the black bag to him. Bank regulations, you know. I had to have the bonds on my person at all times. I got to the station. I forgot I had taken the bag out of the black leather bag. I got on the New York train. On the way, it struck me that I had left the bag in the taxi. I was scared. So I reported the paper bag with the bonds stolen. I said it was in the black leather bag, which I had on my person at all times. That's what happened. So am I in big trouble?" he asked Tom Rose.

"What about the reward?" I asked, before Tom could respond.

The security chief replied, "It's been paid to Agent Donaldson of the FBI."

"When did that happen?" I followed up.

"Shortly after we got the bonds back," the security chief said.

I looked at Tom Rose. He shrugged his shoulders in disbelief.

"Tom, did you know about the results of lie detector test that this fellow took?" I asked, pointing to the courier.

"I never checked the results," he responded.

I took him at his word. I had to work with Tom on this case and probably on others in the future.

The following day, we arranged an appointment with Judge Clark and told him about our meeting with the courier. We both expected the judge to grant our request to dismiss the case. But after our meeting, he informed us that he still wanted to hear the case without a jury.

"I want to hear the testimony of Agent Donaldson under oath." Judge Clark said, looking at Tom Rose. "If what I think happened actually occurred, someone other than Mr. Parker will be a guest of the United States of America," he said. "Tom, I suspect Mr. Donaldson has been up to no good."

Two days before the trial, an article in the *Trenton Times* caught my eye. Stewart Donaldson had been found dead in an apartment in Morrisville, Pennsylvania, a town across the Delaware River from Trenton. The cause of death was a self-inflicted gun shot. I picked up the telephone and called Tom Rose. "Is that our Agent Donaldson?" I asked.

"What about him?" he responded.

"Did you see the article in this morning's *Times*?" I asked.

He hadn't seen the paper yet.

He promised to call the FBI office immediately. A few minutes later, my phone rang. "It's our Stewart Donaldson," he said.

"He leave a note?" I inquired.

"I asked the same thing. No note. So I'm told," he said.

Two days later, Judge Clark convened a perfunctory trial. He asked the United States Attorney to call his first witness. He announced that his witness was not available. The judge banged the gavel and dismissed the case. Alonzo L. Parker was able to take off his jail uniform and walk out of the federal courthouse, a free man.

"What about the reward?" Alonzo asked. "I be wantin' you to be havin' your share. I never shortchanged anyone. I ain't be startin' now," he said.

I inquired about the reward and was told it had been paid to Stewart Donaldson. The Philadelphia Trust Company refused to pay Alonzo a dime. So did the FBI. I urged Alonzo to sue for the reward, for false arrest, and for the suffering he went through in jail.

"Albert", he said, "gotta be movin' on. I be wantin' to move on. No more of this. It be over. You be the best. I be payin' you by the week. Don't you be worryin.'"

I took a good, long look at Alonzo. His thin, long hands were shaking.

Alonzo brought me two hundred dollars a week for an entire year even though I started suit against the bank for the reward it owed him.

A year later, I had convinced the bank to pay the reward and avoid the bad publicity a trial would bring to the bank and the FBI. Alonzo insisted I take a percentage. I accepted twenty thousand dollars and Alonzo L. Parker walked out of my office a free man with eighty thousand dollars.

# STOP LOOK AND LISTEN—WHAT WOULD YOUR MOTHER SAY?

"WHAT WOULD YOUR MOTHER SAY about what you are thinking of doing? A law school ethics professor had urged us to ask ourselves this question when faced with a situation about which we had a doubt.

John Brushman, a detective with whom I worked in the prosecutor's office, listened as I told him about my lunch with Teddy Herman.

Herman was everybody's friend. Advertisements for Herman's business, King Cleaners, featured Teddy's round face bedecked with a king's crown, promising royal treatment to every customer.

Herman had surprised me when he asked me to meet him at Mary Marks, a restaurant that was a converted white Victorian house in an affluent suburban neighborhood in Ewing, a predominately white township on Trenton's northern and western borders. Lawyers, judges, and businessmen patronized Mary Marks. I would have expected Herman to take me to one of the crowded saloons in the "Burg," the Italian neighborhood smack in the center of Trenton, where I had seen him lunch on dishes like roast veal, pasta with clam sauce, or asparagus with olive oil.

I had prepared for a serious meeting, hoping to convince Herman to give me some of King Cleaners' legal work. Leaving my downtown office via Route 29, I had driven behind the State House, passed western Trenton, and the house I grew up in, and then wound along the Delaware River until I reached Lower Ferry Road. I wanted to arrive early so I wouldn't keep Herman waiting. Entering the front door through a canvas canopied entrance, I saw a judge and attorney I recognized sipping martinis. Herman was sitting at a round table in a corner of the dining room. He was chatting with a gentlemen in his mid-fifties, who was barrel chested and wearing a flashy red sweater. I thought that perhaps Herman had decided to sit down with him while he waited for me.

As I approached the table, Herman stood up and greeted me. "Glad you could join us. You're getting a big name around here. Meet my associate, Pat Largo. Pat owns big gas stations. He's got other interests, too. He wants to talk to you about some business."

Herman pulled out a chair next to Pat for me and I wondered why there were four more empty chairs, why Herman hadn't told me about Largo joining us, and why Herman had not told me he was inviting me to talk about something I wouldn't be prepared for. My father thought that an owner of a laundry business would be interested in tax planning, setting up a retirement plan under a new law, and labor relations with the Teamsters Union. When I discovered that, in addition to dry cleaning, King Cleaners supplied linens to restaurants and hospitals, he helped me with some appropriate questions to ask if restaurants or hospitals came up in the conversation. But I knew nothing about the needs of a gasoline station proprietor.

"Some others are going to join us in a while. How about a drink?" Herman asked me.

Four men walked past the bar toward our table. Herman stood up. "Sam, my friend. Angelo, my good buddy. Sal. Tony. Good to see you, fellows." Herman embraced each man as they shook hands. "Glad you could make it. I thought maybe you'd be late coming from Philly. I just ordered the usual for Mr. Stark here and Pat. You fellows look awfully healthy. Miami. The Bahamas. Where you been? Meet our guest, Albert Stark. He's the young lawyer I've been telling you about." Herman motioned to the waitress. "Four tomato juices for the gentlemen, thank you," he told her. It struck me as somewhat odd that everyone was having a tomato juice except for Herman. I had seldom seen men eating with Teddy Herman who were teetotalers. My image of his friends were straight out of *The Godfather*: men with open collars, napkins hanging from their necks, drinking a sip of wine after every spoonful of pasta.

Sam, Angelo, Sal, and Tony settled into their chairs without saying a word. They acknowledged my presence only with a nod of their heads. Sam, probably fifty pounds overweight, had his dark hair cut short and was wearing a knit shirt and sport coat. He was the first to begin. "Pat, you've been very busy lately. Everything okay?" He grabbed a napkin and I noticed a huge diamond pinky ring on his oversized hand.

Pat replied in a deep voice, "Everything's copacetic. Under control. No problems."

"Good to hear," Angelo, a slim man dressed in a sport coat, his wavy grey hair perfectly combed, said softly.

Herman, Sal, and Tony bantered about the racetrack and about how hard the laundry business was becoming now that the unions were making it so expensive to do pick up and delivery.

"This fellow a union lawyer?" Angelo inquired of Herman.

Herman shook his head from side to side.

"Do you have your Pennsylvania bar?" Angelo asked, looking at me.

"I'm admitted in New Jersey," I replied.

"That's going to be a problem," Angelo said, shrugging his shoulders to show Herman his disappointment. Angelo didn't explain what the problem was. Then, the waitress came to the table to serve the drinks and told Herman, "The lunch will be out in a few minutes, Mr. Herman."

I thought it was strange no one had placed an order. I was so uncomfortable that I wanted to get up and say, "Thank you for lunch." I felt like a character in a Greek play where the chorus tells the audience what is occurring while the actors are ignorant as to what is happening to them. I couldn't put my finger on why. I had always seen Herman out with people who were characters. I was scared, yet curious, and I didn't want to be impolite. So I stayed.

Sal, seeing how uneasy I was, asked me very politely, "You single?

Have a wife?"

"Married," I replied. "With two young children."

"So you probably need some law business to feed the family," Sal said with a chuckle.

"Absolutely. I'm always looking for new business," I replied.

Sal turned his head to the others.

"Have any experience with collections?" Tony, a heavy-set fellow who could have passed for a professional wrestler, chimed in.

"I do," I answered eagerly. "When I started practicing, I helped my father with some business clients who were owed money. I'm terrific at getting people to pay."

"Sounds like this kid may have possibilities after all," Angelo commented, flashing a smile at Herman.

The waitress placed large platters of pasta in the center of the table and put plates, which she had already filled, in front of us.

"Mangia," Pat said, twisting his fork in a large spoonful of pasta.

Largo turned to me. "How'd you like to be my lawyer? How's fifteen hundred dollars a week sound? Seventy five thou a year."

Never having had anyone make such an offer before, I replied innocently, "I charge by the case. Seventy-five dollars an hour."

"That's not how I like to do business. I like weekly payments. Helps me keep track of my expenses," Largo chuckled.

"What kind of cases would I be handling?"

"I have a lot of guys working for me. They get in trouble. You know, they get drunk and I need someone to get them out of the mess they're in."

"Well, I am sure I could handle that kind of stuff. But isn't fifteen hundred a week a lot?"

"If you do more and deserve more than the fifteen, you'll get even more. How's that sound, young man?"

"Sounds good," I said.

Largo took an address book out of his shirt pocket and excused himself from the table.

Moving closer to me and patting me on my knee, Herman appeared to be pleased with the answers I was giving to the questions.

I had not eaten any of the pasta because I suddenly had no appetite. The waitress started to pick up the plates in front of us and then put down a platter filled with stuffed cabbage, roast chicken, a pork roast, and a large dish of asparagus, tomatoes, anchovies, and mozzarella cheese covered with olive oil.

"We better stop the kibbitzin' and let the young man eat," Herman joked.

"Don't worry about me. I will be very happy with the roast pork," I said politely. "My great grandfather would turn over in his grave," I added, "He was the first Orthodox Rabbi in Trenton back in the 1880's."

"Kid's got a sense of humor! And class yet," Tony remarked. Because he was chewing his food as he spoke, I wasn't actually sure if he had said "kid" or "yid."

After the others made a gesture agreeing with Tony, he asked, "You like Italiano, eh?"

"You know Johnnie Puccinella?" I asked, thinking that I'd drop a name they might recognize. The four men glanced at each other.

"You've been doing a helluva job against the law," Angelo said sharply.

"Just beginner's luck," I said.

"You know Herman, I like this boy," Tony said, glancing at Angelo.

"Angelo," Sal asked. "You think we got some work for Mr. Stark?"

Angelo looked me squarely in the eye. "Son, we have a lot of work. And, to be quite honest, we're looking for a lawyer like you. Serious. Smart. And loyal. You've got two kids, a wife. You'll also have a bright future if you work with us. We have so much business you'll be set for life. No worries. All the money you'll ever want. Believe me. How'd you like to have a half-a-million in the bank?"

"Who wouldn't?" I responded.

Pat Largo returned to the table. "Did I miss anything?"

"All the good stuff," Sal responded. "Our new lawyer in Jersey is going to be quite a find," he said, forking up another mouthful.

I turned toward Largo. Watching him leaf through the pages of his telephone directory, I noticed that the names on the pages were written in ink, but that the phone numbers were in pencil. "Mr. Largo, how come your book has penciled phone numbers?" I asked seriously, wondering if I shouldn't do the same thing with my address book since our office telephone number had recently been given a different exchange prefix.

"My friends change their phone numbers a lot," Pat whispered loud enough for everyone to hear.

The table erupted in laughter.

After I related the possibility of having enough work for the rest of my life, Brushman smiled. "At least for as long as you live. Do you know who you had lunch with?" he asked.

"Businessmen. Friends of Teddy Herman," I replied innocently.

"Businessmen. That's for sure. Serious businessmen. The Philly mob," he said.

"You've got to be kidding."

"I never knew Herman was connected. But when you mentioned the telephone numbers in pencil, it rang a bell. There's a lot of wiretapping going on so people with something to hide have to keep one step ahead of the law. I had heard the gas station on Princeton Avenue was a mob business where money was laundered. Maybe Teddy's not just into laundering clothes? I had my suspicions but they weren't confirmed until now."

From Brushman, I learned that Pat Largo was "middle management" for the notorious Bruno family from Philadelphia. Angelo fit the description of none other than Angelo Bruno, reputed to be the leader of a family. King Cleaners was a front, a laundry not only for drycleaning but also money laundering. Tony, Sal, and Sam were henchmen for Angelo Bruno who ran the numbers trade, and along with it an illegal adoption and immigration ring. They had contacts in East Asia and brought young girls over to be prostitutes and to have children who were sold for adoption at high prices. "The fifteen hundred was what is called a retainer. You're the family lawyer. And the half-a-million. They'd set up an account in your name. You'd be in the laundry business. Money laundering. Just like Herman. You know there's something nice about the fellows you ate lunch with," John said.

"What is nice about them?" I asked.

John winked. "They hire good lawyers."

That evening, I told Ellen about my lunch. She laughed, thinking I was spinning a tale to amuse her. When I assured her it was true and that I didn't know what to tell Herman, she giggled nervously.

"Remember when we were stopped in traffic on 39th Street waiting to get into the Lincoln Tunnel," she said, referring to a visit to New York City just before we got married, " I told you I didn't want to marry a hard-nosed businessman like most of my father's friends. I wanted to marry an idealist. Tell Herman that your wife doesn't want to be married to a businessman."

The next morning, I called Herman. I didn't think Ellen's explanation would be clear to Teddy Herman. I recalled advice a businessman, who was a friend of my father's, had given me when I first started to practice. He said to steer clear of hiring anyone you can't fire and to make sure you are able to fire any client you don't feel comfortable representing. "I've given some thought to our lunch," I told Herman. "I don't think I want to have any client consume more than ten percent of my time. It would be bad in the long run for me to be too dependent on one client."

"I understand," he assured me. "I was only trying to help. You know Teddy Herman. He's always there to help."

My father came into my office. I related what happened at my lunch with Teddy Herman, but didn't reveal what Brushman had told me.

"I told him I would work for his friends on a case by case basis."

"You did what?" he asked, resting his chin in his palms.

"Cash flow is slow. Overhead doesn't stop. I thought I'd get some business for Richard to take some pressure off you." Richard Shaine was an associate my father had hired to make sure that someone would be able to take over his practice in the future.

My father frowned.

"Come on now, Dad. I'm teasing." Actually, I had ambivalent feelings because I was asking myself when I was going to get out from beneath my father's watch. My mind raced with questions about why I had come back to a place where my family was so well known. I didn't want to be in my father's shadow forever. I wanted my day in the sun.

"I take nothing for granted. I've seen lawyers who are hungry for money, or for fame, do some stupid things," he said.

"What if I did some work for Herman's friends? It's not unethical. They deserve good representation," I snapped argumentatively.

"There are some kinds of work I hope you will avoid doing. And some clients I'd prefer you not to represent. Lawyers have to follow stricter ethical standards than businessmen. It's not always easy. It's not easy to tell which clients not to get involved with. Some of the slickest are the most dangerous."

"You don't have to worry about me with Herman's buddies. I want to be in the courtroom as a lawyer, not in a cell needing one."

My father chuckled, relieved that I was not serious, and that I was still Sidney's son.

# PART TWO

## *REACHING MY STRIDE*

# TURNING POINT—A FIRM OF MY OWN

I WAS FINALLY SITTING AT A MAHOGANY DESK in an office that had room not only for a credenza behind it, but also a small sofa.

While I was sifting through some paper work, the phone let out a ring like an alarm. I picked up the receiver, and Al Buchan introduced himself. "I run John McShain's office here in New Jersey. I'm calling to set up an interview. We have a case against the State of New Jersey. Mr. McShain will be up here from his Philadelphia office on Wednesday."

"Who is Mr. McShain?" I asked, looking at the blank pages of my weekly appointment calendar.

"You haven't heard of John McShain? He's a big contractor. Built the Kennedy Center in Washington, renovated the White House for Harry Truman, and put up almost every Catholic church in the area."

"He wants to interview me?" I blurted out before hastily gathering myself. "What kind of crime is he charged with? I'd be happy to be interviewed, but can you tell me what the case is about?"

"I'm sure he'll fill you in when he sees you. It's not a criminal case. It involves the Yardville Correction Center job," Buchan continued, giving the impression that anybody who was anybody should have known about the Yardville job just as anybody who was anybody should have known John McShain. "How's one o'clock?"

On my last day of work with Governor Hughes, he had taken me aside, "You've done a good job. I owe you one favor. Use it wisely." I had a naive sense that McShain was "the one" Governor Hughes may have been referring to. I called Bill Kirschner, Governor Hughes' counsel, who became enraged when I asked him for information on McShain. "McShain's claiming the state forced him to use some jail builder that went 'belly up,'" Kirschner declared. After telling me that the Yardville Correction facility was a new prison for youth offenders, he continued, "The job was delayed and now he wants the state to pay him all the money it cost him. He asked me to tell the governor to pay him extra money. I told him he was full of you-know-what."

"Bill, why the hell do you think he's interviewing me?"

"God only knows. Crawf Jamieson was his lawyer. He just died. That's all I know. Crawf was a power. An excellent lawyer. He and Dick were close friends. They grew up together in democratic politics. Crawf was old school; his handshake was as good as gold."

I collected as much information as I could in the *Trenton Times* archive describing the dispute. McShain claimed the state had distributed plans for the construction of a prison in which jail cells were to be manufactured according to the specifications of only one jail cell manufacturer, Pauley Jail Building Company. McShain had told the state he would not bid on the project if he had to buy the jail cells, because rumors were rampant that Pauley was on the verge of bankruptcy. McShain wanted to use the Stewart Jail Building Company. McShain alleged that Charles Vogt, the head of the State's Department of Building and Construction, convinced him to bid by assuring him that if a problem arose with Pauley, Vogt would issue a change order for any costs.

McShain won the bid and Pauley went bankrupt.

When I sought advice from Richard Casey, an expert in construction law, and Sam Tauber, the bailiff at the United States Bankruptcy court, they had serious questions about the validity of McShain's claim, because nothing was in writing.

From construction law books in the state law library, I learned that when an owner such as the state insisted that a contractor like McShain use a "unique product" and the "unique product" became unavailable, the owner was responsible for damages. However, there was one exception to that rule. If the contractor knew that the "unique product" was not available and still contracted with the owner to provide it, the contractor could not claim he was locked out.

I pulled into McShain's driveway in front of a stately, Georgian building that reminded me of Independence Hall. A small white sign, with "JOHN MC SHAIN" painted in thick, black letters, stood on the front lawn.

Expecting to enter a plush lobby with leather sofas and brass lamps on antique tables, I was surprised to set foot in a reception area lit with bare fluorescent bulbs. Three armless metal chairs, covered with black Naugahyde sat on a floor of green and black tiles. Black and white photographs of buildings hung on white painted walls. There were no tables, magazines, or lamps.

An elderly woman, with her gray hair combed back and topped with a wrapped braid, greeted me. She picked up the handpiece to a black dial telephone. After putting the receiver down, she lifted her eyeglasses, which were suspended on a chain around her neck. "Mr. McShain will be with you shortly," she said.

A door to my right opened. A portly gentleman with a ruddy complexion, thin, reddish-blond hair, and bright blue eyes, was clad in a red shirt and green, Scotch-plaid trousers. "I'm Al Buchan. Thanks for coming over. Mr. McShain is ready to see you."

A slight, white haired man with a pencil-thin, white mustache sat behind a simple oak desk. He took a bite from a half-eaten sandwich, put it on a paper plate, pushed the plate to the side and slid a cup of coffee toward a black lunch box, like the one I used to carry to elementary school. He raised his eyebrows slightly. "This lad's awful young to handle my case, isn't he?" McShain asked Buchan.

"I'm a fighter, sir," I exclaimed before Buchan could answer.

"Well, Al, I sure need a fighter, don't I?" McShain quipped.

My lips were pursed and my hands nervously squeezed the car keys in my pants pocket.

"Please sit down, young man. I've heard some very nice things about you from Professor Reynolds at the Penn Law School. I understand you went there. He's a good friend of my nephew, Kevin Duggan."

I had not known who John McShain was, what the Yardville job was, and now I did not know why Professor Reynolds would give anyone my name. His courses on contracts and bankruptcy were two of the most unpleasant and uninteresting I had experienced in law school. One afternoon, I was dozing in class when I heard him call my name. My classmates stared at me. Their silence was deafening. He wiped his forehead with the back of his hand and put his index finger on his chin. "Mr. Stark," he said deliberately." Give me your answer."

"The answer to your question is very complex," I said.

"I'll try to understand," Professor Reynolds remarked. Nervous laughter vibrated through the classroom after I admitted that I had not heard the question.

"Do you think a handshake is a contract?" Mr. McShain inquired.

"Shall I answer that question according to the way Professor Reynolds taught me?" I responded. "To me a handshake should be as good as a contract, but legally a contract for any substantial sum has to be in writing to be binding."

"I see." McShain rubbed his chin. "How do you charge?"

I told him I charged seventy-five dollars an hour.

"I don't pay by the hour," he said. "I pay for results. I don't want any lawyer who charges by the hour. There's no incentive for the lawyer except to put in long hours."

"Mr. McShain, this case involves a lot of work. I have come prepared. I read the newspaper reports. I researched lockouts. To do this case for a contingency fee is too risky," I explained. "I don't have the money to finance a case like this one."

"Look at that, Al," McShain said with a sly smile. "He did research. This might just be the kind of case you would want. It's high profile, you know," McShain continued.

I thought that representing a builder of McShain's stature would open doors for me in the big developer's world and would promote my career in urban renewal. I was not going to let an opportunity like this pass. McShain was suing for three million. A one-third contingent fee could net me a million. I had worked for a few small contractors before who had promised me business and none of those endeavors had worked out.

I had to plead with my father to let me take on the McShain case. A product of the Depression, he had a steady, low-risk practice with which he was comfortable. He was also worried that I was going off course. My father had deprecated lawyers who wrote contracts without understanding the terms if the contract became the subject of litigation. We made a decision, which I relayed to Mr. McShain the following morning in Philadelphia. My father reluctantly allowed me to take the case if I reviewed all of the contract documents with him and could persuade McShain to pay a retainer sufficient to cover our costs.

"If you select me to handle the case, I would like you to pay a retainer of fifteen thousand dollars and agree to pay the costs. If I win the case, I will get one third of the recovery and I will credit you the fifteen thousand. My father and I think it's a fair arrangement."

"I'm not going to give you fifteen thousand dollars, but I promise to pay all of the costs," McShain informed me.

"What if I spend a year or two and get nothing for you? As much as I'd like to do this case, I can't put myself into that predicament." I explained again that I was a young lawyer and that I did not have funds to properly handle his case.

"Son, John McShain is a fair man." McShain exclaimed, speaking in the third person. "Don't you worry. When I started out in this business, I laid bricks and block for building foundations. I took a chance. If I did a good job, I trusted the person I worked for was going to pay me. You fight for me, do a good job, and you won't get hurt," he assured me. "Give me someone with a good attitude, and I can teach them anything." His eyes were alive.

If I asked for time to discuss our conversation with my father, I was afraid I would lose any chance I had to get his case. I made the decision. "Okay, it's a deal. A handshake is a handshake," I said.

Mr. McShain shook my hand and confidently said, "You won't be disappointed."

My father was shocked that I was selected and upset that I had committed to a contingent fee. If he had said "no deal" I could have called back Mr. McShain and reneged. Nothing was in writing.

I wrote John McShain a letter thanking him for his confidence and memorializing our contingent fee arrangement. This was my chance to establish my reputation and finally make Sidney Stark, Albert's father. If I blew the opportunity, I would never overcome my frustration. I had to prove myself.

A few days after I received the signed agreement, Al Buchan ushered me into a spacious, windowless room behind the receptionist's cubicle. The floor was covered with the same green and black tile as the front entrance. Flourescent lights hung above a large linoleum topped table that was covered with plans and piles of documents. Stacks of cartons labeled "YARDVILLE" rested against bare, white walls.

"Let me introduce you to your team," Buchan began, walking behind two men seated along the near end of the table. "Meet, Ron Fiori. He was our on-site man in charge of the job. Dick Standiford was the bean counter. He was responsible for calculating costs and submitting invoices to the state. Howard Leake, over there," Buchan said, pointing across the table, "is our engineer. He interprets the specifications." Buchan offered me a chair at the head of the table.

"Howard, why don't you start?" Buchan asked.

A stocky man with a generous crop of white hair and a pink, bulbous nose, Leake opened a thick book and slid it in front of me. He leaned over and pointed, "When all is said and done, the case boils down to what's on this page. Look at this drawing," he said. "See that lock. That's a special lock. It's patented. Pauley owns the patent. No other jail builder can use the lock without Pauley's permission." Turning the page, Leake read a passage underlined in red ink, "'The General Contractor must supply jail cells with the lock specified in Section 3A.' The specs don't say 'equal or equivalent.'"

"That's a good start, Howard," Buchan interrupted. "Ronnie, fill Mr. Stark in on what happened on the job."

Ron Fiori was in his mid-forties and had black, wavy hair, and deep set eyes. He folded his arms on the table. Muscles bulged beneath his short sleeve shirt. "Before the job started, I met with the state people and we agreed on a construction schedule. When we got on the job, we laid the foundations, put up the walls, and set the roof. We were right on schedule. I got word about four months into the job that

Pauley had filed for bankruptcy and wouldn't be able to deliver the cells. So we had to get another jail manufacturer. We found Stewart and got them approved by the state. The schedule had to be changed, causing delay after delay." Fiori stopped and looked at Standiford, "Dick, fill him in from your end," Fiori instructed.

Dick Standiford was the stereotypical accountant. His plain blue tie was clipped to his polyester shirt and his pocket was filled with five pens. His oversized glasses rested near the tip of his nose. "When you schedule a job, you figure the start-up costs. You have to organize the work. That's a big job. Time spent reorganizing is very costly, and it goes right down the line. If the mason can't put in rebars, the walls and floors don't get poured. Then the electrical work gets delayed so the fixtures can't be installed. It's like dominos. Once one goes, the whole row falls down. This job ran over by three million dollars. I submitted invoices to Charles Vogt. He's the head of the Department of Building and Construction. He was supposed to prepare a change order but didn't. I got word that the state was taking the position that McShain knew about Pauley's financial problems and that Vogt wasn't going to issue a change order."

Buchan told me the claim had been filed by Jamieson with the State Legislature and was to be decided by a committee of three legislators at a hearing beginning in March of 1969.

I spent four mornings a week during December and January reading and learning the contents of scheduling documents, start up accounting ledgers, contract documents, plans and specifications, bid documents, architect's approvals, and change orders. Fiori taught me what went into the construction of jail cells, concrete pours, and state inspections.

The Stacy Trent Hotel, a grand building, constructed in the first half of the century, is located on the corner of West State and Willow Streets in downtown Trenton, one block from the state house. In its heyday, the Stacy Trent hosted weddings and inaugural balls. Its main attraction now was the barbershop on the ground floor and a restaurant where businessmen and politicians gathered.

While I was sitting in a raised bootblack chair getting a shoeshine, Vinnie Convery, a lawyer and former law partner of veteran Congressman Frank Thompson, approached me. "When you're finished, stop by the restaurant. I want to share something with you."

I entered the restaurant and saw Vinnie sitting alone at a small table. "I hear you're handling the McShain case," he said when I eased into my seat.

"I am," I replied. "And, Vinnie, to tell you the truth, I think I am a little over my head."

"How so?" he inquired.

"It's so damn complicated. I spend every waking hour thinking and worrying about the case. It's like building the Empire State Building from the ground up . . . and I'm not mechanical!"

"Watch yourself. You may be in more of a fix than you think. There's some heavy duty hanky panky in that Yardville job," Vinnie whispered.

"Hanky panky? What d'you mean?"

"Payoffs. That's what I mean. Watch your backside," he warned.

"What should I do?" I asked.

"Talk to your dad."

My father insisted that I could not cast aspersions at anyone. He told me that if I could not present the case based on the facts, I had to tell Mr. McShain that I could not continue representing him.

I kept my appointment with Mr. McShain at the Olden Avenue office the following Wednesday, and I told him what I had heard. I asked him point blank if he was involved in any payoffs.

"Son, you just go in there and fight," he said. "To me, this is a matter of principle. A million or two to me is not going to make or break me. 'Hanky panky,' as you call it, is not something John McShain engages in. You have nothing to worry about with me. I'm a hardnosed Irishman but an honest one." McShain leaned forward. "There is a twist to this case you should know about. A Republican legislator from Camden County wants to use the case to embarrass Governor Hughes and maybe help out Bill Cahill, who's running for governor next November. Don't worry. You just do an honest job and let the chips fall where they may."

I felt like crying. Mr. McShain's steel gray eyes aimed at mine. "How much time have you spent so far on my case?" he asked.

"About six thousand dollars worth," I told him.

He picked up the telephone sitting on a table to his right. "Mildred, will you please send Dick Standiford in?"

While we waited for Standiford, McShain talked to me about his estate in Killarney and his meetings with the Pope. "Do you know what Truman did when I put an advertising sign on the White House lawn while I redid the White House?" he chuckled. "Harry came to me one day. 'McShain,' he said, 'Don't you think it's in bad taste to put a sign that says 'McShain Builders–Philadelphia' on the front lawn of the White House.' You know what I said? 'Mr. President, every man has to make a living.'" He had thrown his head back and was still laughing when Standiford entered the office.

"Dick, will you cut a check for six thousand dollars to Mr. Stark here?" he inquired.

McShain versus State of New Jersey began. The hearings were scheduled to last twelve weeks. I arrived early to familiarize myself with the hearing room. Morning sun streamed in at an angle onto the floor and walls of the large hearing room. I needed a lift after lugging the sixteen boxes of material from the parking lot behind the State House. I went to the governor's office to get a cup of coffee. Governor Hughes' secretary passed me in the hallway. "I hear you're appearing before the claims committee," she snapped.

Mr. McShain and Al Buchan arrived at nine fifteen. A few minutes later, Fiori, Leake, and Standiford came in carrying Styrofoam cups. We huddled in the rear of the room. A cadre of men from the Department of Building and Construction walked into the room. The attorney general and the state's chief architect, Bob Williams, went directly to the counsel table with a placard marked STATE. Bob Stockton, the attorney general, opened his attaché case and put some papers and a yellow pad on the table. He looked at my table, piled with stacks of paper. As he noticed the cartons lined up behind it, he snarled.

I opened a manila file, which contained my opening statement. I confidently stood up and pronounced, "Good Morning," to Stockton. He did not extend his hand or return my greeting.

The clerk opened a door behind the judge's bench, and revealed three high-backed chairs. "Are you ready to begin the McShain case?" the clerk asked.

"We are, sir," the attorney general and I replied simultaneously. Three men entered and settled in the high-backed chairs. They introduced themselves and told us that they were legislators who would act as judges.

I was the first to speak. "The law of 'lockout' governs this case," I began. "Mr. McShain bid on the Yardville job. The specifications required the use of Pauley locks. Pauley went bankrupt. Because it was impossible to get a unique product, McShain suffered losses amounting to almost three million dollars." For a half-hour, I outlined the basis for McShain's losses. "Richard Standiford filed invoices for extra work required by Pauley's default. No change order was ever issued. This claim is, in reality, a request for that change order."

The attorney general then replied. "This is not a lockout case, but it is rather a simple case in which an experienced contractor gambled and lost. He bet that he could finish the Yardville job before Pauley went out of business. No change order was issued, because it wasn't necessary. McShain is responsible for his own folly."

The Camden County legislator, who Mr. McShain had warned me about, threw the first question at me. "Assuming everything you say is true about Pauley, how are we going to excuse your client for not telling the state in writing that he was holding the state responsible for Pauley's default and failing to submit a change order?"

He wanted me to say that McShain and Charles Vogt had a verbal agreement. "Your question is appropriate, because the answer is going to determine who wins and who loses this case," I responded. "In my briefcase I have a legal brief with cases involving mandatory hiring of subcontractors. Each of them decided the owner was responsible to the general contractor for the failure of a subcontractor, such as Pauley, to perform. I also have the page of specifications that indicates the state is responsible for issuing change orders for work required by the state."

The Camden legislator shifted uncomfortably in his high-backed chair as I handed him a copy of my brief and the specifications.

Charles Vogt, the head of the department of building and construction, was feared by legislators because he approved work done on behalf of the state. Many legislators wanted contracts awarded to their constituents, who, in turn, would contribute to their election campaigns.

If Charles Vogt admitted that he had an agreement with McShain, the contract would be considered unenforceable, and the case would be dismissed.

If I did not prepare a brief discussing legal points, the Hughes administration would be embarrassed by an inference that Pauley had paid off Vogt to obtain a rigged bid to avoid going out of business. If I framed the battle "McShain versus Vogt," I stood little or no chance of winning.

"Do you have a brief in opposition?" the Camden judge asked the attorney general.

"No," he replied, "But I'll get one for you by the morning."

"Please do that," the Camden legislator muttered.

Eleven staff members from the Department of Building and Construction, all of whom were scheduled to testify for the state, sat together in the spectator section.

"I call the state architect to the witness stand," I announced.

"Me?" Bob Williams uttered in surprise.

I nodded.

"I expected Mr. McShain to be your first witness," Attorney General Stockton exclaimed.

"I call the state architect to the stand," I repeated.

Williams, a tall man with thinning, auburn hair, shuffled to the witness stand.

Every bid document and the minutes of each job meeting for two years and five months of the Yardville job was engraved in my brain. The McShain team had taught me how the specifications were developed and how the job proceeded before and after the Pauley bankruptcy. There was only one other person who knew the contract documents and the job progress as well as I did. That person was Bob Williams.

Each judge scanned the numbered exhibits and charts I handed them.

I spent the next six days questioning the state architect, taking him step by step through the Yardville job. When I sensed I was losing the judges' attention due to the boring nature of the subject, I directed them to a particular document and watched carefully to make sure they read it.

At the end of the lengthiest questioning I had ever conducted, the state architect had proved that Dick Standiford had submitted invoices for every piece of work that was required by Pauley's default. Furthermore, I confirmed that there was no provision in the specifications or any agreement at any job meeting that permitted a bidder to use an "equal or equivalent lock."

It was John McShain's turn to take the witness stand. The legislators stood up and greeted him.

"Mr. McShain," the Camden legislator asked, "Don't you think it would be advantageous to all concerned if there could be a settlement?"

"I am open to any reasonable resolution," McShain answered.

I wondered if he was telling McShain he had a weak case and hinting that a small settlement would be a smart move to make. I shuddered when I thought of the inexorable disappointment I would feel if there were a small settlement. I was afraid McShain might decide he was spending too much time at the State House when he could be doing more important things.

We went to lunch at the Stacy Trent, and I discovered that I had lost my appetite. Mr. McShain took out the bag lunch his wife had prepared for him. "You look worried," Mr. McShain said.

Mr. McShain always ate the lunch his wife prepared for him and then left a huge tip for the wait staff.

"I am, sir. I didn't like what the fellow from Camden said."

"Don't you worry. He's only one of three judges. The attorney general is not going to offer me one thin dime. I just wanted to be nice when I said what I did. You just keep on plugging."

McShain admitted that, while he had had conversations with Charles Vogt, he maintained he would not bid if he had to use Pauley. He emphasized that he was not relying on his conversations with Vogt in making his claim. Rather, he was counting on the state to honor the law and the written words in the specifications. When he left the witness stand, I was happy that the three days I spent preparing McShain for his testimony paid off.

The hearings proceeded laboriously as Fiori, Standiford, and Leake testified about the scheduling difficulties and the monetary losses.

Attorney General Stockton called witnesses from the Department of Building and Construction. Each witness presented evidence that McShain's losses were less than what he claimed.

Cross-examining each, I asked if Charles Vogt could have prepared a change order before the Yardville job was completed. Every one of the witness' replied that until the job was complete it was not possible to calculate the loss. My case was building as I had planned.

The state's final witness was Charles Vogt. There was one sure way I could lose. If Charles Vogt testified that McShain told him he knew of Pauley's financial difficulties and bid at his own risk, the law would favor the state under the exception to the lockout law.

"Mr. Vogt is not available today," the attorney general told the judges.

"Very well," the Camden legislator said. "It's a beautiful day. We all deserve a little rest. We'll begin again on Monday."

My telephone rang at home early that evening. Al Buchan told me we were going to Brielle, a seashore town, on Friday night to meet with Joe Keefe, a retired state architect who hated Charles Vogt, because Vogt had fired him.

At dinner, Keefe, through a mouthful of food, gave us some vital information. "Vogt won't testify–not if I'm in the courtroom," he declared vigilantly.

"Why not?" I asked automatically.

"You see, Vogt would be too afraid if I were there," Keefe said as he swallowed a mouthful. "Vogt knows that I am aware that Pauley had promised him a payoff in order to get the specifications written without that 'equal and equivalent" clause.'

"This is definitely useful," Buchan said as he smiled to himself.

"You know what I can do," Keefe began. "I can give you gentlemen the name of a man from Pauley who you could use. Maybe you could call him to the witness stand, because when Pauley went bankrupt, Vogt never received the payoff."

"Now you're thinking like a lawyer!" I declared spiritedly. "But what do you think Vogt's motives are?"

"He wanted to put McShain in a vulnerable position in order to negotiate a settlement," suggested Keefe.

"That would make McShain cover the payoff he had expected from Pauley." I said. The scandal was all coming together.

"You got a glitch though," Keefe started as my heart skipped a beat. "It's really no big deal, but McShain will not meet with Vogt, because McShain believes that he reneged on their handshake."

"So what do you think Vogt will do now?" I questioned.

"He'll try to approach McShain and try to make a deal before his testimony."

Over the weekend, I decided that instead of having Joe Keefe in the courtroom, I would tell Stockton that I planned to call Joe Keefe as a rebuttal witness after Vogt testified.

I arrived early on Monday morning. The attorney general and Charles Vogt were talking quietly to each other. I asked the attorney general if he had a moment to talk with me. "I'm going to call Joe Keefe in rebuttal," I whispered. I motioned to McShain to come sit next to me at the counsel table. Following my instructions, McShain did not look at the attorney general or Vogt.

Shortly thereafter, Vogt left the room.

"Is your next witness Mr. Vogt?" the Camden legislator asked the attorney general.

"No," he replied.

At the end of the state's case, I outlined each claim, its value, and the document backing up the claim. I argued that no change order could have been prepared until the job was completed. Until the state certified its costs and agreed that the specification required the state to have the work that cost McShain extra, Charles Vogt could not issue the change order.

The three legislators sat as they listened to the attorney general's closing argument. He argued that McShain could not recover any money, because he had heard rumors about Pauley's problems and, therefore, took the risk of loss when he bid. Suddenly, the Camden legislator interrupted Stockton. "Why didn't Vogt testify to those facts?"

I almost jumped up from my chair. Stockton didn't answer. I could not control my emotions. My arms reflexively pushed me up and my voice echoed throughout the room. "Mr. Stockton, answer the question."

"Mr. Stark, you are out of order. It's our job to have control." The Camden legislator's eyes bore into mine. "Please take your seat," he said.

Stockton switched his tack and argued that if McShain were entitled to recover, the damages were only one million dollars. He forced a smile and sat down.

Afraid to look up, the silence in the room made me feel as though I were in a vacuum.

"We will take the case under advisement and issue our decision forthwith," I heard the legislators say.

Chairs scraped. A hand was on my shoulder. McShain was standing next to me.

"You did fine," he said. "We're going to get at least a million."

While I packed my documents and files into the boxes I had brought to the hearings, I felt like crying. I had worked so hard and thought I had defeated Stockton until the last moments of the trial.

On the way to my car, I wondered what would happen if the case was not ruled in our favor. I knew McShain appreciated the time and effort that I put into his case, and I could only hope that he would reimburse me for the expenditures I had made and, perhaps, even pay me for the time I put in. But I just didn't know.

Expecting to lose, I looked at the mail everyday. After a month, I had convinced myself I had to move on and prepare myself for the defeat I would suffer. The anxiety nearly paralyzed me as the days passed.

In August, I received the decision. Afraid at first to open the envelope, I flipped to the final page. The legislators awarded McShain

$922,212, the largest claim ever awarded against the State of New Jersey.

There were two steps left to climb. The legislature would convene in September. Money had to be appropriated before the award would be paid. Under state law, payment of a committee's award was not mandatory. Finally, the governor would have to sign the bill.

I was summoned to a meeting with Governor Hughes and the Secretary of the Treasury, John Kerwick.

They greeted me cordially and congratulated me.

"Albert, you know this is the largest award ever made against the state. We have a favor to ask. This is taxpayers' money. Please ask your client to accept fifty percent of the award. We would appreciate it. I'm sure you're aware there is an election in less than two months. The Republicans control the Legislature. They would like nothing better than to embarrass Charlie Vogt. He's an important man in our administration."

"No deal," McShain told me.

Knowing that the legislature had the right not to appropriate the money awarded, I asked, "What if nothing is awarded?"

"You have earned your fee. This is my decision, not yours. I'll live up to my obligation to you."

The governor was not happy with the news. "You're taking a chance," he told me as I left his office.

"Governor, not really," I replied. " I trust McShain and he's taking the chance."

A few weeks later, the Republican controlled legislature approved the payment by one vote. Hughes signed the bill in late November after William Cahill had been elected Governor.

Three political lawyers requested a portion of my fee, claiming they had recommended me to Mr. McShain. I politely refused their entreaties. McShain versus the State of New Jersey presented me with difficult matters. I decided that I would no longer handle cases involving governmental matters that had political overtones, because I was afraid I would not be able to sleep at night. I was worried that I would get caught up in shenanigans that could destroy my reputation and cause me to end up in jail. I also learned something about being successful in the face of adversity. I had not known what I was getting into, especially with respect to the political dimensions of the case. I wasn't sure how these would play out and how they could have jeopardized my career.

I asked Governor Hughes why he thought McShain had hired me.

"Probably because no other lawyer would take the case on a contingent fee," he said. "The country was in a recession. No lawyer in his right mind would have banked McShain. He is a very wealthy man. If he had confidence in his case, he would have been better off paying someone by the hour."

"Governor, was the appropriation bill you signed my one favor?" I inquired.

He grinned but did not answer. I never asked again.

I was sitting in front of my father's desk. Behind him were black and white pictures of Benjamin Franklin and Abraham Lincoln. He held the check for almost a million dollars in his hand. "I've never seen this much money in my life," he said.

"The fee is over three hundred thousand," I added.

"My half will pay me for all the heartache," my father said smiling.

"And Ellen and I can get out of the apartment and buy a house," I responded.

"Don't you think you should use the money wisely? You've told me about the team you had in the prosecutor's office and the team Mr. McShain had. Wouldn't you like your own team?" my father asked.

My father agreed to take a bonus of fifty thousand dollars each, pay the income taxes on the entire fee, and let me use the remainder to build a law firm.

I wondered what it would take to build a law firm and run not only a practice but a business.

John McShain entered the Stark and Stark offices. Janice sat behind her worn desk doing double duty as a receptionist and my father's secretary. She ushered McShain into my office. He sat down and graciously told me how much he appreciated my efforts. Then he endorsed the check I put in front of him.

I called my father on the intercom. As he entered my office, McShain stood up. My father extended his hand. "I'm Albert's father," he said.

# A FORK IN THE ROAD—FROM KID TO COUNSELLOR

WHEN I ENTERED BOBBIE MCKENZIE'S HOSPITAL ROOM, he turned his head on the pillow to see who was coming in. "Hey, kid. Over here. I'm Bobbie," he said, motioning with an arm wired with intravenous tubes.

Bobbie introduced me to Roann. A buxom redhead in her late thirties, with her lips painted a bright red, Roann could be perfectly cast as a waitress at a roadside diner. She told me why Bobbie was in the hospital.

Bobbie worked as a forklift driver at the Chris Craft warehouse in Trenton. He had picked up a wooden pallet loaded with boxes and backed out of the warehouse onto a loading dock as he had done thousands of times during the past eleven years. When he turned his head, he saw a tractor trailer with its rear doors open and its side panel painted with a yellow Criterian Motor Freight logo, its loading bed flush with the loading dock. After slowly turning the forklift around, he revved the engine and pulled a lever that raised the forks. The forklift began to crawl forward after he pushed the gas pedal again and shifted into gear. The front wheels hit a steel ridge at the end of the loading dock. He heard the rumbling sound of the wheels hitting the metal floor of the trailer. Unbeknownst to Bobbie, the trailer began to move away from the dock. The gap between the trailer and the loading dock widened. The rear wheels of the forklift couldn't make it to the trailer and the forklift and Bobbie crashed to the concrete four feet below.

"Oh, man, it hurts," Bobbie said as he closed his eyes. Raising his head from his pillow and looking at me squarely in the eye, he asked, "You with me, kid?"

Before I said anything, Roann said, "I don't know what I'm going to do. Bobbie's going to need months of rehabilitation. I don't know how I'm going to handle this. Who's going to pay the doctors?"

I had seen people in Bobbie and Roann's predicament while taking Ellen and Jared to physical therapy and had heard their complaints about lawyers who were of little help in getting medical bills paid and assisting with rehabilitation needs. Those lawyers were only interested in getting a settlement and taking their one-third fee.

During my third year of law school, a professor encouraged me to go with him as a member of the Legal Peace Corps to establish a new law school in Ethiopia. The excitement of the Ethiopia project and the desire I had to redevelop cities in America caused me to go to Dean Fordham for advice.

"Albert," he told me, "If you go to Ethiopia, it will be at least twenty-five years before you see what you have accomplished. America is a big bear. You can stick it with a pin. Even though it hardly moves if you look closely you can see it move. If you can appreciate that, you get instant gratification."

The Vietnam War was tearing apart the fabric of American society. The urban development team I was putting together with Alvin Gershen, which included a city planner, a retired mayor, and an accountant, was getting stronger, but it had no source for funding its work.

I looked forward to some of that instant gratification when I told Roann and Bobbie I would help them. I also anticipated I would refer the case to an experienced personal injury lawyer.

I had never been on a loading dock at a warehouse. Nor had I ever operated a forklift or driven a tractor-trailer. Out of curiosity, I went straight to the Chris Craft warehouse. Tractors and trailers entered the loading area behind the warehouse, stopped and backed up to a raised concrete platform edged with a thick steel plate. I heard a loud whoosh every time a tractor-trailer stopped. The drivers then walked to the bottom of the loading dock, where they picked up a couple of triangular wooden blocks and carried them to the front of the tractor and put them in front of the wheels. Afterwards, two more wooden blocks were placed in front of the rear wheels of the trailer. The drivers climbed a set of stairs at one end of the platform, walked over to their trailers, opened the rear doors and entered the warehouse. Forklift trucks with loads on the forks came out onto the loading dock, were driven into the trailers, backed out empty, and returned to the warehouse. Truck drivers exited the warehouse, closed the doors to the trailer, descended the stairs, removed the wooden blocks, put them at the base of the loading dock and drove away.

I sat in front of Irving Lewis' desk, cluttered with files, and asked him to help me with Bobbie's case, which didn't seem that complicated. A flamboyant, bald man with a handle bar mustache, Lewis was the lawyer who "got the big settlements" in Trenton. Lewis told me how difficult it would be to win Bobbie's case. When I asked if he would help Bobbie and Roann with their medical bills, he told me, "The doctors will wait for their money." After I asked what would happen if he lost the case, he informed me that because Bobbie had nothing, the doctors wouldn't sue him.

Lewis laughed when I said I was going to handle the case myself. "If you're going to be a jackass," he guffawed, "You ought to, at least, go to a seminar being given by my good friend, Bill Bischoff."

I followed his advice. A South Jersey personal injury lawyer, Bischoff's message was just what I needed to hear. "With preparation you can stand up to the most experienced trial lawyer. Be yourself. Show the jury you believe in your case, how much work you put into your case, and tell them stories that will make them identify with your client's cause. That's been my formula for success in the courtroom."

I visited Bobbie almost every day at the hospital during his stay there. When he was transferred to a rehabilitation facility, I went into the physical therapy room and watched as therapists worked with Bobbie, teaching him how to bend and lift his leg and how to walk again. I tried to cheer him up just as I had when Ellen was depressed about her injuries.

After Bobbie was discharged from rehabilitation, I obtained medical reports from his orthopedist, neurologist, and physical therapists. Terms such as lumbar, vertebrae, fibromyositis, Harrington rods and compression fracture, Steinmann pins, and tibia and fibula were new to me. In order to understand them, I studied the bone structure of the back and legs. I talked to doctors about what I read, and learned there was more to a broken bone than a crack: damaged nerves also caused pain, surgically installed Harrington rods prevented the spine from bending normally, bone deformities irritated muscles surrounding the spine. I followed Bobbie's physical progress by regularly keeping in touch with him and Roann. I tried to figure out what caused each of Bobbie's continuing complaints. He was unable to bend his knees and ankles and had shooting pains into his legs. He couldn't sit or walk except for short periods of time, and was moody and depressed because he was unable to work. I began to look at his injuries and complaints as if they were pieces of a puzzle. When I had a problem fitting the pieces together, Bobbie's doctors answered my questions.

I needed to figure out how to recoup Bobbie's financial losses. The personnel manager at Chris Craft told me Bobbie didn't just lose his weekly wage for six months, but also that his pension benefits were diminished. He calculated the value of the pension benefits that Bobbie would lose during the remaining twenty years he had been expected to work. Because the numbness in his legs prevented him from safely operating the pedals on the forklift, the union agent got him transferred to a less strenuous job at less pay. Because Bobbie was earning less money every week, I had an accountant figure out how much Bobbie would lose in the future.

I sent Bobbie's hospital records, doctors' reports, and lost wage information to the insurance company for Criterian Motor Freight, expecting an offer to settle the case.

Instead of making an offer, the insurance company took the position that Chris Craft, not Criterian Motor Freight, was at fault because on the day of the accident there were no wooden blocks for the driver to use and that the driver had set the air brakes.

"That's bullshit," Bobbie yelled after hearing about the stand the insurance company was taking. "Those chocks have been there for as long as I worked there. And that's eleven years," Bobbie repeated.

"But, Bobbie, I've got to prove that they were there on the day of your accident. Did you see them the day you fell?" I asked.

"Are you kiddin'? All I saw were stars and the ceiling of the ambulance on the way to the hospital," Bobbie replied.

"So how am I going to establish that they were there on the day you fell?" I pressed.

"The shop foreman. He'll know," Bobbie answered.

Bobbie dialed my telephone and spoke with someone. When he hung up he looked stunned. "The asshole gave a written statement to the insurance company that he wasn't sure the chocks were there."

If Criterian Motor Freight was not negligent, Bobbie was out of luck under New Jersey's worker injury laws. Bobbie was limited to receiving small disability benefits and no damages for pain and suffering if Chris Craft was responsible.

I wondered how a trailer could move away from the loading dock if its air brakes were set. I called an experienced trial lawyer, who suggested I contact Professor Jacob Wolf at the Newark College of Engineering because he taught a course to engineering students who wanted to have a career in the air brake industry.

Professor Wolf sat behind a cluttered desk. A stocky, round faced man, Wolf looked like a tackle on a college football team. "So, you want to learn about air brakes, do you? You're in the right place. Tell me about your case," he said self assuredly before he gave me a chance to introduce myself.

I described what happened to Bobbie.

Wolf nodded his head as I gave him one detail after another. He raised his hand, signaling me to stop talking and asked, "Who's the insurance company? Who's the lawyer on the other side?"

"Travelers Insurance Company. Stan Shock's the lawyer," I responded.

"Aha. The red umbrella has the red fox," he said, referring to the Traveler's Insurance Company's symbol and a nickname I had heard lawyers use to describe Stan Shock. "Let me tell you, they're going to argue hard that there were no chocks and that the driver set the air brakes."

I was about to ask what he suggested I do, when Wolf turned to me and blurted, "You got a damn good case, young man. What's your name again? Stark? How do you like to be addressed? Mr. Stark or just Stark?"

"Just call me Al. Or Albert, if that's okay."

"Okay Albert. I'm not comfortable with Stark. You look too wet behind the ears to call you mister. Come over here, Albert." I followed Wolf compliantly to a table. He picked up a piece of black garden hose. "See this hose I have in my hand. I'm going to put my finger in one end. You blow into the hose." Wolf leaned over and put the hose up to my mouth. "Now blow."

I puckered my lips and exhaled.

"Keep blowing. Now put your thumb in the other end and stop blowing." I followed his instructions. Wolf and I were standing about a foot apart, his finger in one end of the tube and my thumb in the other. "Now then, do you think the hose is completely filled with air?" he asked seriously.

"Sure," I said feeling foolish and wanting to dispel the embarrassment I was experiencing because I didn't know something that seemed so elementary.

"You're right. The hose is completely full. But there's an element of pressure. Pressure's important. When you took your mouth off of the hose some of the air that you blew in escaped, causing the air pressure to go down. Here's how an air brake works. When a driver pulls a lever in the cab of his tractor, a compressor pushes air into hoses. As he releases the lever, some of the air escapes with a whoosh. When the truck is running, the air heats up so the pressure goes up. But when a truck is not running, the air cools and the pressure is reduced even more. The truck wasn't running when Bobbie ran his forklift into the truck. The air brake wouldn't have enough pressure to prevent the trailer from rolling a foot or two away from the loading dock if a heavy forklift moved forward into the trailer. Wolf asked if I understood.

"I think so," I responded, even though I was not sure that I did.

"Now about the chocks. They are wooden blocks pointed at one end. The driver of a truck with air brakes has to chock the wheels. You ever see a chock?" he asked.

I said that I had.

"Good. An ICC regulation requires that a tractor or trailer with air brakes have chocks on board. You know what the ICC is?" Wolf inquired.

I shook my head from side to side.

"It's the Interstate Commerce Commission. The ICC controls the road trucks all over these United States. You know why that is? Because air brakes have some give to them unless the motor is running. Suppose the truck stalled on a hill or broke down or the air brake hose sprung a leak. Got the picture? Without chocks, you can never be sure the rig is not going to roll. That's why you turn your front wheels into the curb when you park your car on a steep hill. Even if there were no chocks at Chris Craft, the Criterian driver had to use his own to prevent the truck from rolling. What Travelers and Shock are doing to you is what they do to a lot of lawyers. They're using the air brakes to confuse. Most people think that when you put on your brakes it prevents the vehicle from moving. But this case of yours. It's as simple to understand as blowing air into a garden hose. Or even into a balloon. Everyone's tried to tie a balloon without losing any air. They can't. I can give you lots of other examples if you need them. Simple to understand. Even a lawyer like you can understand it, right?" Wolf asked with more than a slight hint of sarcasm.

I thought about how simple I felt Bobbie's case was when I visited the Chris Craft warehouse that first day. "So, Professor, what am I supposed to do with all of this information?" I asked.

His grin turned to a smile. "Hire me to be your expert witness," he said. "I'm a hundred an hour, and I need three days' notice to testify." Wolf explained that lawyers consulted experts in different fields because, while lawyers were taught how to think legally, they could not possibly know the details of the many situations they were called upon to solve. He told me that while Bobbie and Roann would call me to ease their discomfort about things they didn't understand about their lawsuit, he would be available to answer questions I had that were raised by the "red fox."

For two years, as the case wound its way through the court procedures, Wolf nursed me through the pretrial steps I needed to prove that Criterian Motor Freight was responsible for Bobbie McKenzie's injuries.

I vividly remembered Bill Bischoff taking off one of his shoes. As he limped around the room during his lecture, he explained how he had urged a jury to do the same thing in the jury room so that they could feel what his client, who had a leg one inch shorter than the other, experienced every time he took a step. Bischoff had said that until you let an injured client describe how their injury was affecting them, a lawyer could not be in the shoes of their client. I thought about how I could do something as dramatic for Bobbie. Bobbie told me he could write me stories about his injuries that a third grader would understand.

When the day of trial came, Bobbie had taught me that a personal injury case was personal to the client.

Bobbie McKenzie limped to the witness stand and gingerly took his seat. He gave the jury a broad, good morning smile. A few of them returned the greeting. Bobbie stared at Stan Shock.

Bobbie answered my questions about his experience operating a forklift and what he did the day he tried to load Criterian's trailer. He described his injuries, his disability, and his unsuccessful attempt to work, telling one story after another. He said he was like Humpty Dumpty who the doctors tried to put back together again. He explained that he wanted to work like he used to but felt like the "Little Engine that Couldn't." He told the jury that like the "Little Engine That Could," he wished he could, he wished he could, he wished he could.

He explained the financial difficulties he and Roann had experienced because of his lost wages and the depression that resulted because he could not provide for his wife. He compared himself to Little Jack Horner who sat in the corner.

"Bobby, what have you missed most since you were injured?" I asked in closing.

Bobbie turned to the jury. "Coaching soccer with the neighborhood kids. I can't run around and kick the ball with them anymore. I used to be the president of the West End Soccer Little League, but I had to resign."

A woman juror in the back row started crying.

"When you drove your forklift out onto the loading dock, where did you look?" Shock inquired as he began to cross examine Bobbie.

"I turned around and looked at the Criterian trailer, sir."

"Were the trailer doors open?"

"Yes, they were, sir." Bobbie was following my instructions to answer Shock succinctly and politely.

"Did you rev your engine before you turned to drive into the trailer?

"Yes."

"When you turned the forklift around, you gave it the gas?" Shock's voice conveyed the message he wanted to send to the jury.

"Yes, sir," Bobbie replied.

"You looked at the trailer, didn't you? Shock sneered, showing that his outrage at Bobbie's behavior was evident.

"Yes, I did," Bobbie answered.

I noticed Bobbie's face turning redder. His neck veins began to swell.

"Before you tried to drive the forklift into the trailer, did you look at the wheels to see if they were chocked?" Shock asked in a louder voice.

Bobbie answered, "No sir."

Shock grinned at Bobbie. His teeth shone like a fox's that has just eaten his prey.

Shock started back to his counsel table. Bobbie had gotten up from his chair. His large hands were gripping the rail of the jury box. Leaning on stiffened arms, Bobbie McKenzie looked like he was going to pounce on Shock. "Sir, aren't you going to give me a chance to tell you why I revved it, gassed it, and didn't look?"

"Mr. McKenzie," Judge Leonard warned. "It is the lawyer's job to question you. It is not your right to question the lawyer. If your lawyer wants to ask you questions, he has the chance to do it on redirect examination."

Bobbie was nodding his head up and down. I was concerned it was too late to repair the damage the "red fox" had inflicted. I was almost certain the jurors' minds were made up that Bobbie caused the accident.

"Why did you rev the engine?" I asked Bobbie when it was my opportunity to ask him questions on redirect examination.

"Because you have to rev it to lift the load. It fills up the hydraulics so the forks will go up," Bobbie explained.

"Why did you give it the gas?"

"Because to shift into forward, you have to give it gas. Otherwise, the forklift stalls," Bobbie answered.

"Why didn't you look down at the trailer wheels?"

I waited with trepidation for his answer.

Bobbie looked snidely at Shock and turned to the jury. "Because I looked into the trailer and saw chocks in the trailer. In all my years running the forklift, I had never seen a tractor trailer driver leave a truck without the wheels chocked. All morning the chocks at the bottom of the dock were there. If they weren't there, the driver would use his own chocks. It's a federal law."

I wanted to start clapping.

Shock interrogated the Criterian Motor Freight driver, who swore under oath that there were no wooden blocks at the base of the loading dock the day Bobbie was hurt. He insisted that he had put on his air brakes to keep the trailer from moving.

I made a decision to cross examine with one question. Bischoff had emphasized that the most important aspect of a case had to stand out in the jury's mind. "Strategy. Strategy. Strategy," he emphasized. Learning to develop strategy, I had asked Professor Wolf what he believed was the most important fact in Bobbie's case. "If the jury sees that Criterian has broken a rule, the jury would feel justified in punishing the rule-breaker," he advised.

Following Bischoff's advice never to ask a question on cross-examination to which you did not know the answer, I inquired, "Sir, was your truck subject to ICC regulations?"

He answered that it was.

The owner of Criterian Motor Freight claimed he knew how air brakes worked and that, in his opinion, if Bobbie had not been driving his forklift too fast, the air brakes would have kept the truck from moving away from the loading dock.

After Shock informed Judge Leonard that he had no more witnesses, Judge Leonard inquired, "Do you have anything to present in rebuttal?" .

"I call Professor Jacob Wolf," I said loudly.

The jury sensed the drama. Their eyes were fixed on the professor.

Wolf stood up. He showed the jury a balloon. He tried to tie it. As he did, air leaked out. He then took a hose and put it in his mouth and blew. He put his thumb in the other end. As he did, air leaked out. He explained to the jury how an air brake worked. He told the jury that it was his expert opinion that it was the tractor-trailer driver's job to chock the wheels and that the ICC regulations were designed to prevent what happened to Bobbie.

It was Stan Shock's turn to deliver his summation to the jury.

"Ladies and Gentlemen of the jury," Shock began, "we would not be here today if Robert McKenzie cared about his own safety. Robert backed out onto a loading dock, looked around, and saw Criterian's truck ready for loading. He then gunned the engine, turned his forklift, gave it more gas and rumbled toward the trailer. He tried to bounce into the trailer. He didn't make it because he was in a hurry and the force of a heavy load on a heavy forklift pushed the truck forward, even though Criterian Motor Freight's driver had set his air brakes. If Robert had spent a few seconds looking at the wheels of the trailer, he wouldn't be hurt and he would be working today. He knew that Chris Craft didn't have chocks there. That's why Robert didn't look. This is a simple case. Robert McKenzie and Chris Craft are the reason we are here, not my clients." He looked at each juror and sat down.

Shock had subtly called Bobbie by his formal name, depersonalizing him in the jurors' minds. Stan Shock was the best defense lawyer in Central New Jersey. I felt like a fighter beaten so badly he couldn't stand for another moment.

My knees wobbled as I walked behind Bobbie and put my hands on his shoulders. "If the Criterian Motor Freight driver had put chocks in front of his wheels, I would not have the task of representing Bobbie McKenzie and you, the jury, would not have to decide this case because Bobbie would still be working today." I felt a shot of adrenaline as I described the job that Bobbie McKenzie performed for eleven years, repeated Bobbie's version of the accident, and used the stories to emphasize how seriously Bobbie was hurt. Then, I sat down and closed my eyes.

The jury had retired to reach a verdict, and we waited for what felt like an eternity. In a voice loud enough for Shock and his client to hear, Bobbie said, "Don't worry. Whatever happens, happens. You did a great job for me. The jury knows how hard you worked. You were up against the champ. Like David and Goliath. It's in God's hands now."

The instant Bobbie turned away from him, Shock raised his head. When Shock's eyes fixed again on Bobbie, Bobbie leaned toward him. "You know what, 'Red Fox,' you can take your forty-five thousand and shove it. I'm just lucky to be alive." Bobbie hesitated when I put my hand on his knee. His eyes were bulging.

Five courthouse junkies, who made a life out of going from courtroom to courtroom watching trials and waiting for verdicts, laughed at Bobbie's bravado.

Of the forty-five thousand dollar settlement that Shock had offered after the jury retired to deliberate, fifteen thousand would go into Bobbie's bank account and fifteen would be paid to my firm. The rest had to be paid to Bobbie's doctors and Professor Wolf. The two years since the McShain case hadn't been easy. Expansion had sapped the resources from the McShain case. If it had been my choice to make, I wouldn't have refused the offer.

One of the double doors of the courtroom opened. A Sheriff's Officer poked his head into the courtroom. "You gentlemen ready for a verdict?" he asked, waving an envelope that he held in his hand.

I broke out into a cold sweat. Shock looked at me, smiled and turned to the Sheriff's Officer. "Bring them in," he said confidently. "That forty-five looks pretty darn good right now, doesn't it? It's yours if you want it before the jury comes in," Shock said to Bobbie.

I looked at Bobbie. "What do you say?" I asked.

"Roll 'em, kid," he responded.

The door behind the judge's chair opened and Judge Leonard took the bench. "Gentlemen, we have a verdict. My courtroom deputy will bring in the jury. Twelve jurors, ten men and two women, stood expressionless in front of their seats.

The first juror opened up an envelope and took out a piece of paper after the deputy asked the jurors if they had reached a verdict?

I closed my eyes and heard the Jury Foreman say, "Yes, we have. We find in favor of Robert McKenzie against Criterian Motor Freight in the sum of one hundred and fifty thousand dollars."

When I opened my eyes, Judge Leonard was spinning around in his chair.

The Sheriff's Officer looked at Shock. Shock shrugged his shoulders in disbelief.

Bobbie yelled excitedly, "Wait 'till Ro hears about this. She's at home expecting bad news and now I'm going to call her to tell her we're rich." Bobbie stood in front of the counsel table. "You know what?" he asked.

"What?" I responded.

"I'm not going to call you 'kid' anymore. From here on in, it's 'counselor.'"

What Bobbie had just said rolled around in my mind until I realized the real meaning of what he had told me. Had I evolved from a kid to a lawyer?

The thrill of winning a case for a client who was unable to afford a lawyer and who had put his blind faith in me was indescribable. Never had I imagined that getting money for someone could be so rewarding. Three months after Bobbie and Roann received their money from Travelers Insurance, they invited me to celebrate the new life they had made for themselves. They had opened a tavern located on a corner in a working class section of Trenton. I jumped up and down when I turned the corner and saw the spanking new neon sign flashing the name of the place: THE RED FOX.

I had never felt the sense of accomplishment that came with drastically affecting the lives of Bobbie and Roann. Rebuilding cities, teaching in college, serving in the government. Those goals were fading as I experienced the kind of instant gratification that comes from helping people improve their lives.

# FIRE—SHOULD THE LAW BE FAIR?

ADVERTISEMENTS FOR A NEW YEARS' EVE CELEBRATION at the Nina, Pinta, and Santa Maria Restaurant appeared in local newspapers shortly after Thanksgiving, 1972.

"Alberto and Ellen must be with me for the New Year," Johnnie Puccinella insisted while we were dining before the Christmas holiday. "I have no reservation from you. Look, I put you at my table."

"Johnnie, we would love to come here to ring in the New Year," Ellen explained, "Really we would. But we're going on a vacation to the Bahamas. It's the first time we are going out of the country since Rachel was born." Bobbie's case had given us the opportunity.

"Youra gonna miss a'great time. Wait till you hear the band. Maybe when you get back, eh," Johnnie said with a tone of regret and excitement.

"What's the name of the band? Maybe I've heard them before?" Ellen asked.

"Fire," he answered.

When we got home late in the evening, shortly after New Year's, I called my father and mother to tell them we arrived home safely and to see how the kids made out with their grandparents as babysitters. My father inquired, "Did you hear about the Nina?"

"No, what about the Nina?"

"It burned to the ground the night before New Year's," he replied.

I felt like throwing up.

The trees were bare and the sky overcast as I made my way past strip malls and car dealerships to the Nina.

All that was left of the large white building was a part of the front wall. As I got closer, I spotted Johnnie's bald head bobbing, his broad shoulders and his arms flailing as he talked to men in business suits and overcoats. I thought about just driving by, but decided to park and wait for an appropriate moment to walk over to Johnnie.

He exploded when he spotted me. "Alberto, can you believe it? My place. It's gone. My work . . . . gone." He turned to the men in the business suits. "Alberto, these are the men from the insurance." I shook one of the men's hands while Johnnie continued to talk. "Alberto, they tell me that they will rebuild for me. Just like it was."

"Thank God, I was so worried about you," I said, slapping Johnnie on the shoulder and thinking of the night my son, Jared, was born and that he had done the same for me.

A few months passed. I recognized Sal Scozzari's voice when I picked up the telephone. Sal, Johnnie's business lawyer, was the only lawyer who affectionately called me "Max," a takeoff on my middle name, Maxwell. I had received calls in the past from Sal to discuss cases we had worked on together.

"Max, can I come over? Johnnie Puccinella's with me."

"By all means," I replied, happy Johnnie wanted to come over to say hello.

"How you doing?" I asked after they arrived. That Johnnie's visit was anything but social never crossed my mind. I glanced at Sal when Johnnie didn't respond and saw that his eyes were cast toward the floor. "Good to see both of you," I said again. Johnnie looked up with a blank expression.

"Albert," Sal began in a serious tone. "We're here on business."

"Sit down and tell me what's up." I assumed Johnnie probably needed help with his vendors' bills since collecting insurance proceeds often took time, especially after a fire, because the owner had to supply appraisals and receipts.

Sal began to speak rapidly in broken sentences. "The new prosecutor, Matthews, and the arson investigator, Williams, suspect Johnnie burned down his place."

"Are they fucking nuts?" I responded with disbelief.

"Johnnie told him he had turned the fire alarm on before he left the night of the fire. Williams wanted to take it out to examine it. He said he wanted to help the insurance company sue the alarm company. If the alarm had worked, the fire department probably would have responded in time to put out the fire before the entire restaurant burned to the ground. So Johnnie agreed, not thinking he had anything to be afraid of. Now, the son-of-a-bitch, Matthews, is telling him that the alarm was not in the "ON" position, and that they found a half-burned gasoline can in the rubble. Johnnie was behind in his bills and a million dollar fire insurance policy was taken out two months before the fire. Rumors spread that Johnnie had lost a lot of money gambling. After a Trenton cop, Schultz, said he saw Johnnie driving a few blocks from the Nina while the fire was in progress, they thought that everything put together added up to arson."

Johnnie nodded as Sal spoke.

"Okay. So what are you here telling me all of this for? I'm Johnnie's friend but certainly no arson expert," I told Sal.

"I'm a business lawyer. Our friend here needs a lawyer. He read about that case you won against the cops. The one where the drunk ran a red light and killed Bobby Cunningham. The word is out, Max, whether you like it or not."

Johnnie leaned toward me. "Alberto, why would I burn my a' place? I was sold out for a'New Years."

Sal broke in. "The city building inspector wanted him to tear down the wall after the fire. Johnnie refused. When he rebuilt, he wanted it to be a memorial of the place he and Nora sweated over to make a success. If he burned the place, do you think he would have left the wall standing for two months? Do you think that he'd be stupid enough to leave an alarm box on the wall if he hadn't turned it on?"

I began to wonder. While I understood Johnnie's predicament, I also knew that if I were a prosecutor and I found a gas can in the ruins the first thing I'd assume was what Matthews had. "Where'd the gas can come from?" I inquired.

Johnny shrugged his shoulders. "I have a'no idea. I remember a guy coming to a' fix my roof and he had a'can with him. A red a'can."

It was no secret to anyone that it wasn't unusual for a large insurance policy to be taken out before a troubled business caught fire. "What about the insurance?" I pressed on.

Johnnie responded without hesitating. "Luigi, my accountant, told a'me that I needed it if somebody got a'hurt. I financed."

"Who set the amount?" I continued.

"The insurance. That's what they told me I needed. Talk to Luigi. He knows." Johnnie answered.

"What about the gambling?" Eating at the Nina I saw men in Al Capone attire coming in and going out. Word had it that there was a room with poker tables on the second floor of a store next to the Nina.

"Sure I play. But I don't lose. Not me. Where you think I get the money for all of the improvements? Not from the bank," Johnnie said.

"What about this cop, Schultz? How do you explain that. Why would he lie?"

"The cop. He isn't lying. I was in bed. The phone rang. I pick it up. A voice says, 'Johnnie, your a'place is on a'fire.' I couldn't a'believe it. I throw on a'pants and a coat and run down the stairs and get in the car. I drive to my a'place and a block away I see fire in the sky. I turn to come home to tell Nora," Johnnie explained.

"So how do you think the fire started?" I waited for Johnnie's answer.

"In the cucina, how you say? The kitchen. I was having a problem with the hood. The extinguisher. You know what I a'mean? It's over the stove. In the hood. The hose didn't work. Where the smoke goes. A few weeks ago I had a little fire and had to use the extinguisher from the wall. I called Lavine, the kitchen man. He put the hose in. He never came to fix."

"Why do you want me?"

"Albert," Sal interrupted. "I'm not a trial lawyer. You're his friend. He trusts you."

"I know that. I like him, too. Maybe too much," I responded with a grin, knowing how my judgment was easily influenced by my feelings. "I'm not the most experienced lawyer around here. You know that, don't you?" I warned. I hoped my self doubt would encourage

Johnnie to find another lawyer and I could devote my energies to something that was burning inside: helping people who were hurt. Solving the puzzle of the personal injury case was giving me the ability to change something: the life of a person who's fate had been changed by someone else's carelessness. While criminal cases were challenging, saving someone from losing their freedom didn't seem to be as meaningful as helping someone to regain it.

"Look a'here. You maybe don't wanna take my case because I am on my back a'broke." Johnnie's tone echoed his disappointment.

"No. No. Johnnie. Money will not be a problem if what you're saying is the truth. Believe me. But I have to know everything. That's the only way I can help you. You understand?"

Johnnie nodded.

"Look here. Let me talk to my father. He's my partner. Let's figure out what this is going to cost so nobody's mad at each other later. Let's see if we can make it work for you," I continued, trying to be diplomatic.

"Fair enough," Sal said politely, knowing full well that I was buying time to discourage Johnnie.

Johnnie started to get up from his chair. "You gotta help me, Alberto."

Johnnie's words hit me like a sucker punch, knocking the wind out of my lungs.

"If I can, I will. Remember the night my son was born? I will never forget your help." I walked around my desk, put my hand on Johnnie's meaty shoulder, and whispered in his ear, "Trust me."

I sensed the case was going to be tough. Matthews had political ambitions and would try to portray Johnnie as a pawn of the mob in order to save the insurance company money. A felony conviction for arson would be sufficient evidence in the civil case to stop any payments. Promotion and politics go hand in hand with prosecutors. It was common knowledge Matthews aspired to be a judge.

After discussing Johnnie's case with my father, he told me I would have to drop almost everything if I were going to defend Johnnie. When I told him that I felt indebted to Johnnie, he suggested I charge Johnnie fifty thousand dollars for a trial and five thousand if I worked out a quick plea bargain with his admission of guilt. That way, I would challenge Johnnie to tell me the truth.

Johnnie told me he was not able to afford anything close to fifty thousand. I insisted that he agree to pay for an expert to investigate and if the expert told me I had a good chance to win, I would represent him with the understanding that I would earn one-third of what the insurance company paid him.

Gerald Higgins, a retired state policeman, who had served as New Jersey's chief arson investigator for twenty years, agreed to investigate the case for ten thousand dollars. For ten weeks, Johnnie brought me a thousand dollars each week.

Higgins met me at my office and listened carefully as I described what the charges were and what Johnnie had told me. After hearing about his experience investigating fires, I was confident that if Higgins believed Johnnie was innocent, I would win the case. When he had finished his field investigation, Higgins put a thick red book on my desk: Fire and Arson Investigation by John Kennedy. "Get me the investigative reports from the prosecutor. I want to read them and then meet with Puccinella. Meanwhile you study this book," he instructed.

A few weeks later, Higgins called. "Before I meet with Johnnie, I want to see the alarm box. Where is it?"

"Matthews has it," I replied.

Higgins inspected the alarm box and reported that he couldn't tell whether or not it had been set because it was burned so badly. In all likelihood, Williams also couldn't tell. Investigation reports filed by Detective Williams, the prosecutor's arson expert, revealed that Williams was relying on the alarm manufacturer's opinion that the alarm was not set. "You can discredit the alarm company," Higgins said. "The alarm company has a motive to say that the alarm was not set. If the alarm was set and didn't work properly, the alarm company would be liable to the insurance company for the money they had to pay Johnnie to rebuild his restaurant and for loss of profits due to the interruption of his business."

"I am sure the prosecutor is going to use the insurance policy to prove Johnnie had a motive to burn the restaurant," I said.

"You're right. Interview Luigi Immordino, Johnnie's accountant, and the insurance man who sold Johnnie the million dollar policy. Find out who recommended he obtain the policy and the amount," Higgins instructed.

Higgins also insisted I try to find the roofer with the red gas can because roofers used gasoline to clean tar from their hands. I was prepared to try but Johnnie told me he paid the roofer in cash and that he was a fly-by-night character who was cheap. I checked with seven roofers in the Trenton area, hoping to find Johnnie's roofer from a description he gave to me. While I didn't find the roofer, I found out that roofers customarily used gasoline to clean their hands after applying tar. I was relieved that, even though I hadn't found the roofer, I could call a roofer as a witness so that a jury would have a reasonable explanation that a roofer could have left a red plastic can on the roof. Then, I could argue that when the roof fell in, the can fell into the rubble.

Lavine Products, the installer of the hood over the kitchen stove, verified that the automatic fire extinguisher was broken and gave me a record of a telephone complaint Johnnie made a few weeks before the fire. They also verified that they had not made a service call to repair the problem.

Others backed up Johnnie's story. Vendors told me that Johnnie put them off with various explanations, some about improvements, others about gambling losses. Johnnie explained that he told them about gambling losses because he was ashamed to admit he was a bad businessman. No matter what Johnnie said, Matthews was going to use the debts Johnnie owed his vendors to buttress evidence of his motive for burning down his restaurant and collecting the insurance money. If there were outstanding gambling debts, I assumed that the prosecutor would not be able to prove them since mob members were unlikely to testify.

Nora verified Johnnie's story about the phone call and Johnnie's quick exit from bed in the early morning hours after the fire.

I was feeling very good about the case, when I received a call from Higgins.

"A problem?" I asked nervously.

"You want the truth, don't you?"

"Absolutely. I know enough to know that the worse thing I can do is to bury my head in the sand. I don't want to be one of those lawyers who only desires to hear good news. What's the scoop?" I asked.

"The bottom of the red plastic gasoline can wasn't singed or burned. There were no black carbon deposits. It was found, half melted on a table. The table was next to a wall that was covered with fabric. Albert, you need oxygen to fuel a fire. I want to come over to your office and explain what I am saying. This is very important."

A few hours later, Gerald Higgins put his palm flat on my desk.

Pointing to his hand, he said, "When an object like a plastic can is on a surface like a tabletop, oxygen can't get between the surface of the tabletop and the bottom of the can. Fire needs oxygen to burn. Look at these pictures. See the way the wall fabric is burned above the tabletop, but not below. Fire burns up, not down. Those are signs that a fire actually started near the can." He looked at me to see if I understood what he was saying.

I had carefully read the theories related to the originating sources of fire and patterns of burning in Kennedy's book. Satisfied that I understood, he continued, "If a can with gasoline in it falls from a roof that burned and falls into a fire beneath it, there would be some signs of burning on the bottom." He took out a cigarette lighter, lit it, and then lowered the palm of his hand to the lighter's flame. "And consider the chances of a gasoline can lying on a roof, falling onto a table and landing right side up. They are not very good."

"But," I added, "There were signs of fire origin in the kitchen in the area of the stove hood. Johnnie said that was where the fire started. How can you explain that?"

"A classic sign of arson is multiple spots of fire origin. An arsonist doesn't usually trust a fire starting in one place. There's always a chance that a fire in one place will go out or not spread. Multiple places of origin speed up the blaze so that the fire department can't respond in time to put it out. This is a problem you have to face," Higgins warned.

I felt nauseated.

Although I was listening as carefully as I could, I wasn't entirely sure what Higgins was telling me. Was he telling me Johnnie did it? "Gerald, would you repeat that again?" I asked.

He went over what he had told me but this time, more slowly.

"Mr. Higgins, so what you're telling me is that I can't prove Johnnie's innocence but I can confuse a jury and rebut the prosecutor's allegation that the fire started at the table where the gas can was found."

"You picked up my point perfectly. You must stay with Johnnie's explanation that the fire started in the kitchen. If the jury believes Johnnie, as you do, he will get off. When the prosecutor argues this fire is a classic case of arson, you will counter that the fire started in the kitchen, spread to the walls of the dining room, and burned through the roof, at which point the gasoline can fell into the fire. All you need in a criminal case is reasonable doubt. Let's move on."

"Before we do that, I have a concern. It's about Johnnie being seen near the restaurant while the fire was in progress. Kennedy's book says that arsonists are oftentimes seen at or near the fire."

"You're right. That's a problem. It is common for arsonists to watch the fire. That's how many arsonists are caught. News people take pictures of the fire and there, in the foreground, is the arsonist, smiling. The cop, Schultz, saw Johnnie near the restaurant while it was burning. But the wife's corroborating story should create doubt about the importance of Johnnie being seen nearby."

"Is there anything else that bothers you, Gerry?" I asked.

"No," he replied. "I'm glad I gave you that book to read," Higgins chuckled. "I am happy you believe Johnnie is innocent. Innocence is not being proven guilty beyond a reasonable doubt. I am not convinced he can be proven guilty."

I met with Johnnie after my meeting with Higgins. He asked me about what I had learned from Higgins and as I told him all of the problems we faced, Johnnie became more and more agitated.

"Alberto, am I some kind of genius? Does Higgins think I spend my time on all of those things. I work from a' seven o'clock in the morning until two in the morning trying to run my place."

The alarm company was Prosecutor Matthews' first witness. Testifying that the alarm was not set, the company representatives stuck to their opinions even when I challenged them on cross examination, attempting to show the alarm box was burned too badly to say with certainty that it was set. I displayed the burned alarm box to the jury so they could see the damage with their own eyes. They admitted that, had it indeed been set, their company might be responsible to pay Johnnie's insurance company back for his claim.

Williams, the arson investigator, took the witness stand to present his opinion. He told the jury that there were multiple points of fire origin, that the fire was so hot it may indicate that an incendiary had been used, and that a gas can was found on a table in the rubble on top of a table. He showed photos of the wall against which the table with the gas can was resting as he explained how fire burns up and not down. In his expert opinion, the fire had been started in the dining room by igniting the gas can with a fuse at the end of a string. He conjectured that Johnnie lit the fuse as he left the Nina. Finally, Williams explained to the jury the significance of the gas can's undersurface not being burned.

When I interrogated Williams, he conceded on cross examination that the city building inspector had wanted to condemn the building and tear down the damaged wall on which the alarm was attached and that Johnnie convinced the inspector to leave it up so he could use it to rebuild. When Williams began to say that Johnnie probably thought the alarm was too badly burned to determine whether it had been set, I jumped up and objected on the grounds that the testimony was too speculative. The judge agreed with my position and the jury did not hear what Williams wanted to tell them.

Schultz, the cop, told the jurors that he had observed Johnnie near the restaurant while the fire was in progress. I asked no questions on cross-examination because Nora was going to offer an alibi to counter Schultz's testimony.

The prosecutor called several vendors who testified that Johnnie owed them money and showed the jury the unpaid bills. Representatives of the insurance company explained that they would never have issued the million dollar policy if they had known Johnnie was heavily in debt. Finally, posters advertising the New Years' party where the band "FIRE" was to play were put into evidence to insinuate that Johnnie planned to burn his restaurant, that Johnnie had planned everything including his explanations of how the fire started, and that the New Year's party was a ruse to divert attention from his crime.

After Prosecutor Matthews rested his case on behalf of the state, I called Johnnie to the witness stand. He told the jury how he came from Italy as a teenager, worked his way up from dishwasher, to salad man and then explained how he learned to cook from a local chef. With the help of family and friends, he bought a rundown taproom and with his hard work made the Nina his American dream. He swore that he set the alarm the night of the fire, that his accountant told him why he needed insurance, and how much to buy. He explained the problems he was having with the hood over the stove and that he had called Lavine, who did not come to fix it. He told the jury about the roofer he had paid to fix his asphalt roof. He began to sob when I asked him about the phone call that woke him up and the sight of flames shooting out of his restaurant. I calmed him down and handed him a glass of water. Then, I asked my final question, "Did you burn down your restaurant?"

He looked at me, then to the judge, and finally to the jury, before he cried out, "No, No, No."

Matthews relentlessly cross examined him about gambling debts, inferring the mob was the real owner of the Nina and that Johnnie had taken out the insurance policy to pay off his debts to the mob. Johnnie conceded that he told vendors he couldn't pay them because of gambling debts and that he was just trying to buy time, knowing the money from New Year's would cover the bills.

Richard Lavine, the owner of Lavine Products, verified he got the stove extinguisher complaint.

Accountant Luigi Immordino explained the million dollar policy was purchased because of the many improvements made at the Nina and because business was getting better and better.

The jurors were spellbound as Nora stammered to describe what had happened in her bedroom in the early hours of the morning on New Year's Day, 1973.

Nora corroborated Johnnie's testimony about the phone call.

I had highlighted the testimony of Gerald Higgins in my opening statement. It was now time for him to take the witness stand. As he walked from the spectator's section to the front of the courtroom, the jurors were eager to hear his testimony. Slowly I asked him about his credentials and experience in investigating fires for the New Jersey State Police.

"Mr. Higgins," I asked, "how do you feel about testifying for a defendant in a case brought by the State of New Jersey?"

Before he could answer, Matthews sprung to his feet with an objection. I had made my point.

Higgins testified convincingly that the fire started in the hood over the stove, He said that, because the extinguisher was broken, the fire spread from the kitchen to the dining room walls. It created a hot blaze that burned through the roof, causing the gas can left by the roofer to fall into the rubble.

I sat down after completing my questions and waited for Matthews to interrogate Higgins. Kennedy's book had an entire chapter about hood fires and how difficult it is for them to spread to the interior of a building because of the upward chimney draft. But Matthews, probably following the rule of not asking a question to which you don't know the answer, asked no questions.

The testimony was completed and summations were the next order of the day.

I was exhausted from the nights of lost sleep and from the tension of the battle in the courtroom. As the judge announced that summations would be delivered on Monday, I breathed a deep sigh of relief. Then, the case would be theirs to decide.

On Monday, after the summations, the jury retired to reach a verdict. As hours passed, I paced the courtroom, the hallway, the courtroom, then the sidewalk. Johnnie and Nora sat silently on a bench in the courthouse hallway. When I tried to talk to them they motioned to me to go away. Finally, a Sheriff's Officer informed me the jury had a question. I had waited five hours.

"Members of the jury," the judge began, after he had summoned them back to the courtroom. "You have informed me that you are hopelessly divided and cannot agree upon a verdict. There is no reason to believe that another jury will do any better than you. I ask you to deliberate longer, attempting as best you can to reach a verdict without compromising your individual convictions. I repeat that the state has the burden of proving the defendant guilty beyond a reasonable doubt and that this defendant will wear the cloak of innocence, unless and until, you are satisfied that he is guilty beyond a reasonable doubt."

The jury looked exhausted. Two of the jurors were in tears.

Two more hours had passed when the Sheriff's Officer opened the door to the courtroom and peeked in. "Gentlemen, we have a verdict."

I couldn't catch my breath. I went out into the hallway where Johnnie and Nora sat on a wooden bench. After I gulped water from a fountain, I returned to the courtroom. Johnnie gripped my arm as we made our way to the counsel table.

The judge peered at the jury over his half moon spectacles. "Have you reached a verdict?"

The foreman stood up. Ten of the jurors were sobbing. The two who had been crying stared straight ahead, their eyes red, but dry, their shoulders back. My heart pounded.

"Your Honor," the foreman said with tears dripping onto his cheeks. "We cannot reach a verdict. We are hopelessly divided."

The judge rapped his gavel in disgust. "The Court hereby declares a mistrial. The parties are excused. The jury is excused." He rose from his chair, wheeled around, opened the door behind him, and walked into his chambers, slamming the door behind him.

"What a'happened?" Johnnie asked.

"Nothing, Johnnie. Nothing. Unfortunately nothing," I responded.

"Do I go to a'jail?" Johnnie asked, with fear in his eyes.

"No, Johnnie. But some jurors, maybe even more than one, thought you were guilty. That's the bad news. The good news is that you're still a free man."

"I'm not a'free. I have no restaurant. I have no life. I have no a'justice." He began to sob uncontrollably. Nora patted his face, trying to calm him down. I stood by helplessly while Johnnie yelled, "I gotta no a'justice. I want a'justice. I want my a'place."

The morning headlines the next day read, "Arson Jury Deadlocked in Restaurant Case." The prosecutor called informing me he was going to try Johnnie Puccinella again.

The first trial replayed in my mind over and over. I tried to figure out how anyone could not have a reasonable doubt that Johnnie burned down his life's work. I spoke with Higgins, who told me, "Juries usually are right. But sometimes they do crazy things."

The second trial was a mirror image of the first. And, afterwards, the second jury was once again hopelessly divided. I informed Johnnie and Nora that never in the history of New Jersey had someone been tried three times for the same crime. I thought this mistrial was as good as a victory. The night after the second trial, Johnnie and Nora invited me to their house for a celebration with Gerald Higgins, Luigi Immordino, the accountant, and Johnnie's family. We drank wine and devoured homemade pasta and veal scallopini.

The following morning, I called the insurance company to collect the million dollars. Johnnie had told me he could rebuild for two hundred thousand and that he would borrow one hundred thousand to refurnish. He didn't care about the seven hundred thousand in lost profits he was claiming. I tried to be reasonable and asked the insurance company to settle for three hundred thousand, hoping to get Johnnie back in business and to earn a one hundred thousand dollar fee for my work. The insurance company's representative assured me he was going to recommend a settlement because if there were no third trial, the insurance company would most likely have to pay the entire million. Two days later, my heart fell into my belly after I received a call from the insurance company informing me they were not going to offer anything.

The next afternoon, I received a call from Matthews, who told me he was getting pressure from above to prepare for a third trial. He thought it was coming from the alarm company because the insurance company was asking it to contribute toward a settlement.

Devastated, I felt like I had lost. I questioned the price I was paying for being loyal to Johnnie.

State of New Jersey versus John Puccinella was already two years old when Nora called and asked, "Did you see the morning paper?"

"No, I didn't. What's up? I asked.

"Gerald Higgins died."

My heart fell. How was I going to be able to get Johnnie justice now? I was exhausted and disappointed. Was all of my work in vain? Johnnie had no money. Where was I going to find another expert and energy to prepare for another trial? Slumped over, I shuffled into my father's office.

My father put his elbows on his desk and rested his chin on his palms after I told him, "Not only does Matthews want to try Johnnie again but Gerald Higgins has died."

"You've put your heart and soul into Johnnie's problems. He has to come up with more money for another trial or you have to work out a plea bargain. You can't afford to foot another three week trial and an expert to boot. Loyalty only goes so far. We're not running a charity."

"Where's Johnnie going to come up with twenty grand for an expert and trial costs?"

"Meet with the Puccinellas," he suggested. "They have a lot of friends. Maybe a fundraising dinner would be a good idea?"

"Let me talk to my brother, Antonio," Johnnie said after I told him what my father had suggested.

A few days later, Johnnie showed up at my office unannounced. "Antonio says you agreed to do my case for a 'ten grand." Johnnie put the fee agreement, which said I had agreed to charge only ten thousand dollars and that I would get one-third of any monies I collected from the insurance company, in front of me. I was confused and disappointed that a person I had trusted was throwing my fee agreement in my face after two long years.

"Johnnie, who expected three trials?" I asked.

"Alberto, can you get me some of the insurance money?"

"I don't think so, but I'll try," I replied.

I called Matthews to see if there was room to renegotiate with the insurance company. He responded quickly with an offer. If Johnnie would drop his claim for the insurance money, he would drop the criminal charges.

"But I won't earn a dime for all the work I've put in to this case. It just doesn't seem fair," I exclaimed.

"Can I help it if you made a bad deal? " Matthews hung up before I could utter another word.

"What do you a' think?" Johnnie asked after I explained the offer.

"That you are not guilty. That's what I think. But I see no other choice."

Angry at Matthews and the insurance company and feeling so sorry for Johnnie, I thought about Mr. McShain's handshake. When I had taken an oath to be a lawyer, I had been given a secret handshake. It meant I had to honor the legal profession and honor my relationships with clients. I still felt the same way, but it was becoming more and more difficult to keep that pledge. Without consulting my father, I called Johnnie back and told him, "We're going for it, my friend. Even if it costs me." I faced the dilemma of not being able to hire an expert witness, but lack of funds shouldn't deprive Johnnie of his rights.

"Alberto, how much is the expert we need?" Johnnie inquired.

"About ten grand," I replied.

A few hours later, Johnnie showed up in my office. "My brother, Antonio. He has breakfast and lunch at his place in the 'Burg. He's doing good and wants to help."

Johnnie handed me a wad of bills, ten thousand dollars in cash. "Alberto. You a'listenin to me? I want you to a'tell the prosecutor and the insurance to take their offer and stick it up a'their asses. We're gonna get a'justice. You a'listenin?"

"But, Johnnie. With the deal, there's no risk of jail. You can work somewhere. You're well known. You're a damn good cook. And we could go on with our lives," I said.

"You a'think I came to this a'country to work for somebody? No a'way. Antonio put up the money because you say I'm not a'guilty."

Three hundred people gathered at an Italian social club and raised another ten thousand dollars for their friend, Johnnie Puccinella. The Mayor of Trenton gave an impassioned plea for Johnnie. Both local papers heralded the same headline the next morning. "Mayor Says Johnnie's Innocent."

With the twenty thousand dollars in hand, I flew to Chicago to interview John Kennedy at his office. If I could get the man who wrote the most authoritative book on arson to testify, I was confident I could win the case and get Johnnie the million dollars he deserved.

Over six feet tall, with broad shoulders, Kennedy presented an authoritative and intimidating figure. He appeared even more knowledgeable than Gerald Higgins.

After I explained the case to him, he informed me that he would have to read the transcripts of the two trials before he made a decision to participate in the case. "My reputation is very important to me," he emphasized.

A letter from Chicago arrived. Shivers shot up my spine when I read, "Dear Mr. Stark: I have reviewed the information you delivered to me. I will be able to participate in the trial of State of New Jersey versus John Puccinella. My fee for preparation and testimony will be ten thousand dollars, together with costs of transportation and appropriate hotel accommodations."

I mailed the check for ten thousand dollars the following afternoon.

The following week, Matthews requested removal of the trial to Hunterdon County, New Jersey, the rural county where jurors' prejudice against foreign born people was no secret and where the celebrated Lindbergh kidnapping case, in which Bruno Hauptmann was given the death penalty, was decided.

After the judge granted Matthews' request, Matthews asked me if he could talk to me in the hallway.

"I'm assigning one of my assistant prosecutors to handle the trial," he informed me.

"You son-of-a-bitch. You don't have to try Johnnie again. There haven't been three trials in a criminal case since Washington crossed the Delaware. What is bugging you? You afraid to try it again and lose?"

"I'm not calling the shots on this one. The insurance company and the alarm company are putting pressure on up above," Matthews said.

"I got it. Someone's looking for contributions from them. Let me guess? Lindale? He's looking to run against the mayor."

Matthews nodded.

I was opening the door to Courtroom D on the second floor of the Mercer County Courthouse to start another case, when I heard someone call my name. A tall young man in his late twenties approached me. Tommy Morrison introduced himself. He was the spitting image of Robert Redford. "I'm the one who got assigned to the Puccinella case."

"Nice meeting you," I replied. "I'm sorry I can't say it is a pleasure."

"I understand," he told me.

How could young Morrison understand? He didn't know I had prepared and tried the Bobbie McKenzie case and the first and second Puccinella cases, was strapped for cash, and a case in Oklahoma was sapping my physical and emotional stamina. More and more clients were calling, especially ones injured in accidents. I had to get to know their injuries, their financial problems, their medical needs, and to investigate the accidents. Meeting weekly payroll while handling contingency cases wasn't easy since getting paid took, on average, two years. My father and I had financed the hiring of two lawyers with the money from the McShain case. But that was four years ago. Now nights out at meetings and municipal court, two small children, and a wife were demands I was having a hard time meeting. That the law was a jealous mistress had been pounded into my head in law school, but I never imagined that of the demands of running a practice could be so draining. I was not only juggling my own cases, but trying to supervise our new lawyers, David Botwinick and Richard Shaine.

Because I knew the evidence in the Puccinella case by heart, I wouldn't have to prepare the witnesses. Kennedy was a professional testifier, and I wouldn't have Matthews to battle. That gave me some solace.

While the stress was enormous, what bothered me most was that I was beginning to doubt Johnnie's innocence. The gasoline can wasn't stained or burned on the bottom and I couldn't explain why. Both

Higgins and Kennedy had told me it should have been, unless it was resting on the table by the wall before the fire was ignited. And the chances of that being the case were slim.

After I told Johnnie about my concerns, he vehemently denied torching his restaurant.

"Do you know who did? Do you think someone else did?" I asked.

Johnnie blurted, "You don't a'believe me."

"If you have any enemies, I could use that in your favor by insinuating to the jury that perhaps someone else burned the restaurant."

Johnnie looked at me like I was a crazy man and said, "Alberto, you are out of your a'mind. Alberto, I swear on the Bible. Give me a lie detector."

I did. A lie detector operator entered my office three days later and set up the box with all of its wires. An hour later, he informed me that Johnnie Puccinella showed no signs of prevarication. I felt vindicated and believed in Johnnie's cause more than ever.

Assistant Prosecutor Morrison rose at the beginning of the third trial in March, 1975 and stood before the all WASP jury. In soft, measured words, he began, "All of you know what 'balderdash' means. That's what you are going to hear from the defense in this case." He had used a word equivalent to manufactured bullshit, a word endemic to Hunterdon County. He went on to argue to the jury everything that Matthews had in the first two trials.

Confident that Johnnie was innocent because he had passed the lie detector test, I delivered an even more energetic opening statement than those I had delivered in the first two trials.

I could have closed my eyes and recited what was coming next as Morrison put witness after witness on the stand.

Two days before the state's case was completed, Nora Puccinella collapsed at home, was rushed to the hospital, and put in the intensive care unit. I had no choice but to ask for a mistrial because it was obvious Nora would not be able to appear in Johnnie's defense three or four days later.

"Mr. Stark," the judge said after taking off his glasses and peering at me over his long, crooked nose. "A mistrial. We've had two already.

This is it. Guilty or Not Guilty. This is it. This is the last time I am going to hear this case."

"But, Your Honor," I exclaimed.

"No 'buts.' Do you have anything else to ask?"

"Yes, Your Honor. Can I take a video taped deposition of Mrs. Puccinella in the hospital? That way we can have her testimony as if she were appearing in court," I pleaded.

"So you want to go to a hospital and take the video deposition of your client's wife in a hospital bed with tubes in her arms and oxygen being administered? Mr. Stark, have you considered the sympathy factor and how the prosecution would be adversely impacted by such a procedure?"

"Then what about a deposition without a camera? The transcript could be read," I responded.

"And how will the jury assess her demeanor? Written words don't always tell the truth, do they? It's important to see the witness testify. Request denied. The trial will continue with or without Mrs. Puccinella." The judge impatiently banged his gavel. "Next witness."

"But, Your Honor, in my opening statement to the jurors I highlighted the importance of the corroborating testimony of Nora Puccinella and the conflicting testimony anticipated from Schultz."

"Next witness," he barked.

Faced with an unexpected turn of events and being more comfortable with my ability to strategize, I decided to try something new. Instead of putting my lay witnesses on the stand as I had in the first two trials and then presenting the testimony of my expert, I called John Kennedy to the stand first. After his testimony, people would testify to the facts on which Kennedy relied to form his opinion that the fire started in the kitchen.

Kennedy strode from the back of the courtroom wearing a dark suit jacket with three buttons and a velvet collar. He sat erect in the witness box, turned to the jurors and looked at each one. After he opened his alligator briefcase and took out the exhibits, one at a time, and placed them in a pile, he turned to the judge and nodded. The Sheriff's Officer asked him to stand and put his right hand on the Bible.

Kennedy testified about his education, background, and experience in the investigation of fires. He crisply answered each question while looking at the jury. After Kennedy had explained in detail why the fire was not arson and how it started in the exhaust chimney over the kitchen stove, I turned to Morrison and said, "Mr. Prosecutor, you may cross examine Mr. Kennedy."

Morrison stood behind his counsel table and lifted a thick red book.

"Are you familiar with this book?" he asked.

"Of course, I am. I wrote it," Kennedy replied.

"Mr. Kennedy, are you familiar with the first chapter?"

"Certainly."

"What is the title of the first chapter?"

"How to testify at trial as an expert."

"Let me go through the points you make in your book one by one. Does it say that an expert must walk slowly to the witness stand to give the jurors an impression that he is thoughtful?"

Kennedy answered "Yes".

"Does it say to wear a dark three button suit with lapels, velvet, if possible, to give the impression of success?"

Does it say to sit erect in the witness stand and when answering questions to look at the jurors?"

Morrison went on quoting from Kennedy's book, describing every move that Kennedy had made before the jury.

Morrison sidled over to the jury rail. Changing his tone he asked quietly, "Do you know the definition of 'balderdash'?"

I rose and objected, but was overruled by the judge.

Kennedy looked at me, shrugged his shoulders, and testified, "No, I don't."

"Can you spell that word for me?" Kennedy inquired.

"B A L D E R D A S H".

Morrison smiled at him and proceeded to ask every question Matthews had asked Gerald Higgins. My witness was striking out with the folks from Hunterdon, even though his testimony was similar to what Gerald Higgins had given before two other juries. Johnnie had wasted over ten thousand dollars.

"Jurors," the judge began. "You have heard all of the evidence in this case. It is now time to decide guilt or innocence. I will instruct you about the law. First, let me tell you that you, the jury, are the sole deciders of the facts in this case. While I will tell you what laws of New Jersey apply to this case, you must listen carefully. You must follow the law even if you believe it is wrong. You are the kings and queens of the facts. I am the king of the law." He drolled on for an hour, explaining what was meant by presumption of innocence, credibility of witnesses, and the value of expert testimony.

While I didn't know it, as the jury deliberated, they asked each other why Johnnie's wife hadn't testified. "What wife wouldn't testify for her husband if what he was saying was true?" one of the jurors asked. Another argued, "If he tells a lie about one thing, how can we believe anything else he says?" Seven hours passed before the Sheriff's Officer announced that the jury had a question.

The judge entered the courtroom. "Gentlemen, the jury has a question. They want me to read to them the definition of reasonable doubt."

I looked at Morrison, smiled broadly and thought to myself, "This time it's going to be different."

The judge brought the jury into the courtroom. "I instruct you that the prosecution must prove its case by more than a mere preponderance of evidence, yet not necessarily to an absolute certainty. The state has the burden of proving the defendant guilty beyond a reasonable doubt. Some of you may have served as jurors in civil cases, where you were told that it is necessary to prove only that a fact is more likely than not to be true. In criminal cases, the state's proof must be more powerful than that. It must be beyond a reasonable doubt."

I glanced at the jurors to see what, if any, reaction I could discern. They were all paying full attention to the judge as he read.

"A reasonable doubt," he continued, "is an honest and reasonable uncertainty in your minds about the guilt of the defendant after you have given full and impartial consideration to all of the evidence. A reasonable doubt may arise from the evidence itself or from a lack of evidence. It is a doubt that a reasonable person hearing the same evidence would have."

Out of the corner of my eye, I saw the foreman turn to look at the other eleven jurors. The judge stopped reading. "Do you want to hear more?"

The jury foreman shook his head that they did not.

We went outside the courtroom.

Matthews was sitting on a wooden bench when I walked into the hallway. He motioned for me to come over. "Albert, you ready to settle?"

"Settle, are you kidding?"

"We'll drop the charges if Johnnie will take a hundred thousand from the insurance company. I talked to them and convinced them to make an offer."

I wanted to yell at Matthews for coercing me and threaten him for behaving unethically. But yelling and threatening would not have helped Johnnie, so I said, "It looks good for Johnnie after the jury's question, otherwise you wouldn't be making the offer. Here's a deal I can live with. You put Johnnie on a lie detector. If he passes, the insurance payment is half a million and you drop the charges."

"Lie detectors are bullshit," Matthews snapped. " A habitual liar can pass one any day."

Over my shoulder I spotted Morrison. "You hear what your boss said about lie detectors? You know what? That's just plain balderdash. B A L D E R D A S H."

Morrison pointed his finger at Matthews and laughed. "He's not from Hunterdon. He wouldn't know what that word means."

It was my duty to convey the offer to Johnnie.

The Sheriff's Officer poked his head from the door of the court-room.

"We have a verdict?" I asked.

"Sure enough," he responded.

"We're in negotiations. Ask the judge if he can wait a half hour. We may be able to settle," I said.

Word came back that the judge would not hold up the verdict for the time it would take Matthews to call the insurance company.

The jury filed in. I looked at each one carefully. None of them looked at me as they stood in front of their seats and stared at the judge. It is thought that when a jury does not look at you it is a bad omen. My palms were soaked. I rubbed them on my pants. I couldn't wait to hear the verdict.

"Ladies and Gentlemen, have you arrived at a verdict?"

"Yes, we have," the foreman responded.

"And what have you decided?" the judge inquired.

"That the defendant, John Puccinella is guilty as charged."

My hopes and prayers weren't answered. I could not believe it. I felt faint. I did not believe Johnnie Puccinella was an arsonist. I still don't.

I looked up and saw a tired judge leave the courtroom.

"I'm gonna see my wife," Johnnie said after I explained the verdict. He walked away, his shoulders slumped over like an old man.

I filed an appeal for Johnnie, alleging that the judge's decision not to grant a mistrial after Nora was hospitalized, deprived Johnnie of his right to a fair trial. Johnnie was exhausted and afraid his appeal would be denied.

Matthews agreed to a plea bargain, in return for dismissal of the appeal. Johnnie was resentenced to six months in jail instead of ten years. Johnnie waived his rights to the insurance money and got a job in another restaurant. Nora Puccinella died a year later. On her death bed, she whispered to me, "My Johnnie. He is innocent."

When I see Lady Justice, blind, holding the scales of justice, I see her as human with all of the human frailties. She reminds me of the despair I experienced, knowing there was no justice for Johnnie. I lost even though I was right. Despite my fondness for Johnnie, my belief in his cause, trying as I did, I could not get for him what he wanted.

Morrison had prepared and given a fresh approach to the case. I developed a keener awareness that imponderables inherent in different belief systems influence legal decisions. Time has not dulled those feelings. They still burn inside me each time I prepare and try a case.

I ask if the law is fair and if it should be. Perhaps the law is just a peaceful way of resolving disputes. Perhaps fairness shouldn't matter to lawyers. The oath requires them to represent their clients, within the bounds of the rules of professional conduct, in an adversarial system that encourages different views to bring out the truth. In this case, it failed.

# THE IMPORTANCE OF MEMORY—A
# PERSONAL INJURY DILEMMA

ANNE AND ANTHONY ROSATI WERE REGULARS AT SUNDAY MASS and had
worked hard to pay for their four bedroom Cape Cod. Their home was
around the corner from the church in Hamilton Township, a blue-
collar Trenton suburb. Hoping that Rosa would be the first in the family to go to college, the Rosatis had worked tirelessly to provide their
daughter with a Catholic education.

On the afternoon of October 28, 1974, Anne, forcing a polite
smile and holding her husband's hand, told me what had recently happened to her daughter: "Two weeks ago, Rosa and her roommate at-
tended a weekend religious retreat in Wichita, Kansas, a few hours
away from school. They were freshmen at Stedman University in Enid,
Oklahoma. They returned to their off-campus apartment late Sunday
evening. I think they found their apartment was too cold." She paused
briefly to catch her breath. She appeared to be on the verge of tears.
"So they turned on a wall gas heater in their bathroom and fell asleep.
This is what I have put together so far," she said before she began to
sob. "My daughter. She is dead."

Anthony, with his shoulders slumped over like a weary traveler,
swallowed hard, trying to hold back his emotions that seemed ready to
explode. "And her roommate is in a coma," he said.

"I'm so, so sorry. How did it happen?"

"Carbon monoxide poisoning from the gas heater," Anthony answered in his deep, resonating voice.

Anne bent down and pulled an envelope from her handbag, which was resting on the leg of her chair.

I read it.

October 7

Dear Mom and Dad,

I hope you are all well. We're headed for Wichita this weekend for a retreat. We're helping out a group from Saint Francis Xavier (my local church). I'm looking forward to the trip. It's about 62 with a few clouds. Not bad for October? But we're supposed to get a real cold spell, something that's not very common at this time of year according to the folks here. They told me to take some warm clothes. I didn't think I'd ever need that Irish sweater Dad bought me for my birthday. Can't wait to see ya'll at Thanksgiving. You notice I even write with a southern accent.

Love,

Rosa xxxxx

"I was so happy when I got that letter. You don't know. I was raking the autumn leaves from the front yard when the mailman came. I remember the school bus stopping a few doors away. Kids jumped off. As they scampered by, I opened the envelope. After I read it, I was so happy I smiled from ear to ear. I had been so worried about Rosa being so far away. I missed her. I knew she was homesick when she first started school. You know how it is for a mother. When your child is happy, you're happy. And when they're unhappy, you suffer with them." Tears poured from Anne's eyes. Anne paused and took a deep breath.

"How do you think I can help?" I asked.

She shrugged her shoulders, and then Anthony explained, "The gas company that supplied the fuel for the heater. If they had inspected the heater, they would have seen a yellow flame. They would have known it was bad." He told me he was a union plumber and knew something about gas. He slammed his fist on my desk and exclaimed, "Why didn't they put something in the gas to make it smell bad? And the apartment? Who was responsible for providing heat? I want answers."

I had learned how expensive it would be to investigate and prosecute a case involving a defective heater. I also knew that the death of a child did not command large jury verdicts. However callous it may seem, a parent was not entitled to money for emotional distress.

Since the Rosati's loss occurred in Oklahoma, where I did not know the law or the court system, I had added concern about the difficulties I would face.

" You mean a company has to pay less if they kill someone instead of just injuring them?"

"Mr. Rosati," I replied in an assuaging tone that went from low to high. "I don't agree with the law. But unfortunately, that's the way it is."

"It's so hard to believe. How can you put a value on losing a child? It's so cruel," Anne charged.

"Our law comes from England where no one could sue the king. One day, one of the king's men ran over a boy in a procession. The public outcry was so loud that the king permitted a lawsuit, but limited damages to the actual monetary loss the parents suffered–namely the funeral expense. Our law hasn't kept up with modern times," I explained.

Anne peered pleadingly into my eyes.

"What I can do is call a few lawyers in Enid for you," I said.

Anthony shook his head, nodded to Anne, and said, "If you put us in touch with a lawyer in Oklahoma to investigate what really happened, we would be very appreciative."

When Anne and Anthony left, they appeared much calmer than when they had arrived. I felt I had fulfilled my duty to give them professional advice.

David Botwinick, one of my associates, peeked in to ask his usual "how are you doing?"

"I'm preparing for another arson trial."

"You need any help?" he inquired.

I told him about the interview with the Rosatis.

David snapped, "I'll go down. I went to school in Dallas. I know how those Bible belt Okies think. I'll spend the weekend with a few of my fraternity brothers from SMU and look into things." David, a charismatic fellow with a furrowed brow, penetrating eyes, and a prominent nose, teased, "We've been doing okay since the Bobbie McKenzie case."

"Go back to work," I said with confidence.

After David left my office, I couldn't concentrate, remembering how I felt after Ellen and Jared were injured. The help and support of doctors and therapists at a New York hospital was invaluable. Why shouldn't I help the Rosatis? I had reached out before and taken risks on cases, despite warnings from my father and others. People I had assisted had referred some good cases, because they appreciated my effort. Perhaps the Rosatis would do the same thing. Hadn't I hired David to relieve me when I was too busy?

I walked into David's office. "So you want to go to Oklahoma?"

"Sure do," he replied.

I compiled a list of trial attorneys in Enid from Martindell-Hubbell's directory of lawyers, before I telephoned Donald Jones, a partner in Enid's largest firm. He told me the District Attorney had conducted an investigation and that the case was closed. From what he had learned, he did not think anyone would be willing to take on the gas company on behalf of a student who died since, even on its best day, the case was only worth from ten to twenty thousand dollars. Besides, the student's landlord was Stedman University, to which almost anyone who was anyone in Enid was connected one way or another.

Hamilton James, a single practitioner, agreed with Jones' assessment of the case and explained that in Oklahoma there was no requirement that a gas company put an odorant in the gas used in a heater.

"What about a case against the landlord?" I asked James.

"What's the address again? East Randolph, is it?"

"Yes, 210."

"That row of houses has been there for at least a hundred years.

The university owns the houses on that block. You'll have a big problem bringing a case against a landlord down here."

"What's the problem, if I may ask?"

"Down here, the owner of a building has a lot of rights. You have to prove the landlord had actual knowledge of a defect or problem in order to hold him responsible. I'm sure no one else had the same problem the girls did."

"I'm sure you're right about that," I replied, feeling frustrated. "If they did, they'd be poisoned too.

Mr. James, I understand why you wouldn't be interested in this case, but how about somebody in Oklahoma City. How far is that from Enid?"

"About eighty to ninety miles. You might want to try Harry Rabstein. He's the best plaintiff's injury lawyer down here."

On Saturday, November 16, 1974, David took US Air Flight 873 to Oklahoma City, an hour's drive from Enid.

Billboards heralding "Jesus Saves" welcomed David as he drove through flatland dotted with oil rigs, and passed dark fields which now supported empty grain elevators.

It was a few hours before dusk when he parked his car in front of the No Name Bar on a shady downtown square. Dressed in jeans, a western shirt, ten-gallon hat, and cowboy boots, David looked around at an array of shops. Three brass balls hung from a sign on a pawnshop. There was a luncheonette, a five-and-dime, a clothing store, six bars, and a courthouse. He pulled his briefcase from the back seat and rested it on the trunk. He opened it and looked at a slip of paper. He checked his Polaroid camera and then loaded it with film. A man wearing a red and black wool shirt ambled out of the No Name Bar and tossed a cigarette into the gutter.

"Where's 210 East Randolph?" David asked.

The man pointed across the town square, which had a statue of a man on a horse in the center, and gave David directions. David strolled across the square past a white building with GARFIELD COUNTY COURTHOUSE carved in marble and turned onto East Randolph. The front door at 210 East Randolph, a three story brick walkup, was open. He entered the vestibule, where an insert on one of the three mailboxes read, "Breen-Rosati."

David climbed a dimly lit flight of steps to Rosa and Barbara's apartment and pushed on the door, which creaked as it opened. When he flicked a light switch, an exposed incandescent bulb illuminated a small hallway that led to a bedroom on the left and to a kitchen on his right. He removed the "Rules of Occupancy for College Students" from the door and put it in his briefcase. Two beds faced him as he entered the bedroom. The bed covers had been removed, but the sheets were still in place, eerily unwrinkled. He scanned the room. One window was on the far wall. The bed covers were neatly folded and piled one on top of the other under the window. He took pictures of the scene, pulled the film from the camera and placed it on the bed.

In the bathroom, he observed a wall heater. When he turned the knob, yellow flames jumped up. After taking a picture of the flames, he moved closer and took a shot of soot marks on the enamel cover. Wiping his finger across the cover, he noticed that the soot was fresh. David slid his finger over the cover again. If this was soot from the flames the girls ignited, it should not have been there, assuming the heater was working properly. Clean burning gas shouldn't leave soot on the heater. David rubbed his thumb where he had already wiped his finger. There was no old, hard soot beneath the fresh soot. He thought to himself, "This is not something that has been going on for a long time." Since it was necessary to show a landlord had notice of a danger-ous condition in order to make him responsible, he left the apartment thinking that the lawyers I had spoken to in Enid were right. There was no case for the girls.

The next morning, he met the parents of Rosa's roommate, Glen and Mary Breen, at St. Mary's Mercy Hospital.

"I'm a lawyer from New Jersey. I'm here on behalf of the Rosatis, and I am so sorry about what happened to Rosa and Barbara."

"It's very nice of you to come, young man," Mary Breen responded.

"The Rosatis think the university, which managed the apartment, and the gas company had something to do with this."

After Glen Breen responded, "Right now all we're concerned about is our daughter," David politely bid them goodbye. As he left, a young woman followed him out.

"I'm Dawn Flood," she said. "I have some information you might want."

Dawn told David that Rosa was feeling feverish after she came home from Wichita. When Rosa and her roommate, Barbara, didn't show up for their Monday morning classes, or at the noontime prayer session, Dawn thought Rosa and Barbara might have gotten sick. The weather had changed from hot to cold, and they had been out late at night. After the prayer session, Dawn stopped by to see how they were. She walked up the stair and rang the doorbell. After she received no response, Dawn opened the door and felt heat coming from the bathroom. She then looked through the bedroom door and thought Rosa was asleep. She went over to her, pulled the covers off of her face and whispered in her ear. When Rosa didn't respond, she placed her hand on Rosa's shoulder and shook her. She pulled Rosa's hand from beneath the covers and discovered that her fingers were turning blue. In the other bed, she saw Barbara, covered from head to toe. She pulled the covers off of Barbara's face and discovered that she was not breathing. Petrified, Dawn ran as fast as she could down the stairway and the four blocks to the Dean's Office.

When David returned late Monday afternoon, I listened to what he had learned and carefully examined the photographs.

" Look at the flames," he said peremptorily. "They're yellow. Even the gas grill at my apartment has a label warning against cooking inside if the flame is not clear blue. I recall the manual saying a yellow flame means it's impure and giving off carbon monoxide. Just what Anthony said. The blankets. Look at them. They're folded in a pile. The beds don't have any blankets on them, just sheets. Damn it. These girls came back from Wichita. It was cold in the apartment. So what did they do? They lit the gas heater and went to sleep all bundled up. $CO_2$ is odorless. The apartment filled up with deadly gas. So Rosa is dead and Barbara's in a coma. There's fresh soot on the heater cover. If this case were in New Jersey, it would be a slam dunk because the gas company has to put an odorant in the gas and the landlord has to inspect for defective conditions before he rents a place. All the landlord had to do was turn on the gas. Anyone could have seen the yellow flamé. It's so obvious."

David leaned on my desk before he asked, "What do you suggest we do next?"

I fiddled with my thumbs. "Let's meet with the family and tell them the truth. Let's just tell them to forget about blaming someone and to move on with their lives."

David shrugged his shoulders. His head dropped. I sensed his reaction had more meaning than met my eye.

"David," I said, "I don't want to be hard on you. Don't be afraid to talk back to me. I care about these girls as much as you do."

After I wrote down everything David had learned, I called Anthony Rosati. In an odd way, I was relieved. I had fulfilled my professional responsibility to the Rosatis, to my father, and to the lawyers in my office. I thought that was going to be the last time that I would hear from the Rosatis.

In May, 1975, Father Armand, who the Rosatis had told me was the parish priest helping them deal with their grief, called me to help another parishioner. "The Rosatis told me how nice you were to them," he said.

"How are the Rosatis doing?" I asked.

"Not well, Albert. They can't accept that no one is responsible for Rosa's death. I'm afraid it's always going to prey on their minds. It's a shame the law is so unfair."

"Father, they have a point. I agree with them. I'd hoped they would move on with their lives and I'd move on too. That's God's honest truth. But I'll give it another look. How's the girl in the coma doing?"

"Haven't you heard? The roommate has come out of the coma, and she's in Ohio at a rehabilitation center. I don't know much more than that."

"That's interesting," I muttered, thinking about how my wife and son had experienced a miraculous recovery after some of the best doctors in New York had told me they would both be disabled for life.

I went into the file drawer, pulled out my notes, and called Hamilton

James to get more information about Harry Rabstein.

"He's a character, he is. Wears red linings in all of his suits. Tries to look like a Texas oil man. Came down here from the Bronx. Married a girl whose father owned a department store. He puts on a show in the courtroom. Somehow he wins big ones down here. Tell him I gave you his name and send him my regards," James told me.

Since David and I were now a team, working on all of my cases together, I asked him to come to Oklahoma City with me.

Harry Rabstein's office was on the fourth floor of the Petroleum Building, which had probably been a prestigious property during the twenties, but now was worn by time. With the oil boom in the sixties, downtown Oklahoma City modernized quickly and the Petroleum Building was now a relic of another era. But lawyers still had offices there because it was close to the State Capitol and the courthouses. The thick air vibrated and hot dry winds blew hard enough to slow David and me as we walked from the parking lot to Harry's office.

"Four please," I requested, entering an elevator.

A thin, elderly woman with ringlets of gray hair smiled. She got up from a wooden stool and pulled a lever to close the heavy, steel doors. When the elevator door opened, she exited the elevator and pointed to Harry Rabstein's office door at the end of a hallway.

The waiting room floor was covered with a maroon carpet that was threadbare in places. Wooden chairs needing fresh stain on the edges lined the wall. Articles about Harry's victories hung in black, dust covered frames alongside certificates and plaques acknowledging Harry's community work and legal honors.

Harry, a white-haired gentleman in his early sixties who James had described perfectly, invited us into his office. He sat contentedly in his high-back, green leather chair behind a large mahogany desk. A lamp covered with a Tiffany stained glass shade cast an orange tint on his face. He moved forward and flipped his black plastic glasses up to his forehead.

"Tell me about your case. I have another appointment in an hour," Harry instructed without giving us the opportunity to introduce ourselves.

David passed Harry the pictures he had taken in Enid while I began to tell him why we thought the gas company and the university were responsible for Rosa's death and Barbara's brain damage. Harry slid his glasses down his nose and scrutinized the pictures, one by one. "Old gas heater. Probably from the thirties. Too bad. Oklahoma Natural Gas didn't put that one in. Sure has a yellow flame, doesn't it? You take good pictures, son. Ever need a job, you see me. You hear?" Harry said to David.

"You see the soot marks?" David asked.

Harry moved the pictures closer to his face. "Yes, but I don't see a tag. The gas company puts a tag on heaters they inspect. So this one wasn't on their list. Probably illegal. Probably installed by the owner of the house before it was converted to apartments. Probably connected to the kitchen line without a permit," Harry explained, obviously enjoying the opportunity to display his expertise. "No case against the gas company. What else do you have to show me?"

"Mr. Rabstein. I went to the apartment. The soot marks were fresh. Underneath the fresh marks there weren't any old ones. To me that indicates that nobody had used the heater for a while," David said, pounding out each syllable.

"Good point, but there's no case against the landlord. I'll explain that later. I was interested in the case against the gas company. That's where the big bucks are. That's why I agreed to see you. You fellows sure these girls didn't commit suicide?"

David looked at me. I returned his glance.

David pulled the placard he had taken from the girl's apartment door out of his briefcase and passed it to Harry.

"So you want to sue Stedman, do you? You ever been to Enid?"

David nodded his head.

"Lots of pickup trucks there. You see the gun racks in the rear window? Sue Stedman and you won't get out of town alive," Harry chided.

"But the landlord should inspect. In this case, it's a college. Why isn't it considered a business as it would be in New Jersey and not a landlord?" I inquired.

"A business has the duty to inspect and find defects, which it has to warn a potential customer about."

"We're not so liberal out here. Back in the Bronx or Trenton, yes. In Oklahoma, a man's house is his castle. You know how the Okies got the name Sooners? It was called the Great Land Rush of 1893. And a rush it was. Thousands of would-be landowners scrambled to Oklahoma in hopes of claiming their own sliver of America. Tradition's big out here. I've learned that the hard way. A man can do what he pleases with land. A landlord is a landlord. A business is a business. Stedman is the owner of a house and rents rooms to students. Here you have to show that Stedman had prior notice of a dangerous condition. You gentlemen have this on a contingency?"

"We haven't actually signed the case up yet. But if there's a case, we can get it on a contingency," I told him. "That's why I'm here. I've had some luck with some cases like this. I also think it's important to the parents to have closure when they lose a child. Frankly, I think the university should be held liable."

"You want my advice. Enjoy a day in Oklahoma City. Take in the Rodeo Museum. You'll get a real feel for the Wild West. I'll take you to the Oklahoma Club tonight for dinner if you're staying over. It's a club where anyone who is anybody in this town goes. Then go home and turn this case down. You'll save yourself a lot of grief and aggravation. I'm sure you have better things to do with your time. Nobody here's going to sue Stedman—even if there was a case-and, believe me, there is no case."

Was I getting bogged down in an unprofitable case that would make it impossible to take on the next good one that came along? Maybe Harry had done me a favor? Our law firm was sufficiently in the black to take cases that were risky. We also had the potential to produce financial rewards and do social good. While my idealism about the law and politics was waning in one respect, it was strengthening in other respects. Seeing that thorough preparation led to positive results and involvement with clients led to rich personal relationships, I focused my efforts on becoming a trial lawyer and community activist. I saw that a lawyer didn't have to stop being an idealist to be a financial success. If I didn't have the responsibilities to my family and the lawyers who had hitched their wagons to mine, I probably would have felt that philosophical success was enough. I knew, from the depths of my soul, that I had to fight this case.

Rabstein's office door shut behind us.

Something prodded David to ask the operator if there was another good lawyer in the building.

"Joey Bob Taylor," she said. "Third floor."

"Let's roll 'em. You never know. What do we have to lose? Third floor, please," I said.

David smiled from ear to ear. While I didn't realize the importance of the moment, it was a milestone that soon would prove to be important in my quest for freedom beyond the bar. David was not only an associate but also a person who would act like a partner and permit me to grow as a lawyer, businessman, husband, and father.

The glass door was painted with gray letters. JOEY BOB TAYLOR AND ASSOCIATES. A young looking woman in a plain blue smock sat at a metal desk banging away at an old Remington typewriter.

"Is Mr. Taylor in the office?" I inquired.

"Do you have an appointment?" the secretary asked. Quickly turning in her seat, she grabbed a red appointment book and began to flip through the pages. "I don't see that Mr. Taylor is expecting anyone this late in the afternoon."

"I have a new case to talk to him about," I replied, introducing myself.

"Mr. Roberts is here. He's one of Mr. Taylor's associates. Would you like to see him?" the secretary asked politely.

Barry Roberts was middle aged and balding. He wore a foulard tie, monogrammed blue oxford shirt, and leather suspenders. As he offered us seats, he adjusted his collar and then put an unlit meerschaum pipe on his desk. A framed poster of a skier on a flat surface with an oil rig in the background hung on the wall behind his desk. Bold letters read, SKI OKLAHOMA. I was relieved to see the poster, knowing I was in the office of a lawyer who, despite the pretentious clothes, also had a sense of humor.

After some pleasantries, Roberts asked in a measured voice why we were there to see him. I explained that we had come out to see Harry Rabstein and described my case. "Since my plane doesn't leave until the morning, I thought it wouldn't hurt to get another opinion," I commented.

"At least I know you're honest. Most lawyers wouldn't admit that one attorney had turned down a case during their interview with another one. Harry's the best there is in these parts. He's not going to take any case that's not open-and-shut and big. I agree you can't sue Stedman in Enid, but I'm curious . . . where are your clients from?"

"One's from New Jersey and one's from Ohio," I answered.

"So you have diversity. The girls are from Ohio and New Jersey. The accident happened here," Roberts responded, rubbing his palm on his chin. "A suit in federal court may be possible since the jurisdiction for negligence cases in the federal court is limited to cases worth more than ten thousand dollars and where all parties live in different states. Perhaps the federal court, under a conflict of law theory, would apply New Jersey law and, perhaps, Ohio law? Oklahoma's pretty conservative. But the federal courts are more up to date. The headquarters for the district is in Denver. "

Appreciating Roberts' explanation, I inquired, "Where's the federal court?"

"Here in Oklahoma City."

"Not in Enid?" I asked.

"No. Right here. About six blocks away," Roberts replied.

I decided to take a different approach and see what Roberts' reaction would be. "I realize I'm not going to get a lawyer in Enid, and probably not in Oklahoma City, to take this case. I don't even know if I have a case. But I would like to tell my clients that if, with more investigation, I find out there is a case, I can get a local lawyer to introduce me to the court. In New Jersey, you ordinarily need to be a lawyer who is a member of the New Jersey Bar. Only in extraordinary situations will a court permit a local lawyer to ask permission for an out-of-state attorney to try a case, assuming that the local lawyer sits at the counsel table as the lawyer of record. Is it the same out here? If it is, I'll be looking for a lawyer here who I can pay by the hour."

"Yes. We follow the same practice here. That's an interesting proposition you put forth. There's nothing for me to lose with that kind of arrangement. It's boom-and-bust out here. When you need me, I may be very busy. Right now things are a little slow. Working hourly has its good points at times, doesn't it?"

I took a business card from a wooden holder on Roberts' desk and put it in my wallet.

A week after I returned from Oklahoma City, a young woman in her twenties uncrossed her legs as I entered the waiting room of my office in Trenton. Two black metal suitcases were resting on the gray, tweed carpet beside her feet.

"Can I help you?" I asked.

"I'm Alice Englehart. I'm demonstrating a new product to lawyers. Have you ever seen Lexis?" she inquired.

"Not yet. I've heard a lot about it. What's the story?"

"Lexis is a new computerized method of doing legal research. What reference books do you have in your library?"

"The *New Jersey* and *Federal*," I said nonchalantly.

"With Lexis you can get cases from all fifty states. Would you like a demonstration?"

"How long will it take? I have to be leaving for court in about a half-hour."

"Not that long. Do you have a table near a three-pronged outlet somewhere?"

"So what would you like me to look up for you?" Alice asked after she configured her computer and printer on a table in my office.

"Let's try 'college student dies from carbon monoxide poisoning in student apartment,'" I suggested.

"Let's try 'student' and 'housing' first. It's the broadest type of search. We can narrow it down after if we have to."

She typed "student/housing" on her computer. Cases popped up on the screen. "Let's add 'injured.'" She scanned the screen. "Here are two interesting cases. Let's bring them up." She pushed a few more keys.

"Devin versus Andover Academy. Let's see what it says." Line by line the case printed out on a printer next to her computer. "The case holds a preparatory school responsible for a student's injury in a dormitory because the school was a business. The school exercised complete control over the premises and, therefore, owed the student a duty to inspect and to warn of dangerous conditions that could have been discovered by a reasonably prudent person."

"That's interesting. I thought a school was a landlord and had much less of a duty to a tenant," I commented.

"I'm not a lawyer," Alice related. "I just know how to do searches. The law is up to you."

"Any more like that?" I asked.

"Here's one in Alaska. Let's try it."

The case flashed on the screen.

"Same thing. Private school. Injury. Decides that a school is a business. There's something more here. Let's look."

I craned my neck over her shoulder. Words appeared on the screen. "In order to raise the duty of a school from a landlord to a business, a plaintiff has the burden of proving by a preponderance of the believable evidence that the school administration exhibited the same or similar level of control over the premises that a business owner does or should exhibit over the premises where the plaintiff suffered injury or harm."

"Where can I get hard copies of those cases?"

"Here are the legal citations," Alice said, pointing to the screen. "Let me print the two cases out for you. Souvenirs from Lexis."

A note in my file says it was July 14, 1975, the day I saw the power of technology in the law. I had seen typewriters go from manual to electric, then automatic, and carbon paper replaced by the Xerox machine. But to see cases from all over the country being printed out before my eyes was mind boggling. I was excited to discover a new technology that could give me a competitive advantage.

"David, look at these." I slid the Lexis printouts in front of him.

David looked up after skimming the italicized case summary. His pupils were as big as eight balls. "Holy f . . . . .in' shit. We've got a shot. Let's get these down to Rabstein," he exclaimed.

"Rabstein. Shit! We've struck gold. I want to make a deal with Barry Roberts."

"Are you out of your mind? We'll get skewed and quartered down there. We need a guy like Harry," David insisted, arguing that we would be foolish to take responsibility for a case in Oklahoma.

"O.K." I said, "You call Harry. He's your type, not mine."

A few hours later, David sauntered into my office. "Barry Roberts it is. Harry just turned me down."

On Sunday afternoon, I reluctantly visited with Anthony and Anne to tell them what I had found out.

"I think we have a case against the university," I told them.

"The university?"

"I found some cases, one in Massachusetts and another in Alaska, that may get me around the law that prevents the girls from bringing a case against Stedman."

"And the bad news?"

"The bad news is that the courts down there are pretty conservative. I'd probably lose in the Oklahoma court and have to appeal. The Court of Appeals is in Denver, which, I'm told, is more liberal. But there's no guarantee I can change the law."

"So, what are you saying?" Anthony asked.

"Trouble is I probably should use a lawyer down there. The best one in Oklahoma City turned me down. Something in my gut tells me I can't trust the locals. Everyone's so tight down there. Logically, I should have bailed out of this a long time ago. I know a lawyer shouldn't get so emotionally involved. It's probably not a good thing. But if there's a situation that I should advocate, it's a case like Rosa's."

"That's nice to hear. But honestly, I think you like the puzzle. You want to put it together so bad. The payoff at the end isn't a trifle if you put it together, is it?"

"That's true, if I get the Breen case," I admitted.

"Anne and I will understand if you drop this case. Maybe it's the best thing," Anthony commented.

"Have you told the Breens you have these new cases?" Anne asked.

"No," I replied.

"Maybe you should. People who have had a tragedy want retribution. But they don't want to relive something that is so hurtful, just to lose. That's like dying twice," Anne remarked before she thanked me for what I had done.

"You believe in fate?" I asked David.

"Depends. What're you getting at?"

"A client from Columbus just called and invited me to come to the Ohio State–Michigan game this weekend. The winner goes to the Rose Bowl."

"You mean Palatine?" David asked, referring to our client who had had a construction problem that caused a roof to fall in on shoppers.

"Yes. He's sending me tickets. The game's on the 22nd."

"Hey, this game's gonna decide who's number one," David told me. "Am I on board?"

"He only had one ticket," I teased.

Glen and Mary Breen met me promptly at ten o'clock at the Stauffer's Hotel in Columbus, Ohio. I had called them to tell them I would be in town for the Big Game and would love to touch base with them.

When we sat down in the coffee shop, I had expected Glen and Mary to talk about the 21–14 game that number one Ohio State had won over Michigan, ranked number four.

Instead, Mary Breen began the conversation in a very serious tone. "I'm so glad you called us. We are upset, very upset."

Glen shook his head in agreement.

"Has something happened to Barbara? I heard she was doing much better."

"Thankfully, Barbara has made wonderful progress. She's a real fighter," Mary related. "They started her off with a new kind of therapy. She and I were in a playpen for three months. It's a new way of re-teaching brain cells to do things the cells that were killed by the gas used to do. I started to sensitize her with hugs, then kisses, and before long she was cooing like she had when she was a baby. She's now able to brush her teeth and understand what I say. But that's not what is upsetting."

Glen Breen interrupted. "Stedman is claiming the girls committed suicide. They're saying that the girls were unhappy because Rosa was a

Catholic and Barbara was a Jehovah's Witness. Stedman is saying that the girls didn't fit in and that the carbon monoxide poisoning was intentional. We had taken out a medical insurance policy on Barbara. Not much. Just fifty thousand. The insurance company has written us that if Barbara dies they will not pay until they investigate what Stedman is claiming. If Barbara tried to commit suicide, they don't have to pay us," Glen Breen said with rage. His face was red, and he took a deep, exhausted breath.

"We'd like you to help us if you think you can," Mary Breen said.

Suicide would surely put another obstacle in my way. "This information takes me by surprise. I think I can help you with the insurance," I said. I did not believe for a minute that the girls tried to hurt themselves. There was no note, and the girls had no history of depression.

"You think you can?" Glen Breen asked.

"I think I can," I assured him. I didn't think it would be difficult to get the fifty thousand from the medical insurance because the insurance company would have a difficult time proving the suicide attempt.

When I returned to the office, I immediately informed David about what the Breens had told me at brunch in Columbus.

David was livid when he heard about the insurance company's position. "Remember the remark Harry Rabstein made about suicide? What the fuck does he know? That's bullshit."

"It may be bullshit, but it's another factor we have to consider . . . as if there aren't enough obstacles already in a case against the university."

"So what are you telling me? You're finished? You've heard enough? I smell a rat. A fucking rat. That's what I smell. I never trusted those zealots down there. The holier-than-thou ones. And there are plenty of them down there. I know," David ranted.

"Calm down," I interrupted. " I think we have to be rational and write down all of the things we have to prove to win. The good news is we have the big case. The bad news is we have a bad case. But at least our fee on the insurance case will help defray some of our investigation expenses."

"Okay. We have the Alaska and Massachusetts cases. If we can't get the court to accept them, we're out of court quickly on a summary judgment, because then, the college owes no duty to the girls and there's no case," David said.

"Agreed. We have to get evidence that supports the theory that the university is a business, that the furnace was not on, and that the girls turned on the bathroom heater to get warm. We need a Barbara Breen who is competent and who remembers what happened."

"I'll agree to that. Without Barbara, it's all circumstantial, and you know how that'll go over. That's a tall order," David added.

The phone rang. I recognized the voice immediately.

"Barry. Barry Roberts?" I asked.

"Sure is. I'm in New York City with my wife and the two girls. Just thought I'd call you from the tallest building in the world. We're atop the World Trade Center. Lady Liberty's right below us. How about being the Roberts' guest for dinner? Hit a pretty big one. Malpractice case. Four hundred fifty thousand. Biggest verdict in Oklahoma to date. I have my whole family here. We went to Radio City, saw the Christmas show, and the tree at Rockefeller Center."

"How long you going to be in the city?"

"Leaving tomorrow."

"Where shall we meet?"

"How's the Oyster Bar at The Plaza?"

"Roberts, I always did like your style. David's on vacation. I'll meet you at six."

"The Oyster Bar it is."

The Plaza Hotel is a place my parents used to point out to me as a child as we walked up Fifth Avenue from Rockefeller Center to Central Park. Then ornate horse-drawn carriages waited outside for the guests. Now, shiny black limousines lined the driveway. I tentatively wound my way up the steps past the tall, marble pillars. A doorman in tails and a top hat opened the door. Violinists serenaded diners in a garden-like restaurant in the hotel lobby. I looked around at the elaborate crystal chandeliers, the plush red carpet, and the displays of glistening gold jewelry. I took a deep breath, trying to overcome the intimidation I felt in such an opulent place. I looked for a sign indicating where the Oyster Bar was, but I found none. I timidly approached a woman who was behind a white podium at the entrance to the lobby restaurant. She pointed to my left and told me to follow the hallway with the marble floor.

In front of me, a leaded window embossed with "Oyster Bar" caught my eye. I entered an imposing paneled room and saw Barry sitting at a table beneath frosted glass sconces.

"It's funny you called me," I said after he greeted me.

"Why do you say that?"

"There've been a few interesting developments in the Stedman case."

"There have?" Barry asked with a quizzical smile.

"Well, I . . . "

"Wait!" Barry interjected. "I didn't want to talk to you on the telephone, but I have something to share with you," Barry responded secretively.

"About this case?" I asked, outwardly intrigued.

"Yes."

"It must be interesting if you didn't want to talk about it on the phone."

"Sure is. I was eating lunch at the Oklahoma Club one afternoon last week. John Webster, a fellow lawyer, was at the next table with James Bernard, the dean at Stedman. Webster defends Stedman in all its important litigation and has earned the reputation of being one of the country's finest courtroom strategists. Harry Rabstein stops at John's table and says, in a voice loud enough for half the dining room to hear, 'Web, my buddy, I have to apologize.' Bernard asks John, 'Why would Harry apologize to you? What'd he do, beat your pants off in some case?' Webster guffaws, 'No, no, Harry never has won a case against me.' Then Bernard asks something like, 'why are you apologizing to my friend Web?' Harry says he's apologizing because two lawyers from back east came to see him about taking a case against Oklahoma Natural Gas a while ago. Harry tells them he told the lawyers they had no case against the gas company, but one of the lawyers questioned him about suing the landlord of the building. He assured Webster he discouraged them, then informed him that the lawyer from back east had called him recently about some cases he found. Bernard says to Webster, 'Isn't that interesting?' Then I couldn't hear the rest of what went on. They got quiet."

"Very interesting. Very interesting indeed," I said, thinking out loud.

Barry thought a minute. "So what are you going to do?"

"We have to have a Barbara who is competent to testify. I'll go to Columbus and see how she's doing, and, if there's a possibility she will be competent, I'll ask the Breens to hire me. We'll probably try to argue the Massachusetts and Alaska cases. Even though they deal with prep schools, they will be good precedents."

"I'll bet you a quarter that as soon as you start suit, you'll get an offer. Stedman won't want any publicity," Roberts commented.

"So, you're telling me you're on board?"

"I'm your local lawyer."

"By the hour?"

"By the hour. You ready for dinner? Let me call the wife. Meet me in Room 1406 in about fifteen minutes. I want you to meet the girls. They love room service."

Means Hall is a large brick building on the Ohio State University campus that is used as an infirmary and rehabilitation center. Barbara had been transferred there so that she could be closer to her parents. Glen Breen arranged for me to interview Doctor David Weiss, the physiatrist in charge of Barbara's care.

"She's awake," he informed me. "The next three months are crucial." He took a model of a skull from behind his desk. Pointing, he said, "This is the outer covering. It's bony and hard. Inside is the brain. It's soft and spongy. When the brain is traumatized, it swells up like a sponge absorbing water. Carbon monoxide irritates the brain cells. When the brain cells swell, the brain presses against the skull. Have you ever bruised your knee? If so, you know that it swells and hurts and you can't move it." He stopped his rapid style of speaking and appeared to be concentrating intently on his thoughts. "Then the swelling goes down and you can move it. Something like that has happened to Barbara. She was in a coma because the brain swelled and shut off her electrical system. The only things that were working were her sympathetic nerves. They control breathing. Unfortunately, her roommate lost that function. Well, Barbara's brain is becoming less swollen. Unfortunately, she has lost a lot of cells. They've died. It's called necrosis. We have no idea how many have died. There are millions and millions of them. Right now, she can't talk. She can blink her eyes. She can hear but can understand only a few things. We know that because she is able to respond to some simple commands, such as open your eyes or lift your head. We don't know what she will be able to do, if anything, in the future. But we're doing some important experiments here. We're going to be putting Barbara into a few of them."

I could hardly keep my eyes off of Barbara when Doctor Weiss ushered me into her room. She stared blankly at me while I held her hand. Her face, pale and wan, could not disguise what were the good looks of a college prom queen.

"Can I ask her some questions? Like 'did she go to the cellar to check the heater'?"

"I don't think she can remember something like that. She's only able at this time to recall a state of mind, not actual facts. Maybe sometime in the future. Maybe in six months. Who knows? I've seen patients like Barbara make slow, but steady, progress." I had experienced the incremental improvements Ellen and Jared made; when things stopped getting better, the inexorable feelings of hope and sadness ensued.

After hearing what the doctor said, I met with the Breens, who agreed to a contingent fee arrangement.

I called Barry Roberts. "File the case. I think we have something," I said.

My practice had become almost entirely personal injury. I had learned that if a serious injury could be presented to a jury, a good settlement could be made because the risks to the insurance company were too great to let a jury decide the case. Armed with the dossiers I discovered on Lexis, I thought that, if the case were dismissed on legal grounds, I would not expose myself to a great deal of expense. If I could get the judge in Oklahoma to recognize the Alaska and Massachusetts cases, I had a reasonable shot at getting a good settlement. A jury verdict would be even better because it would launch my career as a national trial lawyer.

John Webster filed the papers on behalf of Stedman University, refuting Barry Roberts' charges that the University was responsible for Rosa's death and Barbara's brain injury. Webster argued that the university was a landlord, that it had no prior notice of any defect in the gas heater, and therefore, that the case should be dismissed pursuant to Oklahoma law.

Barbara made slow, but steady, progress. In March, 1976, Barbara learned to walk on parallel bars. She talked haltingly in a slow monotone. She was able to verify David's theory of what had happened, except for two items. She and Rosa did not check the heater in the basement because the door to the basement was locked. They called Building and Grounds Department to report how cold the apartment was and were told the problem would be resolved in the morning.

I asked Doctor Weiss how Barbara could remember events that happened in 1976 but forget information that I had told her minutes before.

"There's a difference between short-term memory and long-term memory. Most people can't understand why it happens. Some people remember things that happened in their childhood but can't recognize the person they are talking to. That is a simplification. I'll get some books for you. There's a lot of new research being done in the field of brain neurology," he explained.

Barbara's case became an obsession. I read everything I could about brain injuries.

John Webster was sitting in a plush leather sofa outside Judge Delaney's chambers at nine in the morning. In a deep southern drawl, he said, "Welcome to Oklahoma. Better we get rid of this case sooner rather than later." I felt a violent, excruciating pain in my chest.

Judge Delaney's court clerk ushered us into his chambers. A sitting area separated the judge's large oak desk from a large oval conference table, surrounded by eight chairs. Judge Delaney, sitting in short sleeves at the head of the table, rose as we entered.

"Web, my friend, it's good to see you. It hasn't been a week since I saw you last," Judge Delaney began.

Webster turned to me and smiled insidiously.

I was afraid David was right about the closeness of the hometown crowd.

"Barry, it's nice to see you," the judge said, greeting Roberts.

Barry smiled at me, knowing I would be pleased that he had been addressed as familiarly as Webster.

"Gentlemen, please have a seat and let's get down to business. I assume that you are ready for this motion, Mr. Stark."

"Yes, Your Honor. I want to thank you for giving me the opportunity to appear in your court."

"All right then. What we have to do is apply the rule of landlord-tenant," Judge Delaney stated.

"Your Honor, I have filed a brief with your court setting forth my position that the university is a business and that under business law, the university has a duty to inspect the apartment for defects just as it has with a dormitory. I have cited two cases. If you apply them, this case will proceed to trial."

"What do you have to say about that, Web? I have read those cases and they seem to say what Mr. Stark is claiming," Judge Delaney said, winking at Barry. He clasped his hands in a prayer position waiting for Webster's response. I looked at his body language and breathed a sigh of relief because I suspected the judge agreed with the cases I had found.

"Your Honor, under those cases, the university would have to have exclusive control of the premises. In this case, the girls had complete control. They had a kitchen, they cleaned the apartment on their own, and lived just like any other tenants in Oklahoma," Webster argued.

"Your Honor, there's a difference here," I said before the judge could respond.

"I can read," Judge Delaney snapped. "Here's what I'm going to do. Mr. Stark, you have sixty days to take a sworn statement of any three people from Stedman University at a deposition. If you cannot prove exclusive control, I am going to dismiss this case."

"We dodged the bullet," Barry Roberts exclaimed after we exited the courthouse.

"We sure did. Now we have our work cut out for us," David agreed.

At Roberts' office, we decided to take the sworn statements of James Bernard, the head of Building and Grounds, the supervisor of dormitory maintenance, and the person responsible for inspections of University properties.

"I'll get the request off to John in the morning," Barry assured us as we left his office.

When I entered Dean James Bernard's office to take depositions, John Webster greeted me in a businesslike fashion. He then introduced me to Charles Percel, the head of Stedman's dormitory staff. In the middle of the small glass-walled room, I observed a small rectangular table with four metal chairs.

Percel was a heavyset man with a round face. He had bulbous eyes and a wide nose. His midsection was huge and when he sat down his plaid shirttail pulled out of his green work pants.

"How long have you worked at Stedman?" I asked.

"Twenty-six years," Percel responded.

"What is your job?"

"I'm in charge of the dormitories here at Stedman."

"Are you in charge of the heating?"

"Yes," he admitted.

"Is there anyone else responsible for turning on the heat in the dormitories?"

"No."

"Are there any rules and regulations that govern what a student can do with the heating in the dormitories?" I asked short, direct questions, so if Percel changed his story I could use his slander effectively in front of a jury.

"Yes."

"Can you tell me what they are?"

"They're on a placard which we post on the back of the dorm room doors. It's called 'Rules and Regulations Governing Students' or something like that."

"Does it have Building and Grounds Department on the bottom?"

"I think so."

"What do the rules tell a student?"

"Not to mess with the thermostats and if there's a problem to call."

"Who determines when to put the heat on?"

"I do."

"On or about October 13, 1974, did you know that a cold front was coming through Enid?"

He raised his eyebrows toward the ceiling. He looked over at John Webster, who was poker-faced. "Yes," Percel answered.

"What did you do about the heat in the dormitories?"

"I turned on the furnaces."

"Was 210 East Randolph a college apartment?"

"Yes."

"Were the 'Rules and Regulations' posted on the door to the apartments there?"

He looked again at Webster before replying, "I'm not sure."

"Mr. Percel, who turned on the heater at 210 East Randolph?" I asked.

"Oklahoma Gas."

"I have two more questions for you, Mr. Percel. Did anyone, to your knowledge, call Oklahoma Gas to turn on the heat during the week preceding October 13, 1974?"

"I don't know."

"Did you call Oklahoma Gas to turn on the heat at 210 East Randolph at any time immediately before or after you turned on the heat for the dormitories during the week before October 13, 1974?"

"I object to the question," John Webster blurted.

"What's your objection, sir?" I asked.

"This man isn't responsible for 210 East Randolph," he snapped.

"That's not true, sir. I am in charge," Percel interrupted angrily.

"Strike that from the record," Webster insisted in a loud, authoritative voice.

"I'm sorry Mr. Webster. This witness has sworn to tell the truth and he has," I said. "Mr. Percel, I have just one more question. Are you responsible for turning on the heat at 210 East Randolph just as you are in the dormitories?"

"Yes."

"Do you have any questions of Mr. Percel?" I asked John Webster.

"Not at this time," he muttered.

"I'd like Mr. Bernard next," I said to Webster.

James Bernard, the dean of students, stared at me. He pressed his hands against the edge of the table.

I began in textbook fashion delivering the normal information and warnings to Dean Bernard. "Good afternoon, Mr. Bernard. My name, as you know, is Albert Stark. I am here representing two former students at Stedman, Barbara Breen and Rosa Rosati. I am going to ask you some questions. There is a court reporter sitting to your right. She will take down all of my questions and record your answers. Then, they will be transcribed and put into a booklet that can be used in court. If you do not understand a question, please tell me. If you do not tell me you don't understand, I will assume you understood my question. Your lawyer, Mr. Webster, is here with you. If he objects to a question, please do not answer until he tells you to. All of your answers must be stated out loud. The court reporter cannot take down a shake of the head or a nod. Do you have any questions? I see you are shaking your head from side to side. Will you please answer out loud?"

"No, I have no questions," he responded.

"Okay, I'll begin. Did you meet with Mr. Webster before this deposition?"

"Yes."

"Alone or with someone else?"

"With Mr. Percel and Mr. Hodges."

"What instructions did Mr. Webster give you?"

"To tell the truth."

I suddenly realized then how fortunate I was to have forgotten to begin my deposition of Mr. Percel with the usual introductory remarks, warning the witness not to say anything after his lawyer made an objection. Had I done so, Percel would probably not have blurted out "I am in charge" after John Webster's objection to my question. I adopted this unorthodox style in future depositions where I did not want to encourage the witness to put up his guard.

"Was a placard 'Rules and Regulations' posted on the back door of the apartment occupied by Barbara Breen and Rosa Rosati?" I began.

"I don't think so. After the incident, I personally went to the apartment and looked for it. It was not there," Dean Bernard replied.

"How long after the incident passed did you go to the apartment?"

"A month or so, I think."

It was obvious Dean Bernard had gone to the apartment after David.

"Dean Bernard, who is responsible for putting placards on the doors of student housing units to instruct and warn of any problems?"

"That is under my jurisdiction. I make the rules and see to it that they are enforced," he answered.

"Are the 'Rules and Regulations' safety rules?"

"Yes."

"So you are responsible for the safety of students at Stedman University?"

"Unfortunately," he said. I was going to ask him if he saw any evidence that someone else had inspected the soot. I decided not to, because I didn't know what he would answer. If it came out that someone else had touched the evidence, Judge Delaney might throw out testimony about the soot on the grounds that the heater was tampered with. I continued, "Who is in charge of inspecting the furnaces in the dormitories?"

"Joel Hodges."

"Is there anyone other than Stedman University personnel who are authorized to operate the heaters in Stedman University housing units?"

"Yes."

"Who?"

"Oklahoma Gas."

"And who is responsible for calling the gas company to turn the heating on or off?"

"Building and Grounds."

"And unfortunately you assigned Rosa and Barbara to off-campus apartments, didn't you?"

"Yes, I did," he admitted.

"Why?"

"We had more acceptances that year than we had dorm rooms."

"Freshmen don't usually get off campus apartments, do they?"

"No, they don't," Bernard said.

"They sought counseling prior to October 13, 1974, didn't they?"

"Yes."

"According to the records, they were homesick and had some problems adjusting here. Is that uncommon for freshmen?" I asked autocratically.

"Not really," he replied. His terse, sharp answers reminded me of the way my junior high principal spoke.

"Were any medications prescribed for either of the girls?"

"No."

"I have no further questions of this witness," I said sharply.

"Nor do I," John Webster announced.

"Okay, let's do Mr. Hodges," I announced.

"I'd like to take a break. We've been here for an hour and a half," John Webster interjected.

"I have no problem with that. How about fifteen minutes?" I replied, not wanting to give Webster the time to coach Hodges.

"How'd you get so lucky? And what was that about medications?" Barry Roberts asked after we had gone out into the hallway.

"Barry, I forgot to ask Percel the normal questions I ask before questioning. For some reason, I just felt he was going to tell the truth."

"You know, Albert, I've had the same experience with workmen. They aren't going to lie. Not even for their bosses. But did you get the feeling Bernard was hedging?"

"I sure did. He knew there were placards on the doors to the student apartments. I was going to ask him about placards on other doors, but I was afraid of the answer I'd get. If he said there weren't any, I'd have gone into the importance of safety. But I wanted to keep it as simple as I could. In these cases, the defense's job is to complicate things."

"You're on the money there," Barry Roberts exclaimed.

"Let's hope we can stay on the money," I added.

"What about the medications?"

"I'll explain that later. Let's go nail down Hodges."

"You better because Bernard opened the door you closed with Percel."

"What do you mean?" I inquired.

"Didn't you hear him say that Oklahoma Gas had authority to turn on the furnace. You didn't ask about inspection authority. There may have been joint authority between the university and the gas company," Barry warned.

"Good point. Thanks," I said.

After Hodges was sworn in by the court reporter, I started my interrogation. "Mr. Hodges, is it your responsibility to call Oklahoma Gas to turn on the furnace at 210 East Randolph?"

"Yes."

"How do you know when to call?"

"Charlie tells me."

"Charlie who?"

"Charlie Percel."

"Why does Charlie Percel tell you?"

"Supervisor."

"He's your supervisor? I asked.

"Uh huh."

"You mean 'Yes?'"

"Uh huh."

"Did he tell you to call Oklahoma Gas on or before October 13, 1974?"

"What d'ya mean?" Hodges asked.

"I'm sorry if I confused you. On Monday, Tuesday, Wednesday, Thursday, Friday, Saturday, or Sunday before October 13, 1974, did you get instructions from anyone to call Oklahoma Gas?"

"Nah."

"When did you call Oklahoma Gas?"

"When Charlie told me to."

"When was that?" I asked.

"Right after they took out the girls," Hodges replied.

"You mean in the ambulances?"

"Uh huh."

"Were you at the apartment when they took out the girls?"

"Uh huh."

"What was it like?"

"Steaming. Stunk like a skunk."

"How long did it take Oklahoma Gas to come and turn on the furnace?"

"About an hour."

"There were no tags on the bathroom heater, were there?" I knew about the tags because of what Harry Rabstein had told me after he reviewed David's photos.

"Nah."

"The gas company never inspected the bathroom heater, did they?"

"Uh uh."

"Because it was an illegal heater hooked up to the kitchen line, right?"

"How'd you know?"

I looked at John Webster and wondered what he would think if I answered Hodges' question, "A lawyer in Oklahoma City by the name of Harry Rabstein told me."

Webster nodded at the witness.

"Was it hooked up to the kitchen line?" I continued.

"Uh huh."

"Did the University ever get a permit for the heater in the bathroom?"

"I don't know."

I looked at Barry Roberts. He nodded. I assumed he was telling me I had gotten what we needed.

"I have no further questions."

"Me either," Webster said before he pushed his palms on the table, shoved his chair back, and walked hurriedly from the room. Charles Percel and Dean Bernard followed behind. Hodges rose slowly, smiled at me, and then turned and left with the others.

I packed my briefcase, gave the court reporter my business card, and asked if he would send the transcripts to me in Trenton.

"How'd you know about the kitchen line?" Barry asked after we descended the steps of 20 South University.

"Harry Rabstein," I said with a grin.


"So you think you're going to clean my clock?" John Webster asked when David and I appeared at the Oklahoma City Federal Building to begin the trial.

I had learned what to expect from Webster. "I don't know if I'm going to clean your clock but it's high noon on the prairie," I replied.

Webster smiled. "Roberts has been teaching you his Okie humor, has he?"

"Better sooner than later," I replied.

Webster smiled again.

"Wait until you see an Okie jury," Webster continued.

"I know what you're saying, John."

"You do, do ya?"

"Yessir, I do. You might dress like them. But I'll talk like them from my heart. Web, I respectfully think we have you cold turkey on liability. Judge Delaney is going to charge the jury that the university is a business. The damages are horrendous. A million and a half would not be unreasonable."

Webster was taken aback by my addressing him so familiarly. "If he does charge business law, you're buying an appeal for sure. And you'll be waiting for your money until the day hell freezes over. I'm sure you've told your clients about appeals."

"I sure have. They want justice at any price." I knew what I was saying wasn't true, because the Breens wanted me to try to settle for four hundred thousand and the Rosatis wanted forty thousand.

"Four hundred fifty's been the highest verdict ever, and your friend, Roberts, got that one. He had a paraplegic who was wheelchair bound. Your Breen girl can walk and talk. You know brain injured people who make a recovery like her are hard to understand. She looks good and so what if her speech is impaired. That's not worth close to a million. And what is the jury going to think when I ask her about her childhood and high school and she remembers everything? "

"But her memory is impaired. She can't hold down a job."

"You argue that and then tell the jury she remembers everything she did on October 13 and let's see how the jury takes it. You can't have it both ways. I've got some other arguments up my sleeve, but I'm not going to tell you about them until it's my turn in the courtroom," Webster snapped.

"I'm sure you do. You are a seasoned lawyer. I respect that. But my client is an innocent victim and you know it."

"Are your folks interested in talking settlement?" Webster inquired for the first time.

"It depends on the terms. I'm sure they would like to resolve the cases if it is fair."

"Well, what you're asking isn't fair. A million and a half is something you're only going to get from the jury," Webster quipped.

"Well then, we're here and ready to proceed," I said.

"As is Stedman," he replied.

The verbal jockeying continued in the hallway until we were informed by the court clerk that Judge Delaney would like to see us in chambers.

Instead of meeting us at the conference table, the judge was at his desk. He instructed Barry Roberts, David, and me to sit on the side of his desk and had John Webster sit in front.

"Gentlemen, I'm prepared to pick a jury. Before I do that though, I would like to explore settlement. Are your clients interested in a settlement?"

"I'm sure they are if the price is right," I responded.

"I'm sure of that too, counselor. But a good settlement is one where both parties are unhappy."

"That's not my definition, Your Honor," Webster snapped.

"I know it's not, Web. You never know what a jury will do. A bird in the hand is often worth two in the bush. Traveling from the east coast and back again is not inexpensive, either," Judge Delaney continued, looking at me.

"Your Honor, I'm prepared to offer one hundred thousand dollars. Twenty-five to the Rosatis and seventy-five to the Breen girl," Webster stated.

"That's a good start. I'm sure you're prepared to offer more, aren't you?"

"Judge, I have a little more, but not much more."

"Mr. Stark, what is your response to that?"

"Your Honor, I would reject the offer outright. I know I have to communicate it to my clients, but I know what they will say." I had learned that defense lawyers often offer substantially less than they are authorized because they know a plaintiff's lawyer must communicate every offer to his client.

"Why don't you go and talk to them," Judge Delaney suggested.

In a conference room, I explained to the Rosatis, the Breens, and Barbara that the judge wanted to explore a settlement before starting the trial.

"It's an insult," Glen exclaimed. Mary Breen agreed.

"It sure is. We didn't come all the way down here for that. No way am I going to accept twenty-five thousand," Anthony said angrily.

"I've told you what the verdict ranges have been. I think what Webster is doing is giving you a low offer, trying to feel you out. Let's not get upset. I think that when I go back in to the chambers and reject the offer, Webster will try to raise the offer on Rosa's case so he can settle with you and Anne. Then he can focus on Barbara and try to settle with her for about two hundred thousand. I agree we should turn the offers down. They're the first offers. We've never had a cent offered before," I said. I had experienced similar procedures with judges and defense lawyers, but never with the stakes so high.

"You're right about that," Anthony said. "At least they're admitting they're at fault. That means a lot to Anne and me. We have some concerns that we've expressed to you before. For instance, the suicide claim. I'm sure they're going to try to bring that up one way or another,"

"Maybe. But I don't think they'll have a leg to stand on. I got Dean Bernard to admit that even though the girls were homesick, they weren't so depressed that they needed any medication. I'm not worried," I explained.

"That's good," Anne said.

"So what's next?" Barbara asked nervously. It was the first time she had spoken. She usually just sat and listened. I didn't realize she was understanding what was going on.

"I will go back into chambers and tell the judge we reject the offers. Then he will meet with one side and the other, trying to get us closer together."

"Is that the way it works? Sounds like a union negotiation to me," Anthony said, laughing.

"You're right, Anthony. It is difficult to know when to accept a settlement. It's like playing chess. There are pitfalls in almost every move. I've been through this many times, sometimes as a criminal lawyer where someone's freedom was at stake. Here we're talking about money. Nothing's going to bring Rosa back. But money can change the way Barbara lives in the future," I explained.

When Webster and I entered Judge Delaney's chambers, he was fiddling with a pen.

"Mr. Stark, what was your client's response?" he asked curtly.

"They were insulted, Your Honor."

"You do know, don't you, that the death case on a good day can't be worth more than fifty."

"Your Honor, fifty will not settle this case."

"Why not?"

"Because if I try it with the Breen case, it is worth more money. A jury's going to give Barbara more than a million. When they compare her to Rosa, they're going to go high on Barbara. If they give Rosa fifty, they have to award Barbara at least ten times that. She is going to live with her pain and disability for many years."

"That's what you think," Judge Delaney remarked. "But couldn't the jury, following my instructions, give Rosa's parents twenty-five and then say to themselves, 'Well, if a death is worth twenty-five, then an injury like Barbara's is only worth a hundred.'"

"I don't think so, Your Honor. At any rate, my clients are willing to let a jury tell them that, rather than settle. They're willing to take the risk."

"I can appreciate that, but you know a jury verdict will be appealed."

"I've explained that to them. They're adults."

"Web, why don't you excuse yourself and let me talk to the plaintiffs' counsel?" Judge Delaney asked.

"Sure enough, Your Honor," Webster replied, getting up from his chair.

We went back and forth, in and out of the Judge Delaney's chambers, sometimes meeting with him alone and sometimes together. When I was alone with Judge Delaney, in the inner sanctum, he kept emphasizing how horrible it would be for Barbara to walk out of the courthouse with nothing. After the warnings, he tried to befriend me by telling me he would try to get Web to 'raise the ante'. By twelve noon, Webster had offered forty thousand dollars to the Rosatis and one hundred fifty thousand to the Breens. I assumed John Webster had authority to pay two hundred thousand and was saving some ammunition for later.

At twelve thirty, Judge Delaney recessed for lunch and ordered us to be back at one-thirty.

We wound our way back to the Oiler's Hotel. I sensed the Rosatis were ready to settle and go home. All the money in the world wouldn't bring back Rosa. The acknowledgment of guilt was what was important to them, and that had been offered. Before we ordered lunch, Anne turned to Glen Breen. "We would be satisfied with the offer, but we don't want to let you down. We wouldn't be here if it weren't for you joining in this case."

Mary Breen responded, "But you have to do what is right for you. Barbara feels badly that she is here and Rosa is not."

Barbara nodded.

Over lunch, I tried to keep discussion of the settlement at a minimum since I could see my clients were becoming impatient. David helped keep things light by joking about John Webster's cowboy boots and my worn, brown shoes and red and blue tie. The shoes were my trial shoes, which I wore with every color suit, whether it was black, blue, brown, gray, or green. The tie was my way of telling a jury that I was a red-blooded American who respected the flag and justice, something I thought was important, especially in the late sixties and early seventies when hippies, yippies, and Watergate dominated the headlines.

"Mr. Stark, what is your client's position?" Judge Delaney asked when we resumed the settlement discussions.

"Your Honor, one hundred will do it for the Rosatis with a million for Barbara."

"I'm certain it would. If that's your position, I think we better pick a jury," Judge Delaney said. "Albert, there's an old saying: 'The only way you get a million dollar verdict is if the defense makes no offer and your case is worth three million.' Are you ready to pick a jury?"

"I suppose if that's the final offer, we better," I replied.

"Web, why don't you give me a minute with Barry and the 'gold dust twins?'" Judge Delaney asked with a sly grin. Since the judge had called us the 'gold dust twins' in front of Webster, I took the name as a measure of respect.

Webster stepped out.

"I've had a chance to talk to Mr. Webster. I told him to call his insurance company and tell them that one fifty isn't going to do it. He promised me he would. Let's wait and see what he says before we pick a jury," Judge Delaney suggested. I knew that the judge had information that I did not have. I was sure that he was making suggestions to Webster.

"I'm willing to wait a while today, but my clients have come from out of state. I have witnesses with plane reservations," I said, attempting to show the judge I was ready to begin the trial. He had become part of the negotiations. He wanted to complete this case so he could move on to another case and avoid an appeal, in which instance, his rulings would be attacked by either Webster or me.

"I understand. But if I don't charge business law, your clients will go home empty handed and those witnesses won't have to use their plane tickets."

I took the judge's threat seriously. "I understand, but I think Your Honor has a good sense of this case and will apply the right law. You've mentioned an appeal if I win."

Judge Delaney grimaced. judges do not like their rulings to be appealed because, if the case is reversed, it is a bad reflection on the judge. The judge would do everything in his power to get the case settled.

By day's end, I had received offers of forty thousand and two hundred fifty thousand. My offer to settle had stayed at seventy-five thousand for the Rosatis, but at the Breens' insistence, I had reduced my demand to seven hundred fifty thousand dollars for Barbara. They told me they would even settle for four hundred thousand so that they could net a quarter of a million for Barbara, which they would invest at seven per cent. I reluctantly told them I thought she deserved a million or more, but that I was obligated to follow the wishes of my client. I also told them, however, that I could not guarantee that a jury would award Barbara four hundred fifty thousand, nor could I be certain that there would be such an offer.

David and I invited the Breens and Rosatis to an early dinner. They told us they wanted to be alone. I wanted to be with them, because I was afraid they were ready to accept the offers, and I wanted to discourage them. They insisted on being by themselves.

Barry asked us to come to his home for dinner and relax. It was a welcome respite after a tension packed day in court.

The opening statement, which I had rehearsed the night before, played over and over in my head. The next thing I recall was rolling around in my bed at three o'clock in the morning. I tried to go back to sleep, knowing I would need energy for the trial, but I could not. So I decided to go into the bathroom and read the depositions of James Bernard, Percel, and Hodges as I didn't want to turn on the bedroom light and disturb David, who was sleeping soundly.

With the passing of time, I have learned to survive the anxious nights before trials begin. Many lawyers have told me that they experience the same thing, and they claim that if you don't overcome the stress, you are either lazy or lousy.

I returned to bed about six in the morning and got up at seven to shower, shave, and go to breakfast before going to the courthouse. As I walked out of the hotel, the sun hit my face, and I felt dizzy. My head was spinning. After walking about a block, I was running on pure adrenaline. I could have lifted a ton of bricks if necessary.

When I got off the elevator in the courthouse, I saw John Webster pacing the hallway. "I can't believe what's happening," he said when he saw me.

"What's up?" I asked, not knowing what he was talking about.

"Let's go talk."

"What's there to talk about?"

"My insurance company called me at home last night. They want to pay the Rosatis sixty thousand dollars. I can't believe it. But I'm under an obligation to offer the money to you. I disagree with their position, but so it is. It's theirs to accept. There won't be another nickel."

"What about Barbara?"

"No more on that one. I'm afraid they're done."

"I'll relay the offer and let you know," I said excitedly since I had been caught by surprise.

Shortly before nine, Anthony and Anne got off the elevator. I led them to a conference room where I conveyed Webster's offer.

"You've done a good job," Anthony told me. He turned to Anne, "Let's take it and go home."

"What do you think, Albert?" Anne asked.

"I'd be less than honest if I said it wasn't a good offer. But truthfully I would love you to hang in there with Barbara. I know you have your own rights but I think if we stick together we can help Barbara."

"What if they don't offer her more money and we have to go before the jury?" Anne inquired.

"We will make that decision when the time comes."

"Can the insurance company withdraw the offer?" Anthony asked.

"Sure. I can't guarantee they won't, but it's rarely done."

"What do you say, dear? We've come this far. Let's help out Barbara. We wouldn't have gotten this far without her," Anne commented, revealing she remembered that without the Breens' pursuit of Barbara's claim, I wouldn't have handled their case on behalf of Rosa.

"Can we talk by ourselves?" Anthony asked.

"Of course," I said.

I went into the hallway. Webster caught my eye. He opened his arms and mouthed, "Okay?"

I shrugged my shoulders and pointed to the conference room, indicating that the Rosatis were talking.

Webster saw Anthony come out of the room and wave for me to come in.

The Rosatis told me they would follow my advice.

I walked over to Webster. "They want seventy-five thousand."

"Where do they think they are, Las Vegas?" Webster snapped.

"They think they're going to win. You ever work with a stubborn Italian?" I asked.

"They ever see a stubborn Baptist?" Webster retorted.

"Calm down, Web," I said. "They want to stick with Barbara. They really don't care about money at this point." I would never know whether John Webster realized I was not telling him the truth.

"You know something, I've had clients like that," Webster said.

Webster, who often used his insurance client as a foil, had probably used the line hundreds of times. He had bitten at the same bait he tossed, or so I thought at that moment.

David and Barry got off the elevator.

"Hear you had a rough night," Barry joked.

"I'm ready. It's just adrenaline. I've been through this a few times before. Just not two thousand miles away from home," I replied.

"I see Web over there. What's up? Anything?" Roberts inquired.

"I can't talk here. Things are getting warmer."

Judge Delaney's clerk announced that the judge had some emergent matters filed before him that he had to hear and decide, and we were instructed to return at one-thirty. Obviously, the judge had not taken my comments about witnesses and plane reservations seriously. He was prepared to test my resolve and my clients' patience.

Barbara and her parents were getting edgy. They asked me about the chances of losing, saying that they were going to be in debt if they lost. They were also afraid Barbara would clam up on the witness stand. I told them to go back to the hotel and not to come back to the courthouse until I called them. I didn't want them to show signs of their nervousness in front of John Webster.

At one-thirty sharp, the judge's clerk appeared in the hallway.

"The judge is ready for you. He wants to speak to Mr. Stark and Mr. Roberts."

"What about David?" I asked.

"He just said 'Mr. Stark and Mr. Roberts.'"

I was taken aback by the remark. David would feel slighted. He had been so important to this case. I thought about not going in without David, but I was too anxious not to follow the judge's order. I had reached a point in my career where I had learned to read a judge's opinion or attitude and not stand on ceremony or principle if it didn't serve my client's interest. I gleaned from the judge's remarks that he wanted to put pressure on John Webster and me and bring closure to the case. He saw that our egos were clashing, and that the best interests of the Rosatis, Breens, and Stedman University would be served by finality.

I entered the chambers with Barry. Judge Delaney was sitting in his high back chair.

"I've decided that from here on only Mr. Stark will be able to participate. Only one lawyer can be introduced to the court."

Judge Delaney was obviously losing his patience with me.

He instructed his clerk to bring in Webster.

"So where are we, Web?"

"I can't believe it, Your Honor. My company's willing to pay sixty thousand to the Rosatis."

"I'm sure that will satisfy them, Mr. Stark," Judge Delaney remarked.

"No, Your Honor. They've given me instructions to accept no less than seventy-five thousand."

"Very well then. How about the Breen girl?"

"Nothing more there," Webster replied.

"Web, let me talk to you alone. Gentlemen, will you excuse yourselves," Judge Delaney ordered, looking first at Barry and then at me.

We exited the chambers. After five minutes, we were invited back.

"Gentlemen, here's where we are," Judge Delaney said as Barry and I entered his office. "I've considered this case very carefully. Mr. Stark, you have a very seriously injured young lady. I believe she is an innocent victim. You've done a yeoman's job getting this far. Don't press your luck. I have recommended to Mr. Webster that he get seventy-five for the Rosatis and four and a quarter for the Breen girl, for a total of a half million. You know four fifty is equal to the largest single verdict for a victim in this state, and fifty is the highest for an infant death."

"I know that, Your Honor. Mr. Webster has made a point of telling me that numerous times," I said tactfully.

"Mr. Webster is going to the telephone and will be back in a while. Meanwhile, I would like to talk to your clients and have them tell me whether they will accept the offer if Mr. Webster follows my request."

"Your Honor, that's not fair. To pressure them is not appropriate. That's my job," I replied anxiously, knowing that my clients would accept the offer.

"As you like it," Judge Delaney said. "I'll take care of things from here. Tell Mr. Webster to come back in."

"Mr. Webster has come back with some good news," Judge Delaney told me after he conferred with John. "He has sixty-five for the Rosatis and four ten for the Breen girl."

I knew immediately that he had the seventy-five and four and a quarter. He wasn't going to disappoint the judge with whom he had an ongoing relationship. Besides, he needed him to rule in his favor if I refused to settle.

The negotiations proceeded. I kept prodding the Rosatis to stick with the Breens, and they reluctantly agreed with the proviso that if the case didn't settle by the end of the day, they were going to accept the offer. An additional ten thousand would not make that much of a difference to them, and they did not want to risk either a jury trial or alienating the judge.

I told the Breens that if we began the trial and got the case to the jury, Webster would come up with seven hundred fifty thousand. I had the feeling that Stedman did not want publicity and that Webster was beginning to feel sympathetic toward the Rosatis and Barbara. The more he saw the Rosatis' devastation, the more he understood that they were not just money-hungry. He was also understanding the difficulties Barbara was going to face for the rest of her life. By repeating that the case could bring more than a million from a jury, Webster, in my view, was beginning to believe it.

It was just before four-thirty when John Webster asked me to come into the judge's chambers for the last time.

"Your Honor," began Webster, "I have been instructed to tell you that if the Breens will accept five hundred thousand dollars, the claims manager in Tulsa will call New York, where the main office is located, and recommend it. I can't assure you he'll get it, but I have every reason to believe he can."

"What do you say, Mr. Stark?" Judge Delaney inquired.

"Let me talk to my clients," I said, smiling at the judge to show that I appreciated what he was doing.

He returned the smile.

I explained to Glen and Mary that I thought Mr. Webster had authority to pay five hundred thousand. I told them if they said they would accept it, he would offer less. Glen Breen understood what I was saying and agreed to let me negotiate. We agreed that if the insurance company did not offer five hundred, then we would tell the Rosatis to settle and go to trial alone without the Rosatis. Barbara began to cry. The pressure was getting to her. She wanted to get on with her life, whatever it was going to be. All the money in the world would not make up for what she had gone through.

I conveyed to Webster that the Breens were stuck at seven fifty.

He banged his fist on the wall. "Dammit, I don't usually cave in like this, but there's five hundred thousand on the table. Take it or leave it."

The case was settled.

"I'll see you in the morning, gentlemen," the judge said. "I want to put the settlement on the court record and make sure the Breen girl understands the terms. If not, I may have to appoint a guardian to review the settlement and make sure her interests are protected. Parents sometimes have their own agenda, which may not be good for the child. I will approve it under any circumstances. I was not going to charge the jury that Stedman is a business."

Webster's shoulders slumped over and his chin dropped to his chest.

At dinner, we celebrated.

"It's not the money that matters to us," Anne remarked. "The settlement is vindication. No amount of money can replace Rosa. I want to set up a scholarship fund so other youngsters can get an education."

"The toughest thing is that during this case it was as though my daughter was still alive. Now she's gone. I know I fought for her. And so did you fellows," Anthony added.

Mary Breen began to cry and then embraced Anthony and Anne.

At that moment, I realized that Anthony and Anne would not have risked a trial because they did not want to experience Rosa's dying twice. I could only imagine what it would be like for Anthony and Anne if a jury returned to the courtroom and declared them losers. I had that happen in less serious cases, and I knew the anger that the losing client felt toward the judicial system and their lawyer. I took a deep breath, looked Anthony and Anne in the eyes, and felt like hugging and kissing them both because they were such wonderful people.

In an august, oak-paneled courtroom in the Federal Building in Oklahoma City, Judge Charles Delaney spoke to Barbara Breen: "The half-million dollar settlement you have received is the largest in the history of Oklahoma." He also addressed Anthony and Anne: "Mr. and Mrs. Rosati, the seventy-five thousand dollars you are being paid by Stedman University is the most any parents have ever been paid in Oklahoma for the death of a child."

I was exhausted, somber, and unhappy when an American Airlines 707 lifted off from Oklahoma City's Will Rogers Airport into a setting sun. At four o'clock that morning in a strange hotel, I was left wondering why I had taken a case so far away, and doubting if I would physically make it to court.

I had rehearsed my opening statement to a Bible belt jury in front of a closet door mirror. I had learned how important it was to rehearse, to develop a strong theme at the beginning of a case, because a jury remembers the first words they hear from a lawyer. I wanted to indelibly implant my powerful premise into the jurors' minds: "They broke their own rules. Now Barbara Breen's life is broken. And Rosa Rosati is dead. Her parents' hearts are broken." I watched my face in the mirror as I turned my shoulders toward where John Webster and Dean Bernard would be sitting in the courtroom.

During the day, I had negotiated and expressed my disappointment to David that our clients had accepted settlements rather than risk a jury trial for which I had steadfastly prepared.

Fiddling with my fingers, I impatiently shifted back and forth in my airplane seat while I downed a few scotches. A winter snowstorm blanketed the Great Plains. The pilot announced that Chicago's O'Hare Airport was closed, to expect turbulence, and to be patient because the flight would be delayed at least two hours. He had to fly in a holding pattern before being cleared for landing in Milwaukee.

Suddenly the airplane rollercoastered in the sky. A few minutes later, a man sporting a railroad worker's cap and a black and white striped shirt, wobbled down the aisle, grabbing one seat back after another, bellowing, "I'm Casey Jones. You'd have gotten home faster if you had taken the train." As Casey passed me, I broke into a smile when I noticed the tail of a pilot's jacket protruding from beneath his striped shirt.

I wasn't sure about the advice Irving Lewis had given me when I discussed the case with him before I had gone to Oklahoma. Lewis, a prominent Trenton trial lawyer, had told me that the best-tried case was a settled case, because it saved the client from the stresses and uncertainties of the legal system and brought a case to an end. I had put so much effort into the case that I had convinced myself I was going to win a large jury verdict.

I was sitting at my desk after a hectic day at the Trenton courthouse. Why, I asked myself, was I so unfulfilled and moody a month after a settlement that I should have been proud of? I had wanted to present the case to a jury. If we had been awarded a million dollars, I would have launched a career as a national trial lawyer. I felt I might have been acknowledged by Webster and the judge. I questioned whether I was too weak to withstand the rigors and pressures placed upon me by our court system. I had desperately wanted to change the law so that others wouldn't suffer the fate Rosa and Barbara had. Because it had settled, the case got no publicity. Other victims would have to take difficult risks to get justice for themselves and others.

I saw Sam Lenox, Senior., a defense lawyer known for paying injured plaintiffs as little as he could, eating lunch by himself at a restaurant across the street from my office.

After I asked if I could join him, he listened while I told him what was bothering me about the settlement I made in Oklahoma.

"Our profession is an art, not a science. The system's not perfect by a long shot. But it's the best that man has devised," he said. He tilted his head a bit and leaned forward. "Look here, Albert. You've had some good luck. You did okay out there in Oklahoma, where none of us would have dared to tread. You have to make a decision. You can pocket the cash and live a nice life. That's what I would probably do. Or, you can use it to take some risks. Some will pay off. Others won't. Good lawyers are like Sherlock Holmes. Always trying to figure something out, putting the pieces of the puzzle together. Life in the law is a never ending search—not always for justice, and not always for money."

My mood began to improve as I considered the cases that I had taken. I had fought for a dead inmate at the State Hospital just as the Rosatis had for their daughter. I had settled a case that provided enough money to bring things into Barbara's life that could compensate for much of what she had lost, just as I had done for Bobbie McKenzie. I had discovered that personal injury law could change more than the life of just one person. The Rosatis had set up a scholarship fund. A few days later, I received an envelope from Mutual of Omaha Insurance Company. In it was a letter that said that they had completed their investigation into the case of Barbara Breen. Enclosed was the settlement.

I wrote thank you notes to the doctors, nurses, and therapists who had helped me prepare the medical evidence. I picked up the telephone. I wanted to call Harry Rabstein and thank him, too. I put the receiver back on the hook.

David poked his head in the door and asked his usual question, "What's up?"

"You really want to know?"

David nodded his head up and down.

"My career as a traveling trial lawyer is over," I said.

"Until the next one comes along," he replied.

When I received a call from Barry Roberts six months later, he told me that Oklahoma Natural Gas was putting an odorous agent in their gas.

Now, at least in Oklahoma, what happened to Barbara and Rosa would not happen again.

# FREEDOM ROAD—MAKING THINGS HAPPEN CLOSE TO HOME

MY FORTIETH BIRTHDAY, MAY 3, 1979, WAS ON A WEDNESDAY. Cards congratulating me on reaching the big one jokingly reminded me that I was over the hill. I was looking forward to a party. I became teary-eyed sitting at my kitchen table, thinking about what had happened to my ambitions and my idealism, and where I had fallen short. I was neither a successful urban development lawyer nor financially secure. I had invested the McShain money into building a law firm and let it slip away being loyal to Johnnie Puccinella. I tried to assess what I had achieved representing individuals who had to face an uphill battle in life and in the courtroom and whether it was worth it to have hired two associates. Then, I started to think about where I wanted to go from there, wondering if I would ever discover a road leading to my own identity, to financial and intellectual independence, and to inner satisfaction.

My father and I were going to a dinner the following Wednesday to hear retired Supreme Court Justice, Arthur Goldberg at the University of Pennsylvania Law School. His topic was "Can We Afford Freedom?" Goldberg and my father were contemporaries. I knew he admired Goldberg's brilliance and his rise from a local labor lawyer to national and international prominence. My father was proud of my success in Oklahoma. Perhaps he wanted to proudly introduce me to his law school friends? I couldn't think of why he would be taking me to a dinner for Benjamin Franklin Society members, the law school's major donors.

The late afternoon sun was setting on the river as my father and I drove down the interstate from Trenton to Philadelphia. I stared into space, watching the boats on the river, thinking about the days when my father and I had a motorboat. Now tug boats slowly pushed barges and speedboats skimmed the surface, churning up waves whose crests flashed when the setting sun hit them. The radio was tuned to 90.9, my father's favorite public radio station. He talked back to the radio, then fiddled with the sun visor.

I was about to break an uneasy silence and start talking about the fun we had had together when my father and I were younger. Instead, I asked him, "Do you think I was stupid to tell everyone I didn't want a party?"

"You got your wish, didn't you?" he answered matter-of-factly.

As I thought about what he was thinking, my mind began to race. I said that I didn't want to have a party because I was ashamed I had lost sight of my original goals. I was too insecure, or perhaps, even too conceited, to revel in my accomplishments as a trial lawyer, prosecuting, defending, and now representing accident victims. I questioned whether the countless nights developing a reputation as a young community leader, preparing questions for witnesses, writing openings and closings, oftentimes neglecting my role as a husband and father, were worth the price I was paying. But I could not imagine how I could have gotten to where I was by leading a so-called balanced life. I wasn't free. The trials and tribulations of building a law firm, paying the bills, growing or dying, were overwhelming. Janice, once a secretary, was now the office manager. The firm, now five lawyers, was outgrowing her, causing insecurity among the lawyers and staff. My loyalty to her was becoming counterproductive. I had never had to fire anyone before. I couldn't imagine hurting her and felt as if I'd rather quit. My father was seventy–two, ready, at least in the minds of others, to retire. Associates wanted a leader to follow. And I wasn't confident I knew where I was going, let alone, if I had the ability to get there. Thinking about the future and how to create it was taking its toll on me.

My father glanced at me. I had the feeling he knew exactly what I was going through. A few minutes passed. I wanted him to say something. Anything. Didn't he know I was becoming more and more uncomfortable? Finally, I couldn't take the silence any more and angrily blurted out, "You know what! I feel really empty because Ellen believed me. My birthday was ten days ago. I thought for sure that last Saturday or Sunday night there would have been some kind of surprise."

Gruffly, he challenged, "Why would you think that? You made it perfectly clear you didn't want a party, no fuss. Did you think that Ellen wouldn't respect your feelings? You made your own bed."

I couldn't bring myself to believe that Ellen would really think that I didn't want a celebration, a party, an affirmation of some sort, especially because she knew I got my energy and spark from other people. I couldn't believe my father would either.

"How'd you feel when you were forty?" I snapped.

"Me? Forty? Let's see. It would've been in forty-eight. Just after the war. I had just started practicing again. Everything I had built during the Depression had evaporated. I was struggling to survive. I didn't have time to feel. It was work and family. Looking after you. I was involved with Jewish causes. Israel became a state that year," he said with a quiet dignity.

"You make me feel like a jerk worrying about not having a fortieth birthday party. You know why I said I didn't want a party? I thought a party would remind me of aging. Time is passing faster and faster every year. I've heard so much about the forty crisis. The forty crazies. I guess I thought by not having a party I could avoid it all."

"Well, Albert, you'll look back at forty as a milestone. You've experimented with different kinds of law. You've had your successes and setbacks. You've found a niche for yourself in the courtroom. You've begun to build a law firm. You've got a loving wife and two wonderful children. The time for the party has passed. You got your wish. Now let's move on. We have a treat in store for us tonight."

"How has it been for you working with me?" I asked.

"You haven't been easy." I noticed a little smile. "If you want to know the truth, you've reacted instinctually, sometimes too emotionally for me. When you resigned from the prosecutor's office because the police were beating yippies, I was disappointed. When you took the case where the policeman was killed by the black accused of being drunk, I thought you were nuts. The McShain and Oklahoma cases gave me the shivers. I lost more than a few sleepless nights thinking we were going to take a financial bath on them just as we did on Puccinella." My father grinned. "I probably would have slowed down by now if it weren't for you. You've kept me on my toes."

I hadn't realized how my choices had affected him. I felt my anger toward my father dissipating.

"You know what?" I asked without waiting for an answer. " If mother hadn't become ill and hadn't needed so much support because of her kidney disease, I would have been teaching college students today. When I told Professor Wilson at my fifteenth reunion how upset I was that I wasn't working to change cities, he offered me the opportunity to teach local and state government at Dartmouth. I thought of leaving the law, and you. Academic freedom seemed like a good way to escape."

He nodded in agreement. "I knew when you graduated from law school in 1963 that the furthest thing from your mind was returning to New Jersey to practice. I wasn't sure I was that happy about your return either. I was very satisfied just practicing at my own pace, helping my business clients grow. You planned to go to Denver, where you could learn the ins and outs of municipal finance. Look how Denver has grown. You'd be a rich man by now. You could probably even support me."

"Maybe not," I joked. "Maybe I'd be bankrupt like my grandfather." The economy fell out of bed after the Bay of Pigs, the Cuban missile crisis, and JFK's assassination. After Daniel Greenfield from the Ford Foundation asked me to work with Governor Hughes, I got to write a housing law that has enabled seniors in New Jersey to have comfortable places to live in. Now, I wanted to do something in personal injury law that would change the lives for more than just a victim and his family.

"I'm sure you will find your way. You've seen that political life isn't all it's cracked up to be."

I nodded in agreement, then said, "Hopefully, someday, I'll develop my career to the point I truly enjoy it. I know so many lawyers in their fifties and sixties who hate what they're doing. They get caught up with blaming it on the system. It's easier to do that than blaming themselves for not adjusting to the roll of the dice, to the law as it changes. I feel fortunate. I love to come to work every day. I only wish I could think and do as I please."

"Controlling or creating your own destiny isn't a picnic, is it?" My father steered the car on to the cut-off that led to the law school.

I was disappointed. We really were going to a dinner at the Law School.

"We're both in for a treat tonight. We may not be celebrating your fortieth at a party, but we are going to hear someone who epitomizes the highest principles of our founding fathers. In Philadelphia, no less. How's that for a fortieth birthday celebration?"

I thought my father was being too coy, that there was going to be a surprise party at the Law School for me, when he said, " I'm looking forward to meeting and hearing Arthur Goldberg. Arthur Goldberg. Now there's a fellow who started at the bottom, fought the wars with the labor unions, became an Ambassador to the United Nations, was appointed to the Supreme Court, and then found it was too confining and resigned. Can you imagine resigning from the Supreme Court?"

Playing into his repartee, I replied, "I never wanted to be a judge. I'd be terrible. When Joe Merlino became a state senator he wanted me to go on the bench. I refused. That's the best decision I ever made. Can you imagine me on the bench? I'd be trying every case for the lawyers. I'm dogged when it comes to preparation. I'd be helping the guy I thought was getting the shaft. Judges are supposed to be neutral and let the lawyers try their cases. I hate it when a judge jumps into the fray. And, as you know, being neutral is tough for me."

My father listened and smiled. "Truthfully, I was sad when you turned down the judgeship. I would have liked you to be a judge. I wanted to be a judge, but by the time I could afford to do it I was over the unwritten sixty-year-old age limit. That's one of my regrets."

We were silent while my father stopped, started, and weaved in and out of the traffic on the narrow West Philadelphia streets. After we parked the car in a lot on Chestnut Street, we walked to the brown brick building in which both my father and I had gotten our legal education. The three years we had spent in the classrooms there gave us a common bond. My father was proud that I had gone to his law school and so was I.

We walked up a double flight of marble steps toward imposing wood-paneled doors that were twice our height. My father pulled one of the doors open and motioned me to enter. To my surprise, I wasn't greeted by friends and family yelling "Surprise."

Instead, men in dark business suits were chatting familiarly, holding wine glasses in their hands. Ladies dressed in black uniforms with white collars were passing canapés. "Hey, Sid. Great to see you. How've you been?" A tall, gray-haired gentleman turned toward my father and extended his hand. I had seldom heard my father called "Sid." For as long as I could remember, his friends and colleagues called him Sidney. Only his two younger brothers referred to him as Sid.

My father approached some of the gentlemen who had greeted him. "Good to see you, Max. I want you to meet my son. I've told him a lot about you. Albert, this is Max Rosenn, an old friend. Sits on the United States Circuit Court up in Wilkes Barre. Tonight he's the chairman of the event." My father often referred to Rosenn as "my friend Max Rosenn, the scholar and lawyer's lawyer."

A black man dressed in a tuxedo walked through the rotunda ringing a bell and asking people to go into the dining room for dinner. "Sid, I have you sitting at my table," Max said.

Max led us to a round table at the front of the dining room. In the front was a podium faced with the red and blue seal of the University of Pennsylvania. I waited, patiently and politely as Max counted the seats and looked at a list which he held in his hand. "Sid, this is for you," Max said pointing to a seat one away from where he was standing. "Let's see, we'll put the dean next to Sid. I'll sit here. We'll put Justice Goldberg next to me. And Albert, you sit here." Max pulled out an empty chair to the right of the one he had designated for Arthur Goldberg.

Chairs scraped on the floor as the hundred or so guests found their way to the tables and were seated. I looked around and saw that I was probably the youngest person in the room. Max sat down. "I feel honored to be sitting with you. But I have no idea what to say to someone like Arthur Goldberg. I hope I'm not too intimidated by him."

"Don't worry about that. First, we have to get him in here. Neither he nor the dean has arrived. He was supposed to be here at five. We got word that he missed the four o'clock shuttle from Dulles. The dean personally went to meet him and bring him in from the airport." Max stood up and scanned the room.

The doors at the rear of the dining room opened. Heads turned. Coming through the doors was a tall, broad-shouldered man, Jefferson Fordham, dean of the Law School. At his side was a short, somewhat stocky gentleman with a distinctive crop of curly white hair. All eyes fixed on Arthur Goldberg.

The dean stopped at each table, greeting the alumni, exchanging pleasantries, and introducing Arthur Goldberg. By the time he reached our table in the front, Max was standing. Taking a cue from Max, my father and I and three other gentlemen rose and stood behind our chairs. Upon seeing Max, Arthur Goldberg immediately walked up to him, opened his arms wide, and embraced him. He then whispered something that I could not hear. The dean took his seat next to Max and Max escorted Goldberg to his seat beside me.

"Well, look who is here," Dean Fordham exclaimed, when he saw me. My law school mentor and I exchanged pleasantries. "How's your urban development going?" he asked.

Not having seen him since I went to him for advice fifteen years ago, I sheepishly told him it was on hold, that things had taken a different turn, and that I would fill him in more about it after dinner.

Now that Arthur Goldberg was sitting next to me, I was more nervous than ever. I felt faint and a sudden heat rushed into my temples. Max walked to the other end of the table and asked my father and the three gentlemen sitting at our table to come over and say hello to his good friend, Arthur. The four of them walked with Max over to Arthur Goldberg. Goldberg stood up, and the four men exchanged greetings.

"It's a pleasure meeting you," one said. "I've followed your career for many years now," said another. "It's wonderful of you to come to talk to us. I'm looking forward to hearing what you have to say. I'm intrigued by the topic 'Can We Afford Freedom?'" I wanted to say that I wanted to know what freedom cost before I decided if I could afford it.

My father and Goldberg shook hands without saying a word. I noticed their bright blue eyes meet. They seemed to connect even though I knew they didn't know each other.

A gentleman at the table introduced himself to me. "I'm David Berger."

I recognized his name immediately. Berger was the senior partner at a venerable Philadelphia law firm and one of the largest contributors to the Benjamin Franklin Society, a collection of major givers to the law school. He told me about his son, an up and coming urban development professor. I recognized his son's name. He seemed pleased that I had heard of his son.

I talked to Berger about the days when I aspired to do what his son was doing, I was relieved I was not being put into a position where I had to talk to Justice Goldberg. I thought about how intimidated I had been by my professors in college when I first met them and how strange I felt being asked questions by law school professors who practiced the Socratic method of teaching. After I got to know the professors, I lost my fear and awe of them and saw them as people. But I had not yet met a Supreme Court Justice. I wondered if my resignation from the prosecutor's office would be of interest to Goldberg when and if I had the opportunity to talk to him.

Dean Fordham rose from his chair and walked to the podium. The conversation and banter stopped. He welcomed the attendees and thanked them for their generous contributions to the law school, each of which, he said, exceeded five thousand dollars. He told the gathering that they were being rewarded for their generosity with the privilege of hearing a "good friend of lawyers, Mr. Justice Arthur Goldberg."

The audience rose and applauded as Dean Fordham finished. Goldberg approached the podium.

Justice Goldberg thanked the Dean for the introduction and without further ado began his talk. "Can We Afford Freedom?" he asked in a strong, sonorous voice. "The answer, my colleagues, is 'Yes'. Electronic surveillance is depriving Americans of freedom. Eavesdropping on Russians and criminals is too big a price to pay to fight a cold war and catch criminals."

David Berger smiled at me. In the background, I heard snickers and mumbling.

"It is better to use more tedious methods available to achieve our goals of ridding the world of communism and mob-rule in our own country. Reverse audits are available to show that a person or organization spent more than they earned. With reverse audits, the Internal Revenue Service can root out criminal activity. We don't need to invade our citizens' privacy."

Some clapped, but the clapping did not spread.

Goldberg's voice got louder. "Snooping gadgets will get into the wrong hands. Businesses and organizations will eavesdrop on their employees and enemies. I fear citizens will become detached from one another, afraid to speak openly. I fear good young people will think twice before getting involved in public life."

I wanted to applaud, but since no one did, I did not. My father and Max smiled. Others at the table tightened their faces.

"A trend toward 'big brotherism' and 'big business' is unavoidable unless we, as lawyers, fight to see that technological changes that rob people of their privacy and right to free speech are declared unconstitutional and banned."

Goldberg finished. Eyes darted at each other. While I loved what the Justice had said, the skeptical expressions on many faces told me others didn't.

The hour's drive home seemed like it took five minutes. My father reminded me that he had observed the Francis Gary Powers trial in Moscow in August, 1960. I remembered the letter he wrote me: "Can you believe it? My hotel room is bugged. Something like this could never happen in our country?"

"Times are always changing but authority is always battling individual freedoms," my father said.

Something changed for me on that ride home. I realized it was not my father who had held me back from achieving freedom. I had to free myself from myself. All the distractions that were holding me back such as my father's aversion to risk and my disillusionment with politics and authority were mine.

When, two years later, I was asked to be the prosecutor of Mercer County, remembering what Goldberg had said, I said I would not wiretap to catch underworld criminals. Needless to say, I was not appointed. If I had changed fields, it would have been devastating, not only to me, but also to my father and the lawyers and staff who were working with me. I had opened up to myself and to those around me and my professional life was opening up, too.

I was going through my appointment book a day or two after the Goldberg talk, when I saw an entry that looked different from my handwriting or that of my secretary. It looked like one of my partner's handwriting. The entry indicated that on May 24, I was scheduled to play tennis with three of my regular partners at a tennis club. I went to the club for the scheduled match, something we had done on many occasions. But while I was playing, I heard a noise above me and looked up. A helicopter was descending from overhead. As it came closer and closer, I could feel the churning of the air from its blades. My three tennis cronies and I began to run away. The helicopter veered from above the court. I stopped running and watched it land. A door on the side of the chopper opened and I saw the pilot motioning me to come to him. I thought the chopper was in trouble so I ran over to it. The pilot was yelling, but the noise of the blades and motor prevented me from understanding what he was saying. "I can't hear you," I said.

He took off his headphones and cupped his ears. "What?" he yelled.

"I can't hear you," I replied.

I walked closer, lowering my head as far as I could, afraid of decapitation from the whirling blades.

"Get in. I need help," he yelled, extending his arm. He grabbed my hand and pulled me up and into the bubble of the chopper. "Where's the Italian American Sportsman Club? I'm lost. I have to pick up a passenger there."

Before I knew it, the chopper was lifting off of the ground. The pilot must have seen the look of fear and confusion on my face. He said, "Relax, Albert. Just relax."

I looked around, trying to get my bearings. How did he know my name? I had been to the Italian American Club many times for lunch and dinner and knew there was a large soccer field next to the main building. I began to point to where I thought the club was.

"Are you sure it's that way?" he asked.

I shrugged my shoulders. I can't recall what I was thinking.

"Will you recognize it from the air?" he inquired.

"I'm sure. Can't miss it," I replied.

"I'll bring you right back. Show me the way, will you?"

Despite having been in a helicopter only twice in my life, I said, "Sure."

I looked down at the tennis court as it became smaller and smaller. We continued ascending until we were high enough to see some distance. I pointed the club out to the pilot and he flew toward it. When the chopper was over the grounds of the club, I saw a lot of people beneath the trees that bordered the soccer field. As we got closer to the ground, I began to recognize some familiar faces. "Son-of-a-bitch," I said to the pilot. "She really got me this time."

He turned and smiled, pushing the nose of the chopper toward the ground.

When we landed, I was greeted by over two hundred people: colleagues, office staff, judges, policemen, prosecutors, detectives, some clients, friends, and my family.

"Surprise," they yelled as I got out of the chopper.

I danced with a belly dancer, accepted the congratulations of judges, and exchanged stories with detectives from the prosecutor's office. I laughed with the many people who had made the first fifteen years of my law career what it had been. Pete Antonuccio, a fellow who went out and bought a video camera to take the first videotaped deposition admitted into a trial in 1974, presented me with a Captain Video costume. The detectives who had helped me gather evidence for criminal trials gave me a large, wrapped cardboard box which contained smaller and smaller boxes, all of which were marked with the names of cases I had tried. Judges who taught me how to listen to them and watch them put on plastic, three dimensional glasses and held up a sign, "What you see is what you get!" I saw my mother, frail and fallow, smiling at me with satisfaction. I was given a watch and airfare for me and Ellen to go to Switzerland for a two week vacation.

Ellen and I were dancing when the band stopped playing. Two of my friends, both of whom were builders, were behind a microphone. They asked me to come over to them. They had a gift. They talked about me as a caring lawyer and friend. They handed me a gold-plated mason's trowel. Inscribed were the words, "Your 40's are building years."

My father came up to me and asked, "Enjoying the party?" I hugged him and gave him a big kiss. "You got what you didn't want, didn't you?"

The Swiss Air jetliner taxied down the Newark Airport runway. Ellen held my hand tightly as it took off. When it leveled off and I felt her hands relax, I asked, "So where do you think we'll be in another fifteen years?"

She turned toward me with a big smile. "I'm only sure of one thing," she said.

"What's that?" I asked.

"It'll be a surprise," she said.

A few minutes later, she was fast asleep.

Moonlight slanted through the window next to me. I peered out at an indigo sky drilled with stars and propped my chin on my palm.

I wondered what the next ten years would bring and whether I would have power over my own mind. I wondered if I could afford to achieve freedom: identity, financial independence, and the ability to think as I pleased.

A cart with drinks was being rolled down the aisle. "May I offer you a drink?"

"A double scotch, please?" I answered the stewardess.

I twisted open the cap on one small bottle. I poured the scotch over ice. I did the same thing with the other bottle. I stirred the ice for a moment or two. I lifted the plastic glass and stared at it. "Here's to hoping, someday, I can afford freedom," I mouthed out loud.

Ellen's eyes opened. I told her about what I had been thinking.

"Albert, remember the story you tell about your father and the

Parcheesi game?" Ellen whispered.

I smiled, recalling the day when I was five and the men were all over the game board. My father had leaned over, picked up the box and began reading me the directions. I was more concerned about how the dice were going to role.

"Of course," I responded.

"You went to law school to use the law to accomplish something, to change the status quo in urban development. Have you thought about how free you will feel when you can say you are a trial lawyer that used the law to change things, for even one person, and better yet, for society?" Ellen asked.

I raised my glass again, leaned over, and kissed her. I knew what I could not afford to do. I could not afford to be what I was. I had more questions than answers.

# MORE QUESTIONS THAN ANSWERS—ON TO THE NEXT STAGE

GAZING UP AT THE MATTERHORN IN THE SWISS ALPS from a glacier in a valley, I saw a dark line connecting dots. On closer reflection, I realized that the line was a safety rope connecting climbers as they trudged up to the summit. I thought about the journey I had taken during the first fifteen years of my law career, my formative years, and wondered about the perils I would encounter making a name for myself, achieving financial independence, and becoming intellectually independent.

From my first assignment as a public assistance lawyer, I had wandered through a maze of legal challenges and the clients and adversaries that went with them. I had begun with a view that legal knowledge could be used to make the world a better place, convinced that it was possible to be both a good lawyer and a compassionate person. Pitfalls and disillusionments in my path had changed that vision.

After I returned from the trip, I told my father about the Matterhorn experience. My father chuckled as I told him how it felt to be called Sidney Stark's son while standing in front of Judge Light the week I passed the Bar Examination, and how my lack of political savvy had disrupted my quest to become an urban renewal lawyer. Then, in a tone that spoke incredulity, I said, "If anyone had told me I would be a personal injury lawyer, I would have told them they were crazy."

"Most lawyers never end up doing what they set out to do after graduation," he responded seriously. "I didn't think you'd become a trial lawyer. But fate seems to have steered you into the courtroom. One thing seems to have led to another. It sounds like you've become something you were not when you graduated from law school. You have changed, haven't you?" I shrugged my shoulders before he continued, "I'm not being humorous when I say, by trial and error, you've established an identity for yourself. Where do you want to go from here now that your are no longer your father's son?"

"I wish I knew . . . Having the freedom to express my thoughts and ideals as Arthur Goldberg did at the Franklin Society dinner would be wonderful," I answered.

"On my watch, I've seen many lawyers grow like you have. If you want freedom, like Arthur Goldberg has, you have to develop your career and your firm in a way that fits your principles. "

I asked, "How do I do that?" My father leaned forward and cupped his chin in his palm. A moment later, he told me, "Think about where you came from and how you got to where you are. Then create a vision of where you want to go and figure out how to get there."

We continued talking about the stories I had lived beyond the bar.

My father was engaged. He looked me straight in the eye. "When I started in the depths of the Depression, most lawyers practiced alone. There were no such things as the billable hour, time-sheets, or hour requirements. Lawyers actually put their feet on the desk, lit up a smoke, and thought about a legal problem. You could put something in the mail and not worry about a response for a month. You could ask the other side for just about anything. You billed clients when you thought about it. Clients paid bills for 'professional services rendered' and associates learned by following a partner around. You knew most, if not all, of the lawyers in your bar association. Things are different today, and they're going to become even more complex. The law is more complex and, especially in the beginning, more personal than most fields. The challenges can be greater. So too, the rewards can be greater." My father turned his head away, then back to me. "When I graduated from law school, I wanted to be a professor and then an appellate judge. But times were tough. Your grandfather lost his grocery store and I filed his bankruptcy. I filed bankruptcies for many of his friends. That's how I began to represent businessmen. I learned from their mistakes."

"Today, the practice of law is becoming a business where big cases and big money are the bait. Big city firms are paying exorbitant salaries to law school graduates and demanding sweatshop hours. Corporate mentality has inculcated a stress filled culture into the workplace. East Coast firms are beginning to compete with those on the West and vice versa. How can I compete with them?" I asked.

My father paused, then said softly, "You don't have to," he replied.

Two days later, Sidney, David Botwinick, Richard Shaine, and I were talking about my trip. They laughed as I described how slippery it was to walk on the glacier and how funny it looked to see climbers tied together. Our conversation turned serious. After we talked about the journey we would like to take together, we joined hands, agreeing to build a law firm that would respond to, and try to satisfy, the legal needs of the people in Trenton, New Jersey; not just the injured, but also those who needed legal help in building their businesses. We pledged to help each other along the way to our dream.

Consultants assisted us in defining and pursuing that goal. They taught us to face, not fight, the realities of law as a business, suggested formulas for budgeting, taught management skills, marketing techniques, and the importance of long term planning.

Bill Colson, Craig Spangenberg, John Shepherd, John Elam, and other trial lawyers with national reputations helped me sharpen my skills in the courtroom.

When the law did not fulfill my expectations, lawyers like Bill Bischoff, Samuel Lenox, Sr., Joe Merlino, and Irving Lewis were there at every turn to help me find the strength and develop the stamina to climb to a higher level. A lawyer's future usually grows with his or her physical health, and, many times, declines with it. It is my hope that veteran lawyers who read *Beyond The Bar* will be inspired to interact with and develop young lawyers, thus perpetuating the legal profession's progress.

I devoted myself to representing the seriously injured, especially victims of brain trauma, and the building of a law firm that didn't suffer the maladies that makes a law career a chore instead of a choice.

Adopting a strategy to develop a culture where climbers felt secure as they ascended to more risky terrain, my partners and I have not tried to copy any other firms. We have tried to treat our lawyers and staff like clients. Being creative, focusing on our strengths, and doing the things we did well, we have strived not to be all things to all people or so specialized as to be too narrow. Today, we are proud of a law firm that fulfills the roles of a good citizen and a place where we enjoy working.

I have met a Shakespearean cast of characters: cops and robbers, judges and prosecutors, rich and poor, all of whom were caught up in the web we call the legal system. They have changed me.

The obstacles I encountered are not much different today than those my father faced in the Great Depression and during the rigors of the Second World War. My career began in the aftermath of the Bay of Pigs and the Cuban missile crisis. Vietnam influenced my past thirty years. Now, September 11, 2001 has changed the world.

Who could have imagined there would be metal detectors in the courtroom as there are today? There were no fax machines, e-mail, voice mail, word processors, cellular phones, Internet, Palm Pilots, or laptops when I graduated from law school. As I sit in my office and look around, I see mementos of past achievements and notes of appreciation from clients I never dreamed of representing.

Over the years, I have shared my experiences with young lawyers navigating beyond the bar. Many have told me that I helped them to overcome the obstacles that would have made them unhappy, bitter, or burned out. That my experiences have changed them has been the inspiration for this book.

I reveled meeting those who have been with me on my voyage, traveling from idealism to reality, bouncing between ethics and practicality. With the help of family, partners, friends, lawyers, judges, and clients, I have become free beyond the bar. My quest for freedom in a world of conflict has been worthwhile. Trying to use the legal system to implement change, the law has changed me.

# SUMMATION

It is satisfying to look back at the forty years I have been traveling beyond the bar. The intimate friendships and interaction I have had with lawyers and judges have given me deep satisfaction. I can recall but a few instances in my relationships with lawyers, which, at the end of a case, did not find us better friends than at the beginning.

And now, having had my "day in the court of public opinion," having submitted my best case, I am hoping for a favorable verdict, a verdict that announces that you have a better appreciation of the challenges a young lawyer faces.

# ACKNOWLEDGMENT

I COULD NOT HAVE WRITTEN *BEYOND THE BAR* WITHOUT THE HELP AND GUID-
ance of Carolyn Farrington, my teacher and editor, who nudged me
like a good shepherd so that I stayed focused on my work. To her, I
give the biggest "thank you."

My father, Sidney Stark, my uncle, Amel Stark, and attorneys like
Samuel Lenox, Sr., Bill Bischoff, Irving Lewis, Ernest Glickman, and Joe
Merlino were mentors who taught me many of the lessons I share with
you. I have strived to emulate their wisdom and professionalism.

The lawyers at Stark & Stark gave me the opportunity to write.
David M. Botwinick, John Sakson, Lewis Pepperman, Frank Orbach,
and John McDonald encouraged me to be honest and frank when ex-
posing my shortcomings.

Nancy Karlosky, my secretary for thirty five years, has lived most
of these moments and events. I thank her for her patience, good humor, and loyalty. Florance Malone, my legal assistant, cared for clients
while I was immersed in thought as I wrote.

Dr. Fred Gottlieb, Jack Howard Klein, Jr., Abigail Pollak, the late
Michael S. Arcieri, Bob Levitt, Cecelia Rosenblum, Herbert W. Hobler,
Richard Rosenberg, Denise Forrester, Lorena Miller, Michael Foster,
Lisa Rough, Sam Gaylord, Michael Donahue, Sandy Durst, Matt
Lehman, Scott Unger, Ross Urken, my son, Jared, and daughter, Rachel,
have been marvelous readers.

I owe a deep debt of gratitude to Johannah Rodgers, Claire
Zuckerman, and Mark Stevens for assisting me on putting the finishing
touches to my work.

E. John Wherry, my longtime colleague, adversary, and friend gave me the courage I needed to aspire to publish *Beyond the Bar*.

Bill Tipton, Tony Nocito, Beverly Seche, Michael Sherman, Claudia Jackson, Karen Shaw, Debbie Graiff, Sylvia Mura, and Pam Hoover bailed me out of the many jams I experienced using my computer.

My wife, Ellen, has been the inspiration for my writing. If she had not encouraged me to enroll in a fiction writing course at the Arts Council of Princeton, I would never have been able to develop whatever writing skills these stories exhibit. She has lived through my moods: enthusiastic, frustrated, depressed, aloof. She has prodded me when necessary to "get real" and laughed at me when I became so enthralled with a story that I became a shadow of the lawyer I really was. I thank her also for removing whatever it was that hid the lawyer and person I was during the formative stages of my rich career.

And to the Shakespearean characters who played a real life role in *Beyond the Bar*, I thank you for playing a role in my life.

Albert M. Stark

September 26, 2002

# ABOUT THE AUTHOR

A GRADUATE OF DARTMOUTH COLLEGE AND THE UNIVERSITY OF PENNSYLVA-nia Law School, Albert Stark is a partner in the Stark and Stark law firm in Princeton, New Jersey. He practices in the firm's Personal Injury Group where he concentrates on seriously injured clients, particularly those who suffer from severe brain injuries.

Stark is a member of the Mercer County, New Jersey, and American Bar Associations. He has been qualified as an Arbitrator with the U.S. District Court and has been certified by the Supreme Court of New Jersey as a Certified Civil Trial Attorney. Prior to joining Stark and Stark, he was a Ford Foundation Fellow and an Assistant to the Governor of New Jersey.

At present, he is the host of "In the Public Interest" on WIMG radio and WZBN-TV, a program bringing topics of current importance to the community, as well as appearing as a Comcast Newsmaker.

The New Jersey Trial Lawyers Association recognized Mr. Stark with its Trial Bar Award in 2000. He has been named one of The Best Lawyers in America.

He lives with his wife, Ellen, in Princeton.